Introduction

The purpose of this book is to introduce children to phonetic readiness skills by providing activities that combine all areas of the curriculum while utilizing a thematic, multi-sensory, whole language approach. By participating in exciting "hands-on" activities built around different consonant sounds, your students will experience success and therefore gain confidence while developing listening, speaking, reading and writing skills.

Each chapter is organized into categories which encompass writing, reading, poetry, dramatization, science (including ecology), math, social studies, cooking, art, music and games. Appropriate activities are described in each area which can be used as a springboard for unit study. Holiday activities are also included when applicable. There are literature suggestions relevant to specific activities as well as a comprehensive list at the end of each chapter.

Through our combined 78 years of early childhood teaching and administrative experience, we, as authors of this book, have found that the more modalities provided for students, the greater the percentage of skill mastery. Based on this conviction, we have developed the materials in this book as a demonstration of this philosophy.

This book is not intended to replace current curriculum, but rather to enhance, expand and supplement it. It is compatible with any early childhood curriculum.

Suggestions for Using This Book

As you introduce each letter, read through the appropriate chapter and select the activities that would best suit the interest and abilities of your class. Be sure to stress the initial consonant sound with each activity. The "B" chapter is much longer than any of the other chapters because there are several activities which can be applied to all the other consonant sounds. (See the list of these activities on page 4.)

Most chapters include a group of pictures pertinent to the consonant sound being studied. These pictures can be enlarged, colored and cut out to make flash cards or incorporated into bulletin boards depicting the current consonant sound. As each new sound is completed, incorporate the new flash cards into a set to use as a means of reviewing and distinguishing between the different consonant sounds. Copies of the pictures could be distributed to the students for them to make their own sets of flash cards or to be used in various art projects.

Also included in this book are ideas for in-school "book publishing." These ideas involve classroom books as well as individual children's books. Suggestions for laminating and binding are included as well. We are confident the hands-on, multi-sensory activities in this book will help make learning exciting for you and your students.

Cooperative Learning

Frequent opportunities are provided for cooperative learning experiences in order to enhance young children's self-confidence. When forming the groups, make certain that children with different skill levels are included in each one. Put extremely shy children with those who are outgoing and have more nurturing personalities.

Parent Connection

As you begin each letter unit, make copies of the note to parents on page 3. (Make one copy first, fill in the blanks and then run it out for each child to take home.) Parent involvement in, and awareness of, what is taking place in the classroom has been proven to be a very positive influence on the educational growth of students. Many of the chapters include suggestions for field trips which will help expand young children's background knowledge. These field trips offer excellent opportunities for parent involvement.

_____
date

Dear Parents:

We are beginning a unit of study on the letter ____ . We are very excited about the learning that will take place across the curriculum as we study our letter. You can help at home by:

    a. reading books to your child to reinforce the letter sound. (See book list attached.)

    b. helping your child create the letter from clay, with paint or by tracing it in sand.

    c. helping your child find magazine pictures to cut out that begin with the featured letter. Have your child paste the pictures on paper to form a collage.

    d. asking your child to tell you about the special letter activity he/she worked on in school today.

Our special author is _____ . You may want to read books written by him/her.

We need your help in school! If you can contribute in any of the following ways listed below, please check and return the form.

Thank you for your continued support.

_____
teacher

- -

I can do one or more of the following:

☐   read a book to the class

☐   help with a letter project

☐   read a book to individual students

_____   _____
date   parent

Chapter B

The following activities in the "B" chapter can be used with any letter of the alphabet.

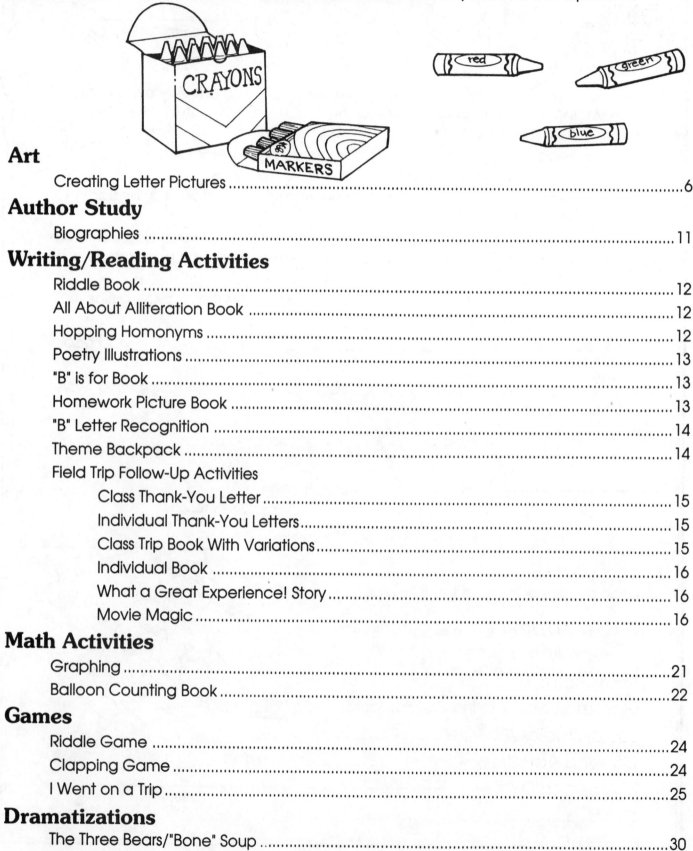

Art
Creating Letter Pictures 6

Author Study
Biographies 11

Writing/Reading Activities
Riddle Book 12

All About Alliteration Book 12

Hopping Homonyms 12

Poetry Illustrations 13

"B" is for Book 13

Homework Picture Book 13

"B" Letter Recognition 14

Theme Backpack 14

Field Trip Follow-Up Activities

    Class Thank-You Letter 15

    Individual Thank-You Letters 15

    Class Trip Book With Variations 15

    Individual Book 16

    What a Great Experience! Story 16

    Movie Magic 16

Math Activities
Graphing 21

Balloon Counting Book 22

Games
Riddle Game 24

Clapping Game 24

I Went on a Trip 25

Dramatizations
The Three Bears/"Bone" Soup 30

Table of Contents

Creating Letter Pictures

Balloon Basket

Art

Materials: crayons, markers, paper with "B" and "b" on it

Directions: Emphasize the words basket, balloon, big and baby. Give each child a paper with a capital "B" and a small "b" written on it. Model for the children how to make a big basket of big balloons and a baby basket of baby balloons. This works best as a directed lesson.

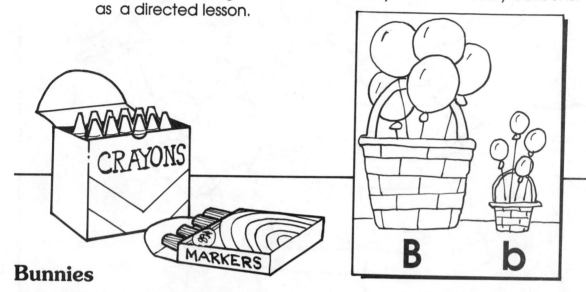

Bunnies

Objective: To create bunnies from capital "B" and small "b" (The children will learn which direction to make the small "b.")

Materials: crayons, markers, paper with "B" and "b" on it

Directions: 1. Tell the children that they will create bunnies from capital "B" and small "b."

2. To help the children learn the direction of writing lower case "b," tell the following story as you model the drawing of the picture.

"The mother or father bunny and the baby bunny are taking a walk. They always walk and face in the same direction. They never look at each other." (Embellish the story as you continue to complete the picture.)

This works best as a directed lesson.

6

Paper Bag Bunny

Art

Materials: paper bags, paint, paintbrushes, 9" x 12" and 12" x 18" sheets of oaktag, crayons, scissors, 9" x 16" sheets of orange paper, green cellophane, crêpe paper, tissue or construction paper, colored construction paper, cotton balls, newspaper

Directions: Have the children bring paper bags from home. The size of the bag will determine the size of the bunny.

1. Have the children paint both sides of the bag. (Pastel stripes are nice for spring.)

2. Using 12" x 18" oaktag, have children draw and cut out a bunny head with ears. Discuss shape, size and the position of the head on oaktag. Be sure to leave room for the ears. (See sketch.)

3. Use 9" x 12" oaktag to make the hands and feet. You should draw these and have children cut them out. (See sketch.)

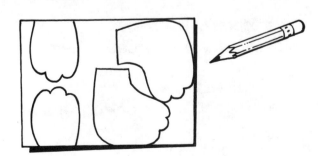

4. Give children a 9" x 6" piece of orange paper. Have them draw and cut out a carrot. Attach two or three green strips of construction paper, cellophane, tissue or crêpe paper.

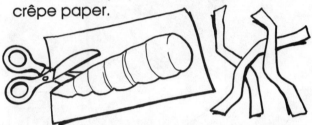

5. Give children a piece of 9" x 12" colored construction paper to make a bow tie. Have them draw, cut out and decorate as they wish.

6. Stuff the paper bag with newspaper. Assemble the bunny as follows: Close bag and staple two feet to the bottom flat part of the bag. Staple two hands to the sides of the bag. Staple the carrot in the bunny's hand and bow tie under head. Paste cotton balls on for tail.

Beautiful Butterflies

Art

Materials: 9" x 12" colored paper, scissors, paint, paintbrushes

Directions: Fold paper in half. Have the children trace a pattern of a butterfly wing with the straight edge on the fold, and cut it out. Have students be sure to keep the paper folded. Discuss the terms "half" and "symmetry."

Children paint one half of the butterfly and quickly press the wings together to imprint the other half. Point out that the butterfly's wing design is symmetrical.

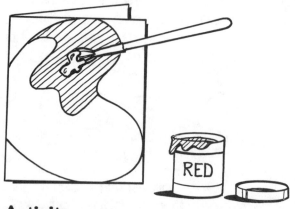

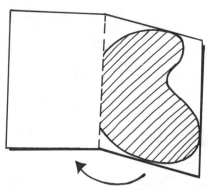

Fold and press.

Extension Activity

Materials: books, charts, pictures and filmstrips

Method: Discuss the life cycle of a butterfly - egg to caterpillar, pupa to adult. Discuss cocoon. Discuss the differences between the bodies of a butterfly and a moth. (The butterfly has a long, slender body and antennae, whereas the moth has a short, fuzzy body and feathery antennae.)

Suggested Reading: *Where Does a Butterfly Go When It Rains?*

Button Collage

Materials: large collection of multi-colored buttons of different sizes and shapes, assorted patterns of items beginning with "B" such as ball, bell, bird, etc., one piece of oaktag (12" x 18") for each child, black markers, glue

Directions:
1. Each child chooses a pattern.
2. Children trace their pattern with a black marker on a piece of oaktag.
3. Fill a number of trays, bins or cups with mixtures of buttons.
4. Children glue one button next to the other inside their traced pattern picture until the picture is filled.

Extension Activities:

Children can write the name of their picture, in pencil, on the oaktag. The word can then be traced with a thin marker.

Play **"Button, Button, Who Has the Button?"** (See page 25.)

Beach Scene

Art

Materials: sand or rice, glue, crayons or paint, paintbrushes, shells (pasta), Bristol board

Directions: Develop an awareness of a beach ecosystem and create a beach scene. After discussing what you might find at a beach, (or after taking a trip to the beach if possible), give each child a sheet of Bristol board. Have students draw a line toward the bottom of their boards to mark where the sand will be placed. (Model this first.) Next, have the students color or paint the water, sky, sea gulls, etc. Then, have them use a paintbrush to spread glue on the bottom of their papers. Sand or rice should be put on top of the glue next. Have students let their pictures sit for a count of ten. Then, they shake off the excess sand or rice. Tell the students to glue on the shells.

This can also be done with a shoe box to create a diorama.

sand

Shake off excess.

Build a Bus

Materials: yellow and black construction paper, scissors, pencils, paste, white crayons

Directions: Give each child a pre-cut yellow rectangle, and a pre-cut yellow square. Have them paste the two together to create the body of a bus.

Next, have them fold a black piece of paper in half, and draw one circle. When the children have cut the circles out, they can paste them on. Or, if you'd like, you may fasten them on with paper fasteners so they move. The children can add windows, doors, a driver, children, etc. Have the children write "bus" on the bus.

Extension Activities: song - "The Wheels on the Bus"
discussion - bus safety rules

Bunny Basket

Art

Materials: one half-pint milk carton for each child, construction paper (white and a variety of colors), scissors, stapler, crayons or markers, grass (commercial or thin strips cut from green crêpe, cellophane or tissue paper), small balls of cotton

Method:

1. Cut the tops off of the milk cartons.

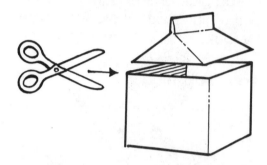

2. Cover the outside of the carton with construction paper.

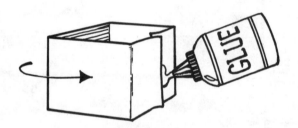

3. Cut 1/2" wide strips of construction paper for the handles. The children should decorate their handles. Attach the handles to the inside of the milk carton with a stapler.

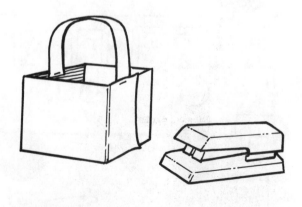

4. Have children make a bunny face on a piece of 6" x 8 1/2" piece of white paper. Cut it out.

5. Glue the face to the front of the carton.

6. Children should paste or glue a cotton ball on the back of the carton for the tail.

7. Put grass in each basket.

Biography

Objective: In order for the children to think of themselves as authors, they need to think of authors as people. This activity is intended to introduce the children to the meaning of the word biography, and to reinforce the letter sound "B". Under the Suggested Reading section, you will find the proposed authors, accompanied by a short biography, as well as a list of several books each has authored.

Materials: several books written by each author

Suggested Reading:

Brandeberg, Franz

Franz Brandeberg lives in England. He has two children, Jason and Alexa. His wife has illustrated and written many books. Her name is Aliki.

A Secret for Grandmother's Birthday
Aunt Nina's Visit
Leo and Emily and the Dragon
Leo and Emily

Branley, Franklyn

Franklyn Branley lives in Sag Harbor, New York. He has written many science books. His birthday is June 5.

Tornado Alert
Floating and Sinking
What Makes Day and Night?
Sunshine Makes the Seasons
Mickey's Magnet

Burmingham, John

John Burmingham lives in London, England. He hass written 27 books. He has lived in many parts of the world and has worked at many different jobs. He has over three million copies of books in print in several different languages. He co-authored *Chitty Chitty Bang Bang* with Ian Fleming.

Suggested Authors:

Berenstain, Jan and Stan
Bridwell, Norman
Burton, Virginia Lee

Riddle Book

Objective: To illustrate and assemble a riddle book

Materials: construction paper, markers/crayons, stapler or book rings

Directions: Play the **Riddle Game** as described on page 24 to introduce your students to riddles (or to give them practice with them).

Then, have each child make up a riddle whose answer begins with the sound for "B." The children will illustrate their riddles and then dictate them to be written on the drawing. Put the answer on the bottom of the page under a flap. (Answers can also be written on the back of the page.)

Assemble all the pages and bind, staple or use book rings to form the book.

Circulate the book among the children in the same manner as a library book. Be sure to discuss the care of books with them.

An Alliteration Book

Objective: To use adjectives beginning with "B"

Materials: drawing paper, markers/crayons

Directions: Play an introductory game. Name an adjective beginning with "B" (beautiful, big, blue, etc.). Children take turns adding a noun beginning with "B" (big ball, brown bat, blue bird, beautiful bee).

Each child then chooses one of the objects named in the game. Children can then draw a picture of their chosen "B" object adding the "B" adjective (example: blue bird).

Have children label each picture.

Make a cover and title the book, **Our Beautiful Book**. Bind the pages with a bindery machine if available, or punch holes and use book rings.

Hopping Homonyms

Objective: To illustrate homonyms beginning with the letter "B"

Materials: crayons, paper, chalkboard, chalk

Directions: Illustrate an example of a homonym on the chalkboard. Be sure to print the word under each drawing. Next, generate a word list from the children or provide them with words from the list below and ask for two meanings for each word. The children can then choose a word they would like to illustrate. The illustrations can be compiled to make a class book.

Word List: back, band, bank, bark, base, bat, bill, block, bolt, break, buck

12

Poetry Illustrations

Writing/ Reading

Objective: To interpret a poem using illustrations

Materials: a poem, crayons, paper (preferably 12" x 18")

Directions: Allow children to become familiar with a short poem by reading it several times over a few days. After the children have become comfortable with reciting it with you, ask them to close their eyes and imagine what a character or setting may look like. Ask specific questions. For example: Are the trees tall or short? What color do you think Bill's shirt is? etc. After they have had time to think about your questions, read the poem again. Next, give them paper and crayons. Ask them the same questions again, except this time, stop after each one so that the students can put their "answers" on paper.

Suggested Poem:

"Early Bird" by Shel Silverstein

Possible Questions:

1. What color do you imagine the bird to be?
2. Where do you think this bird would have breakfast?
3. Can you imagine a bird eating from a plate?
4. Where is the worm sleeping?

"B" is for Book

Objective: To enhance students' vocabulary of nouns beginning with B

Materials: a copy for each student of an 8 1/2" x 11" sheet of paper with "B is for ___."

Directions: Children will select a noun beginning with the sound for "B" and illustrate it. You or the children can label it. Papers can be assembled to make a class book.

Beautiful Babies Book

Materials: photo album

Directions: Mount children's baby photos in an album. Write the child's name under each photo. Encourage children to read each other's names.

Title the album, **Beautiful Babies**.

Homework Picture Book

Materials: magazine pictures, construction paper, glue

Directions: Have each child bring in pictures from magazines that start with the sound for "B."

Collect the pictures and mount them with their name written under the picture. Arrange them as in a collage. Assemble the pages into a class book.

Writing/
Reading

"B b" Letter Recognition

Directions: A student wears a "B b" necklace for a day. This could be a child whose name begins with B, the birthday boy, etc. Another possibility includes creating several necklaces so that a group of children can wear the necklaces on Monday, a second group on Tuesday, and so on. This way, each child gets a turn. To make the necklace, put "B" and "b" on a round piece pf cardboard. Punch a hole at the top of the cardboard. String yarn through the hole and tie a knot. Be sure the yarn is long enough to fit over a child's head.

Materials: letter B, b cutouts, hole punch, yarn, cardboard

Extension Activity: Allow students to decorate the letters.

Big Books

Objective: To introduce big books if you haven't already If you have utilized big books, you can simply stress the initial consonant sounds in the words "big" and "book"

Suggested Reading:

Hairy Bear by Gardiner and Elizabeth Fuller
The Three Billy Goats Gruff by Paul Galdone
How Big Is Big? by Avelyn Davis
Who Sank the Boat? by Pamela Allen
Billy Balloon by Blackburn and Handy
Mrs. Wishy Washy by Joy Cowley

Theme Backpack, Bag or Box

SUSAN SAVES

Objective: To stress that backpack, bag, box and book all begin with the letter "B"

Materials: a bag, box or backpack, thematic books

Directions: In a bag, box or backpack, place several books on one subject relating to an area of study you are currently working on. (For example, if you are working on community helpers, place books about community helpers in the box/bag.) You can include fiction, nonfiction and periodicals.

Suggested Reading:
The books in your bag, box or backpack!

A "B" Field Trip and Follow-Up

Objective: To use the field trip as motivation for several writing activities

Suggested Trips:
bakery
bagel bakery
beach
barn
bank

Class Thank-You Letter

Materials: large chart paper, markers/crayons

Directions: Discuss the trip. Encourage the use of complete sentences. Encourage the expansion of vocabulary. Ask students questions like, "What did you see? What did you like? What did you find out? Who showed you around? How can you say thank you? How do you write a letter?" Discuss the form of the letter. Have the children contribute (dictate) sentences for the letter. Write them on a chart. Have the children sign their names.

Individual Thank-You Letters

Materials: construction paper, markers/crayons

Directions: Discuss the field trip as described above. Have each child draw something relevant to the trip (i.e. "What did you enjoy most?"). The children may either dictate a sentence or two to be written on the drawing page, or they may use invented spelling to write their own words or sentences.

Class Trip Book

Materials: construction paper, markers/crayons

Directions: The pages described under **Individual Thank-You Letters** can be laminated and bound to form a book. If a laminator and bindery are not available, the pages can be put together with book rings or just stapled together.

Variation on a Class Trip Book

Materials: construction paper, markers/crayons

Directions: After the class discussion about the trip, the children can dictate a story about the experience with each child contributing a sentence. Each child will then illustrate a sentence of the story. This can be assembled into a book with the pictures and sentences on a page.

A "B" Field Trip and Follow-Up continued

Individual Books

Materials: construction paper, markers/crayons/pencils, binding materials

Directions: After class discussion about the field trip, each child can dictate his/her own story about the trip and then illustrate it. An individual book is then assembled for each child. This will produce a number of books that can be circulated "library fashion" among the children in the class. It is a good idea to make a cover, title page and author page. On the author page, write some information about the author.

> i.e. Allison is in kindergarten. She is five years old. She lives in _____ with her mother, father and sister. She likes to ride her bicycle. Allison wants to be a doctor when she grows up. This is her first book.

A photograph of the author next to the biography makes this a very special "publication."

What a Great Experience! Story

Materials: chart paper, markers

Directions: The children dictate a story about the trip and you write it on large chart paper. Write each sentence in a different color. This makes it easier to read and re-read with the children.

Movie Magic

Objective: To make a movie from children's story and illustrations

Materials: construction paper, markers/crayons, opaque projector, two rollers from aluminum foil or something similar

Directions: After much discussion about the class trip, the children will dictate a story about the experience. This should start with leaving school and getting to the destination. Each child will illustrate several parts of the story. There should be several pictures for each sentence or paragraph (i.e. if you take a bus to the destination, there should be about three bus pictures).

After the illustrations are complete, tape the pictures together in reverse order. The tape should go on the back. Include a title page, credits page and author page. Place one blank sheet at the beginning and end. Tape the end of the story to a roller.

Roll up the "film pictures" and tape beginning pages to the second roller.

BUS 14

We rode across town in our school bus.

Use an opaque projector and a screen. It would be helpful to have two people operate the "showing of the film" - one to read the story and to unroll the film and the other to roll up the film as it is moved across the projector.

Invite parents to a film showing. To have a real film party, have children make butter, bread, brownies, bananas and butter cookies to serve to guests.

Blowing Bubbles

Science

Objective: To allow children to experiment with air and water

Materials: straw, bucket of water

Directions: Blow through a straw in the air. What do you see? feel?

Blow through a straw in water. What do you think is in the bubbles?

Beans and Bulbs

Objective: To teach students about planting, comparing and classifying beans and bulbs

Materials: bulbs (onion, tulip, radish), beans (lima, black, navy, pinto, garbanzo, lentil, kidney), soil, potting containers, water, paper towels, chart paper, crayons

Directions:

1. Display all beans on a table. The students can then compare and classify the beans by shape, color and size. Repeat the activity using the bulbs. (Depending on the class size and/or time restraint, you may want to work this activity with small groups.)

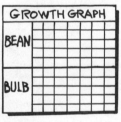

GROWTH GRAPH

BEAN								
BULB								

LIMA BEAN

TULIP BULB

2. Next, plant a bean and a bulb. Through this activity, you can teach children what plants need to grow. To bring in math, graph the growth of the two plants over a month's period of time.

3. With a remaining bean, you can show demonstrate a seedling. Place a bean in a wet paper towel. Over a number of days, the bean will sprout and grow.

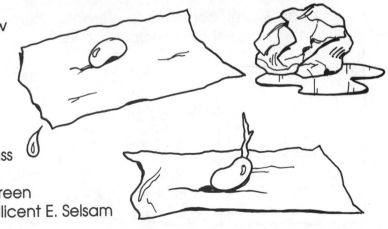

Suggested Reading:

The Carrot Seed by Ruth Krauss
Jack and the Beanstalk
The Plant Sitter by Graham Green
Seeds and More Seeds by Millicent E. Selsam

Balloon Experiments

Science

Objective: To predict outcomes and make observations

Materials: balloons, pin, bucket of water

Directions:

1. Have a student blow up a balloon.
2. Ask the following questions:
   What happened to the balloon?
   (It got bigger.)
   What do you think is inside?
   Can you see it?
   Can you feel it?
   Can you smell it?
   Can you touch it?
   Can you taste it?
   Can you hear it?
3. Have students let the balloon go.
   Ask students what happened and why.

4. Have a student blow up another balloon. Have him/her stick a pin in it. Ask what happened and what came out of the balloon.
5. Have a student blow up yet another balloon. He/she should let the air out in a pail of water. Ask the students: What happened? What do you see? What do you think is in the bubbles? Why do you think that?

Buoyancy

Objective: To discover that some materials are buoyant

Materials: banana (sliced), bead, button, bow (ribbon), toy boat, brass paper fastener, bag, water, container (preferably a clear one), large sheet of paper, marker

IT FLOATS
1. toy boat
2. banana slice

IT SINKS
1. paper fastener
2. button

Directions: Fill the container with water. One by one, drop the listed items into the water to test for buoyancy. Make a list of items that are buoyant and those that are not.

Suggested Reading:
Who Sank the Boat? (Big Book) by Pamela Allen

The Balance
Science

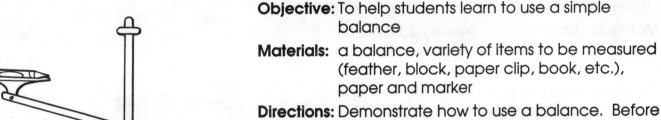

Objective: To help students learn to use a simple balance

Materials: a balance, variety of items to be measured (feather, block, paper clip, book, etc.), paper and marker

Directions: Demonstrate how to use a balance. Before weighing materials, have the children predict which object will be heavier, and which will be lighter. Record the results. After working with several items, place the balance and new objects in a center so that the children may experiment with the balance on their own.

Bird Feeder

Objective: To observe the construction of a simple bird feeder, to learn how to care for a bird feeder and to observe birds feeding

Materials: a large plastic bleach bottle, an aluminum pie tin, scissors, glue, string, birdseed

Directions:

1. With scissors, cut an arch-shaped opening into the side of the bottle.
2. Glue the pie tin onto the bottom of the bottle.
3. Tie a sturdy piece of string around the neck of the bottle.
4. Ask students the following questions:
   Where will the food go?
   Where will the birds perch?
   What kind of foods do birds like?
   Where shall we hang our bird feeder? (Encourage children to suggest a place near a classroom window.)

Extension Activities:

Observations of feeding can lead to further discussions of bird identification and habitat.

Feeders can also be made from pine cones rolled in peanut butter, plastic baskets, milk cartons and tin cans.

Suggested Reading:

Bird Talk by Roma Gans
Birds in Wintertime by Allen Eitzen
The Good Bird by Peter Wezel

Buzzy Bees

Science

Objective: To learn about the lifestyle of the bee

Materials: book - *Honeybees* by Janet Lecht (Books for Young Explorers National Geographic Society)

Directions: After reading the book, discuss the various jobs of bees.

Discuss the meaning of the expression, "Busy as a bee."

Button Classification

Objective: To sort or classify various buttons by shape, color or size attributes

Materials: buttons of assorted sizes, shapes and colors

Directions: Have students sort or classify buttons according to color, size, shape, pattern, etc.

Bear Week

Objective: To become familiar with several kinds of bears and to have the opportunity to share favorite bears with the others

Directions: Discuss various types of bears:
brown bears
grizzly bears
polar bears
panda bears
koala bears (not really bears)

Have a Teddy Bear Day at school. Encourage children to bring their teddy bears to school to share.

Suggested Reading:

Buzzy Bear Goes South by Dorothy Marion
Bears in Pairs by Niki Yektai
Baby Bears and How They Grow - Books for Young Explorers National Geographic Society
Brown Bear, Brown Bear by Bill Martin, Jr.
Blueberries for Sal by Robert McCloskey
Ira Sleeps Over by Bernard Waber

Extension Activity:

Have children draw a teddy bear out of circles. (See sketch.)

Block Blueprint

Math

Objective: To construct a block building by following a blueprint

Materials: a large sheet of paper (18" x 36" recommended), markers, blocks

Directions: To create a blueprint, lay the sheet of paper on the floor of your block-building corner. Create a structure, laying each block on its side on top of the sheet of paper. Trace each block in its place. You now have created a blueprint! Hang it in your block corner and ask the children to reproduce it. When every student has had an opportunity to construct the building, create a new blueprint. (For those who have had difficulty, lay the blueprint on the floor and have them match the blocks directly on the blueprint.)

Graphing

Objective: To become familiar with graphing techniques

Materials: large chart paper, crayons, markers

Directions: Select a graphing idea. (See below.) Discuss the choices with the children. One by one, have the children indicate their choices. Provide a simple method in which students can record their choices. For example, if you are creating a color graph, have students make a brown X if their favorite color is brown, a blue X if their favorite color is blue.

Graphing Ideas:

1. Favorite colors - <u>br</u>own, <u>bl</u>ack, <u>bl</u>ue
2. Lunch - Did you <u>br</u>ing or <u>bu</u>y?
3. Favorite breakfast food - bagel, egg, cereal, waffles, pancakes or French toast
4. Birthday - Make a chart of the months of the year. As each child is able to remember his/her birthday, place a star next to the month and write the child's name under the star. When all the stars are completed, have children compare the stars on the graph to see which month has the most, least or equal number of birthdays.

Birthday Chart			
Month	**Boys**	**Girls**	**Children in All**
Jan.			
Feb.			
March			
April			
May			
June			
July			
Aug.			
Sept.			
Oct.			
Nov.			
Dec.			

Balloon Counting Book

Math

Materials: 4 1/2" x 5 1/2" sheets of white paper (one per student), crayons, stapler

Directions: Write a numeral on the bottom of each piece of paper. Children then draw the correct number of balloons corresponding to the numeral printed on the bottom of each page. Assemble pages in order. Staple or bind them into a book.

Suggested Variation:

1. Provide papers with numerals from one to however many students are in your class.
2. Give one to each student.
3. Students draw the number of balloons and write the numeral that you gave them.
4. Put the pages in numerical order before you bind the book.

Bead Patterning

Materials: colored beads, string

Directions: As a group, create a simple pattern (i.e. 1 blue bead, 1 brown bead, 1 brown bead, 1 blue bead, 1 brown bead, etc.). Have students create other patterns until you feel they are ready to work independently. Have the beads accessible to the children so that they may use them during "center time."

Before and After

Objective: To learn the concepts of before and after (as related to time)

Directions: Tell a short story.

Example:

Tom went to the supermarket with his mom. First, he helped her buy fruit and vegetables. Next, his mom picked up two cans of soup. That was all they needed, so they paid for the food at the check-out counter. After leaving the supermarket, Tom and his mom went to a restaurant and had hamburgers for lunch.

Before and After continued

Math

Then ask students questions. For example: What did Tom and his mom do **before** they bought soup? What did they do **after** they left the supermarket? What did Tom's mom get **before** she checked out and paid for the food?

Or:

Amy came to school. She put her things in her cubby. She got out her crayons and some drawing paper. Amy drew a picture. She showed the picture to her teacher. Amy's teacher hung her picture on the bulletin board.

Ask similar questions as with the first story.
What did Amy do **before** . . . ?
What did Amy do **after** . . . ?

Big and Little

Objective: To become familiar with the concept of "opposite" in terms of size

Materials: concrete objects such as large and small crayons, blocks, chairs, scissors, etc.

Directions:
1. Present children with one big and one little block.
2. Ask students how these blocks are different and how they are the same.
2. Guide students into telling the difference in size, using the terms big and little.
4. Use other materials in the same manner.

Extension Activity:
Give each child a piece of drawing paper. Ask each to draw two similar things - one big and one little. Encourage the children to keep their drawings simple; a big circle and a little circle, a house and a skyscraper, etc. Label the pictures using the terms "big" and "little."

Suggested Reading:
Goldilocks and the Three Bears by Janet Stevens
Big Ones, Little Ones by Tana Hoban

Riddle Game

Games

Objective: To answer riddles and make up riddles

Directions: Tell the children that you are going to ask them a riddle. There may be lots of answers to the riddle, but the answer is correct only if it begins with the sound for "B".

Examples:

1. What can you wear on your feet in the snow? (boots)
2. What flies from flower to flower and says, "Bzzz"? (bee)
3. What can you throw? (ball)
4. What can you sit on in the park or at the playground? (bench)
5. What can you hit a ball with? (bat)
6. What can you go on to cross over a river? (bridge)
7. What builds a nest? (bird)
8. What builds a home in a river? (beaver)
9. What can you do to an egg? (boil it)
10. What can you do to your hair? (brush it)
11. What can you do to an apple? (bite it)
12. What is something you can eat? (beef, beans, buns, bread)

You can have children make up their own riddles, but they must remember that the answers should begin with the sound for "B."

This activity can be used with all letters and can be followed by writing a class riddle book.

Clapping Game

Objective: To respond to words that begin with the sound for "B"

Directions: Say a word. If it begins with the sound for "B," the children clap one time. If it does not begin with the sound for "B," the children sit on their hands.

This game can also be played using pictures and objects instead of saying a word.

"Button, Button, Who Has the Button?"

Games

Objective: To respond to words that begin with the sound for "B"

Materials: button

Directions: Children sit in a circle. One child is "It" and sits in the middle of the circle with his/her eyes closed. The others pass the button. When the teacher calls, "Stop," the child who is "It" has three chances to guess who has the button. If the child guesses correctly, the child holding the button becomes "It." If the child does not guess correctly, the teacher selects a name out of a bag. This child is now "it."

I Went on a Trip

Objective: To concentrate using words beginning with the sound for "B"

Directions: Children sit in a circle with you. You begin by saying, "I'm going on a trip and I'm taking a ball." The child next to you continues saying, "I'm going on a trip, and I'm taking a ball and a bat." The next child continues in the same way, " . . . and I'm taking a ball, a bat and a bell." Continue around the circle with each child repeating the items previously mentioned and adding a new "B" item.

Beanbag Basketball

Materials: beanbags, wastebasket

Directions: Mark the floor at an appropriate distance from the basket.

Children take turns throwing the beanbag.

Extension Activities:
Math - keep score
Social Skills - teamwork

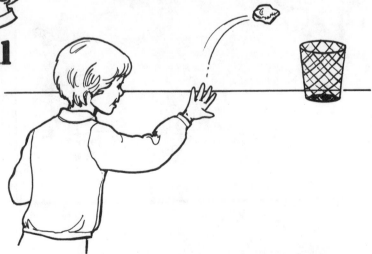

Social Studies

Boats for Columbus Day

Objective: To cut, paste, draw and color the *Niña*, the *Pinta* and the *Santa Maria*

Materials: drawing paper (12" x 18")
paste
scissors
crayons
3 Popsicle sticks (per student)
3 half-circles (per student)
3 sails (per student)

Directions: 1. Read a story about Columbus. Emphasize the names of his three boats.

2. Demonstrate what the children will be doing or have a picture already made that you can look at with the class and discuss.

3. Children paste half-circles on drawing paper.

4. Distribute 3 Popsicle sticks to each child.

5. Children paste a stick on each half-circle.

Model the following steps:

1. Paste 3 half-circles on construction paper to represent the hulls of the ships.

2. Paste a Popsicle stick on each half-circle. These will be the masts.

3. Paste the sails on the masts.

4. Write the name of one of the 3 boats on each boat.

5. Children may use crayons to enhance their pictures by adding water, sailors, birds, signs of land, etc.

Election Day Ballots

Social Studies

Objective: To become familiar with a ballot and how it is used

Materials: two storybooks (See Suggested Reading below.)

Directions: Provide students with two familiar stories. Ask them to decide which book they like best. Students can campaign for their favorite. To do this, provide each student with a ballot. Next, have them cast their vote. Choose electioneers to help you tally the votes. Discuss the results. Read the story that wins.

Suggested Reading:
The Last Basselope by Berkeley Breathed
Bears in Pairs by Niki Yektai
Golden Bear by Ruth Young
The Berenstain Bears and the Trouble with Grownups by Stan and Jan Berenstain

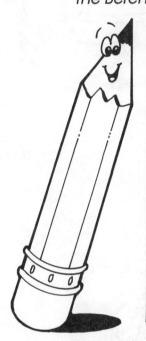

BALLOT . . . Vote for one book.

***The Last Basselope* by Berkeley Breathed**

***Bears in Pairs* by Niki Yektai**

BALLOT . . . Vote for one book.

***Golden Bear* by Ruth Young**

***The Berenstain Bears and the Trouble with Grownups* by Jan and Stan Berenstain**

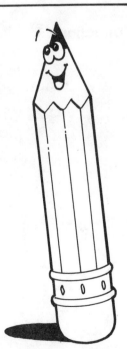

Banana Bread

Cooking

Materials: 1 3/4 cups flour
2 1/4 teaspoons baking powder
1/2 teaspoon salt
1/3 cup shortening
2/3 cup sugar
2 eggs
1 1/4 cups mashed ripe banana
mixing bowls, spoons, measuring cups,
measuring spoons, bread pan, oven

Directions: Sift flour, baking powder and salt and set aside. Blend shortening and sugar. Add eggs and banana. Add dry ingredients and mix. Pour into greased bread pan. Bake at 375 degrees for 40 minutes. Bread is done when toothpick is inserted into center and comes out clean.

Bread Sculpture

Objective: To create sculptures from a bread mixture

Materials: 3 cups flour
1 1/2 cups salt
3 teaspoons oil
5 tablespoons warm water
paint and paintbrushes
cookie sheets
acrylic spray
oven

Directions: 1. Mix the ingredients above with hands. Give each child a portion to shape. (Perhaps the children could make "B's.")

2. When sculptures are complete, place them on a cookie sheet.

3. Bake at 275 degrees for 25 minutes on the lowest oven rack.*

4. Let them stand overnight before painting.

5. For a final finish, you may want to use an acrylic spray.

*Thick pieces may need to bake longer.

Bone Soup

Cooking

Objective: To make a pot of bone soup based upon the book, *Stone Soup*

Materials: book - *Stone Soup* by Marcia Brown
vegetables such as carrots, celery, parsley, potatoes
1 onion
soup greens
1 beef soup bone
large pot with cover
hot plate or stove
peeler, knife, spoon
small dishes and spoons (for each child)
bread
butter

Directions:
1. Read *Stone Soup* to the class.
2. Discuss with the class the reasons for using a bone rather than stones.
3. Have children bring the necessary ingredients to school.
4. Put a beef soup bone in the soup pot.

5. Peel and wash the vegetables with the children.
6. Children place all the ingredients in a large pot.
7. Cover the contents of the pot with water.
8. Place the pot on the hot plate or stove, boil, cover and simmer until done.
9. Serve to the children in small dishes with bread and butter.

Poems and Finger Plays

Little Boy Blue by Mother Goose

Little Boy Blue
    come blow your horn!
The sheep's in the meadow,
    the cow's in the corn.
Where's the little boy that
    looks after the sheep?
He's under the haystack,
    fast asleep!

Bo Peep by Mother Goose

Little Bo Peep, she lost her sheep
And didn't know where to find them.
Let them alone and they'll come home
Wagging their tails behind them.

Bats in the Belfry by Michele Gunther

1 bat was hanging in the belfry.
When a bat joined him, he did soar.
That made 2 bats, in the belfry,
Hanging upside-down, above the floor!

(repeat, 2 bats were hanging in the belfry
          3 bats were hanging in the belfry
          4 bats were hanging in the belfry
          last verse

5 bats were hanging in the belfry.
When the bells rang, they flew out the door.
That made 0 bats in the belfry,
Hanging upside-down, above the floor.

Dramatizations

The Three Bears/"Bone" Soup

Objective: To provide a few simple props and some space in your classroom to allow children to re-create a familiar story, and express themselves

Materials: 1. book - _The Three Bears_
             3 plastic or paper bowls and spoons
             3 chairs
             3 carpet squares (beds)

This porridge is <u>too hot</u>!

          2. book - _Stone Soup_ - Your students can adapt the story _Stone Soup_ to "Bone Soup." Provide a plastic bone, a mixing pot and spoon, and plastic vegetables. Or, this could go along with the cooking activity on page 29.

Directions: Be sure to read and re-read the story you are providing props for. Perhaps you'd like to put it on tape. Be specific and set limits for your drama corner.

Another great book for dramatization to illustrate the "B" sound is Bill Martin's book, _Brown Bear, Brown Bear, What Do You See?_

Band

Music

Activities: Ask your school band director's permission to have your class sit in on a band rehearsal. Attend a band concert. Create a rhythm band in your own classroom! Discuss which senses the children will utilize most. Ask the children to name as many instruments as they can.

Rhythms

Objective: To respond physically to music

Materials: piano, guitar, tape recorder, phonograph, etc.

Directions: Have children name animals, insects, vehicles, etc. that begin with "B." Then ask students appropriate questions such as: How does a bunny move? How does a buffalo move? How does a bird move? How does a bear move? How does a butterfly move? How does a bee move? How does a bus move?

Select and have music prepared to fit the movements of the animals, insects and vehicles (i.e. music that suggests hopping, flying, etc.).

The Wheels on the Bus

1. The wheels on the bus go round and round,
   Round and round, round and round,
   The wheels on the bus go round and round,
   All through the town.
   (Roll hands over each other.)
2. The doors on the bus go open and shut,
   Open and shut, open and shut,
   The doors on the bus go open and shut,
   All through the town.
   (Hold palms forward and turn hands out and in.)
3. The money on the bus goes clink, clink, clink,
   ("Twinkle" or flutter fingers on both hands like coins falling.)
4. The driver on the bus says, "Please move back."
   (Make "move to the rear" gesture.)
5. The windows on the bus go open and shut,
   (Move hands up, then down - or however the windows on the buses in your community move.)
6. The horn on the bus goes beep, beep, beep,
   (Pretend to beep the horn on each word "beep.")
7. The children on the bus go bump, bump, bump,
   (Bounce up and down as if on a bumpy ride.)
8. The daddy on the bus tips his hat,
   (Tip hat.)
9. The baby on the bus goes, "Wah, wah wah!"
   (Pretend to cry like a baby, wiping tears with fists.)
10. The mother on the bus goes, "Shh, shh, shh."
    (Put index finger to lips.)

Book List

Ancona, G. (1979). *It's a Baby!* New York: Dutton.

Barton, B. (1986). *Boats.* New York: Harper and Row.

Barton, B. (1973). *Buzz, Buzz, Buzz.* New York: Macmillan.

Berenstain, S. and Berenstain, J. (1971). *The B Book.* New York: Random House.

Berenstain, S. and Berenstain, J. (1987). *The Berenstain Bears on the Job.* New York: Random House.

Berenstain, S. (1964). *The Bike Lesson.* New York: Beginner Books.

Brown, M. (1962). *Benjy's Blanket.* New York: Franklin Watts.

Brown, M. (1989). *Big Red Barn.* New York: Harper and Row.

de Paola, T. (1979). *Big Anthony and the Magic Ring.* New York: Harcourt Brace Jovanovich.

Flack, M. (1958). *Ask Mr. Bear.* New York: Macmillan.

Freeman, D. (1977). *Beady Bear.* New York: Penquin Books.

Galdone, P. (1985). *Three Bears.* Ticknor & Fields.

Gans, R. (1971). *Bird Talk.* New York: Crowell.

Gibbons, G. (1983). *Boat Book.* New York: Holiday House.

Hoban, R. (1960). *Bedtime for Frances.* New York: Harper and Row.

Ipcar, D.Z. (1972). *The Biggest Fish in the Sea.* New York: Viking Press.

Kellogg, S. (1991). *Jack and the Beanstalk.* New York: Morrow Junior Books.

Lamorisse, A. (1957). *The Red Balloon.* Garden City, New York: Doubleday.

Lionni, L. (1959). *Little Blue and Little Yellow.* McDowell, Obolensky.

Marino, D. (1961). *Buzzy Bear Goes South.* New York: Franklin Watts.

Martin, Jr., B. (1983). *Brown Bear, Brown Bear.* New York: Henry Holt & Co.

Mayer, M. (1980). *Bubble Bubble.* New York: Macmillan.

McCloskey, R. (1977). *Blueberries for Sal.* New York: Viking Press.

Parish, P. (1963). *Amelia Bedelia.* New York: Harper and Row.

Rice, E. (1981). *Benny Bakes a Cake.* New York: Greenwillow Books.

Ueno, N. (1973). *Elephant Buttons.* New York: Harper and Row.

Vincent, G. (1985). *Breakfast Time, Ernest and Celestine.* New York: Greenwillow Books.

Wezel, P. (1964). *The Good Bird.* New York: Harper and Row.

Wildsmith, B. (1981). *Bear's Adventure.* New York: Pantheon Books.

Wildsmith, B. (1974). *The Lazy Bear.* New York: Franklin Watts.

Yektai, N. (1987). *Bears in Pairs.* New York: Bradbury Press.

Zolotow, C. (1960). *Big Brother.* New York: Harper and Row.

Table of Contents

*Remember to check **B Chapter Table of Contents** (page 4) for additional activities.

"Fold in Half" Cats

Art

Objective: To create a cat without patterns using one sheet of paper

Materials: 9" x 12" construction paper, crayons, scissors, paper fasteners

Directions:
- Fold a 9" x 12" piece of construction paper in half in either direction.
- At the open end, draw a half circle and cut it out. There will then be two half circles. (The folded paper will become the cat's body.)
- One of the half circles will become the head. (Draw eyes, nose, mouth and whiskers on it.)

- From the other half circle, the children will cut a curved tail and two triangular ears. Paste the ears onto the head.
- Draw paws, stripes, spots, etc. (Use black paper and white crayons for Halloween.)
- Assemble the head and tail using paper fasteners. Open the paper slightly and the cat will stand.

The size of the heads, ears and tails will vary depending on the size of the half circles.

Canary in a Cage

Materials: 9" x 12" sheets of construction paper (any color), 4" x 6" sheets of yellow construction paper, construction paper scraps, yarn (optional), crayons, scissors, stapler, staples

Directions: Cage: Fold a sheet of 9" x 12" construction paper in half down the long side and draw lines as shown.

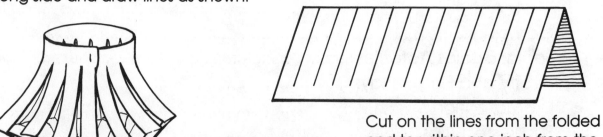

Cut on the lines from the folded end to within one inch from the edges. Open the paper and staple the ends together at the top and bottom to form a ring on the top and bottom.

Canary in a Cage continued

Art

Canary: On yellow construction paper (4" x 6"), draw and cut out one large and one small circle for the head and body of the canary. (The size should be appropriate for the cage size.)

Add a beak, wing and tail. Attach the bird to a "perch" cut from construction paper scraps. Slide the bird and the perch through the bars of the cage.

Add a handle made of construction paper scraps or yarn so that the children can carry their canary in a cage.

Creative Collage

Objective: To encourage individual creativity in art media

Materials: paste, construction paper, scissors, assorted materials such as scraps of colored construction paper, tissue paper, ribbons, corrugated paper, packaging materials, fabrics, etc.

Directions: Explain to the children that a collage is an art form. Model how to create various designs by cutting the scrap materials into the size and shape desired and pasting them on a piece of construction paper. (This is a good time to introduce the children to abstract art.) Explain that the finished product does not have to represent objects such as a house, tree, flower, person, etc. You might want to show the children works by Paul Klee, Georges Braque or Pablo Picasso.

Some children may be more comfortable with more conventional types of work. Model how to use the scrap materials to create houses, people, trees, flowers, cars, etc.

After the children have created several collages, encourage them to move away from a completely flat presentation. A house can have a door that opens. A bird can have wings that can be moved, etc. In the more abstract representation, folding, twisting and curling of the scraps can be used to create three-dimensional creative collages.

Suggested Reading:
Pezzetino by Leo Lionni

Class Cookbook

Materials: paper, pencils, book rings, construction paper

Directions: Discuss with the students what a recipe is. Using rebus pictures, write a simple recipe (such as cream cheese and crackers) on the board. Demonstrate how the recipe is followed. To create your classroom cookbook, you can:

1. Ask students to bring in a favorite recipe from home. The students can then illustrate the dish or some of the ingredients.

2. Ask students to write or dictate to you the directions of something they know how to make. Ask them what their favorite food is. Ask how they think it is made. Next, have students illustrate their pages.

Make a copy of each recipe for each student. Have him/her design a cover on construction paper. Bind recipes together with book rings.

"C" Word Caterpillar

Objective: To create a word caterpillar, using words beginning with "C"

Materials: pre-cut circles of various colors, pencils and markers

Directions: As a class, create a list of words beginning with "C." Have each child choose one of the words from the list. Give each child a pre-cut circle. Each child will write his/her "C" word on his/her circle in pencil. After the spelling has been checked, the student can trace over the word with a marker. Place the circles in a chain fashion to form a caterpillar's body. Create a face on a larger circle, add antennae and place it on the left side of the caterpillar's body to promote left to right progression.

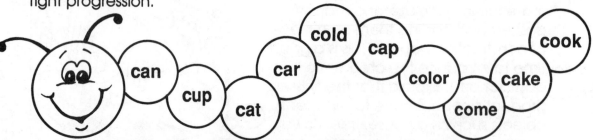

Author Study - Eric Carle

Activity: Refer to **Biography** (page 11).

Materials: books written by Eric Carle

Background: Eric Carle was born in the U.S., but lived in Germany for many years. He now lives in Massachusetts. He is married and has a daughter and a son. When illustrating, Mr. Carle cuts shapes out of paper to match the sketch he has created, and pastes them down with rubber cement.

Suggested Reading:

The Grouchy Ladybug　　　　　　*The Very Hungry Caterpillar*
The Mixed-Up Chameleon　　　　　*The Secret Birthday Message*
Do You Want To Be My Friend?　　　*Papa, Please Get the Moon for Me*

Clouds

Objective: To become familiar with three major types of clouds

Materials: 18" x 12" sheets of paper (oaktag if available), cotton balls, kosher salt, white paint, dryer lint or grey flannel, glue, crayons

Directions: Have students place the papers horizontally and divide into three equal parts by drawing two thick vertical lines. Demonstrate this on the chalkboard. Then, label the top of each section "cumulus," "stratus" and "cirrus" for the students to copy.

Students will create cumulus clouds at the top of the cumulus section of their paper by gluing on cotton balls. Under the clouds, have students illustrate what they could do on a day when cumulus clouds are present.

To create stratus clouds, mix white paint with the kosher salt. Have students paint the clouds in long streaks. (Discuss the presence of ice crystals in the clouds because of the clouds' height.) Again, students can illustrate under them.

To create cirrus clouds, have students glue dark dryer lint that you have collected or grey flannel. Have students illustrate under them.

Suggestion: Do not work on more than one type of cloud per day.

Suggested Reading:

It Looked Like Spilt Milk by Charles Shaw
The Cloud Book by Tomie de Paola
Cloudy With a Chance of Meatballs by Judi Barrett

Extension Activities:

1. Have students write and illustrate the following title on a poster: "If Clouds Rained _____ ."

2. Create "rain" in your classroom. Place ice cubes in a saucepan to represent a cloud. Place the saucepan over the steam of a boiling kettle of water. When steam hits the bottom of the cold pan it condenses and forms water droplets. When the droplets become too heavy, they drop to the ground. Rain!

Carrot Top Experiment

Science

Objective: To find out what will happen if a carrot top is put in water

Materials: two or more carrots, water, 2 dishes

Directions: Cut off the tops of two carrots. One should have some green sprouts, and one should not.

Place each top in a separate dish with enough water to just reach the top of the carrot.

What happens to a carrot top when placed in water?					
What happened to water level?					
DAY 1	2	3	4	5	6
7	8	9	10	11	12
What happened to each carrot?					
DAY 1	2	3	4	5	6
7	8	9	10	11	12

Record the changes on the chart daily:

What happened to the water level?

What happened to each carrot?

Variables can be added by placing one carrot in the sun and one in the closet.

Suggested Reading:

The Carrot Seed by Ruth Krauss

Conservation

Objective: To discuss the meaning of conservation and why it is important

To demonstrate the meaning of conservation

Materials: cup, pitcher, water, large sheet of paper, marker

What can we do to save water?

1. Take showers, not baths.
2. Put a brick in toilet tank.
3. Turn off water while brushing your teeth.

Directions: Explain to the students that conservation means saving by eliminating waste. Next, hold up the cup and a pitcher of water. Ask the students, "What would you do if you were thirsty?" After the students have responded, pour some water into the cup, allowing some to spill on the floor. Ask the students, "Can I drink the water off the floor?" (NO) The water on the floor is waste. Water has not been conserved. Next, make a class list that tells ways to conserve water and/or electricity. Be sure to discuss the importance of conserving our natural resources.

Color Graph
Math

Materials: poster-size graph paper, pre-cut cars in several colors, glue or tape

Directions: Discuss the purpose of a graph with the class. Show the children a prepared graph with each row designated by a different-colored car. One at a time, have children select a car in their favorite color and attach it with glue or tape to the graph in the corresponding row. After each child has had a turn, count the cars in each row to determine the most favorite and least favorite color. Note any ties.

Explain that color graphs may be used to survey many different color preferences. For example: favorite color of shoes, favorite color of house, favorite color of crayon

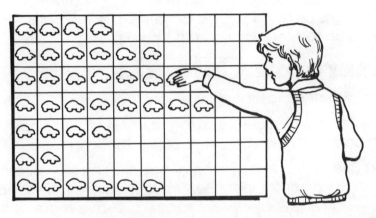

Clock

Objective: To make a clock

Materials: teaching clock, paper plates, paper fasteners, crayons, pre-cut paper clock hands, chalkboard

Directions: Draw a circle on the chalkboard. Model for the children where to put the "corner numerals." Write the numerals in this order: 12, 6, 3, 9. Then, show the children how to write the remaining numerals in their correct places.

Give paper plates to the children. Using crayons, have children write numerals in their proper positions as you just demonstrated. Then, help them attach pre-cut long and short hands to the center of the plate with paper fasteners, placing the longer hand on top.

Have the children demonstrate time by the hour individually using their clocks. Write verbal (ten, four) time and digital times on the board. Have students show the times on their clocks.

Suggested Reading: *The Grouchy Ladybug* by Eric Carle

Cookie Counting Book

Math

Materials: drawing paper, crayons, stapler, staples

Directions: On each sheet of paper, write a number from one to the number of children in your class. Children draw and decorate the correct number of cookies corresponding to the number on their page. Children may want to write the number word as well as the number. Have the children put the pages in numerical order. Add a cover and staple pages into a book.

To make the activity more fun, have children draw their favorite Cookie Monster on their page. Have some cookies on hand to pass around while the class is working on their cookie counting books!

Classroom Calendar

Objective: To count with the classroom calendar

Materials: large rectangular piece of oaktag or construction paper, 30/31 small squares of oaktag or construction paper, markers, masking tape

Directions: Make a grid on the large piece of paper using six vertical lines and four intersecting horizontal lines. Be sure to measure first so that the lines are equally spaced. Leave room at the top of the paper for the month and the days of the week. With markers, write the days of the week at the top of each vertical column. Above this, in very large letters, write the name of the month. You may want to decorate the top of the calendar with seasonal or holiday pictures. Hang or display the calendar grid so that the children can reach it.

With a black marker, write the numbers from 1 to 30/31 on small squares (or use the pattern below). Place them in a stack in numerical order. The calendar is now ready to help you teach the months of the year, the days of the week, numerical order, etc.

Select a different child each day to attach a numerical card to the calendar. Using a piece of masking tape, help the child put the numeral in the appropriate place. Help the child recognize the numeral and remember the day, the month and the year. Encourage all of the children to recite the numerals, in order, as you point to them.

When several weeks have been completed on the calendar, ask the class to tell you all the numbers that were Fridays in the month. Repeat the question, changing the days of the week. This is a great way to review numeral recognition and introduce children to a fun experience with a calendar.

Concentration

Materials: "C" pictures, oaktag, 6" x 9" index cards or construction paper

Directions: After a discussion of words that begin with the sound for "C," have students bring magazine pictures to school that begin with the sound for "C." Mount each picture on an index card and write the name of the object under each picture.

On another card, just write the name of the object. Start the game with about five pairs of cards. Turn them face down on the floor. The first child will turn over two cards. If they match, the cards are out of the game and the child scores two points. If they do not match, turn the cards face down again. Gradually increase the number of pairs in the game.

Cookie Jar

Objective: To reinforce the sound for "C" (This is a good activity for learning classmates' names.)

Directions: Students sit in a circle. Tell students that they are going to pretend that there is a cookie missing from an imaginary cookie jar. Tell the students that you will name someone in the class and say that they have eaten the cookie. Instruct the children to respond as follows:

> Stephen ate the cookie in the cookie jar.

Teacher:	William ate the cookie in the cookie jar.
William:	Who me?
All:	Yes, you!
William:	Couldn't be!
All:	Then who?
William:	Stephen ate the cookie in the cookie jar.

The game is repeated until all students have had a turn, or until time permits. Until the game becomes familiar, the teacher will need to supply the students with their "lines."

Community

Objective: To become familiar with the buildings/services that make up a community

Materials: shoe boxes, paint, scissors, mural paper

Directions: Lay the mural paper flat on a table or on the floor. Draw the main street(s) in your town (or make up your own), leaving enough room for "shoe box buildings." After a discussion or community walk, have students choose buildings in the community to create. (Some buildings to include may be the firehouse, police station, grocery store, school, park, city hall, etc. You may want students to work in pairs.) Students can paint the shoe boxes and add windows, doors, etc. Next, place each building on the mural paper accordingly.

Suggested Reading:

Dan, Dan the Flying Man by Gardiner and Elizabeth Fuller
Katy and the Big Snow by Virginia Lee Burton

Christopher Columbus

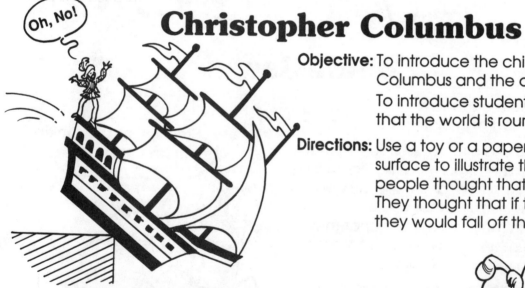

Oh, No!

Objective: To introduce the children to Christopher Columbus and the discovery of America

To introduce students to the concept that the world is round

Directions: Use a toy or a paper boat on a flat surface to illustrate that years ago, people thought that the world was flat. They thought that if they kept on sailing, they would fall off the end of the Earth.

Use a globe to illustrate to the children what Christopher Columbus wanted to do and how he "bumped" into America before he could get to the Indies.

Suggested Reading:

A Book About Christopher Columbus by Ruth Belov Gross

Suggested Art Activity:

See **Boats for Columbus Day** page 26.

Social Studies

Canada

Objective: To be introduced to large maps and the concept of our neighbor to the north

Materials: a large map that shows the U.S. and Canada

Directions: Begin the discussion by asking what city, state and country they live in. They will probably need help in understanding the difference. Find their city on the map, then their state and then identify the boundaries of the whole country.

Show them the country of Canada on the map. Say the word together. Write the sentence, "Canada is our northern neighbor." Tell the children that since they live in America, they are called Americans. Ask them what they think people from Canada are called. Say together: If I live in America, I am an American. If I live in Canada, I am a Canadian.

Caution

Objective: To understand the meaning and symbols for CAUTION

Materials: two traced 3" yellow or orange circles for each child, worksheet for each child, red crayons

Directions: Discuss with students the fact that they may come across areas that could be dangerous, and that the way they are warned is with the word CAUTION. Write the word on the board. Discuss it's meaning. Ask students if they could name times or places when they may see this word. Next, show them the symbol for caution. Again, discuss where you may find this symbol (i.e. on a traffic light, at a construction site, near a public floor that has just been washed, near a damaged sidewalk, etc.). Discuss what children should do when they see the sign/symbol.

Create a "caution horse." Use the worksheet. Cut out the circles. Glue two to each end of the sawhorse. Place stripes on the sawhorse with a red crayon. Trace the word CAUTION at the top of the page.

Extension Activity:
Dramatize a situation in your classroom in which a caution sign or symbol would be needed (a wet floor, a broken chair, wet paint, etc.). Place the sign, symbol, or both in the area in which it is needed.

CAUTION

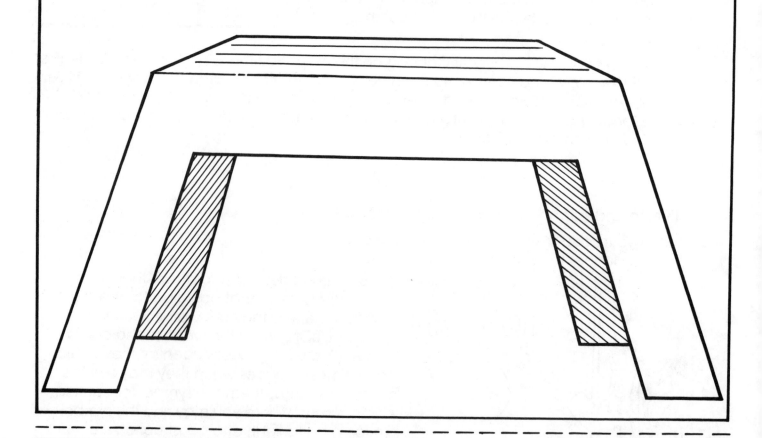

yellow

Be Careful!

yellow

Finger Play

Poetry

Cats-A-Counting

One little cat looking for some milk
Her fur is smooth, smooth as silk. (Stroke hand.)

Two little cats on the run. (Run two fingers.)
They are looking for some fun.

Three little cats walking into town.
    (Walk three fingers.)
Two are striped and one is brown.

Four little cats and a fifth one too,
They are out looking for you and you and you.
    (Point to children.)

by Ada Frischer

Suggested Reading:
    Poems - "The Owl and the
    Pussy Cat" by Edward Lear
    - "Pussy Cat Pussy Cat
    Where Have You Been"

Caps For Sale

Dramatization

Objective and Directions:
    Refer to **Dramatizations** page 30.

Materials: book - *Caps for Sale* by Slobodkina,
    several Frisbees

Frisbees stack very well and can make
excellent caps and promote balance as well!

Community Walk

Suggested Trips

Objective: To walk around the community
    and make a class book about
    the experience

Directions: See **A "B" Field Trip** (page 15) activity
    4, Variation on a Class Trip Book.

Suggested Reading:
    *And To Think That I Saw It on
    Mulberry St.* by Dr. Seuss.
    Willie's Walk by Margaret Wise Brown
    Dan, the Flying Man by Gardiner
    and Elizabeth Fuller

45

"No Cook" Candy

Cooking

1. Wash ✋🤚 .

2. Mix 2 🥄🥄 of 🥫 peanut butter
   and 1 🥄 of 🍯 honey.

3. Add 2 🥄🥄 of 📦 powdered milk.

4. Mix in 10 🍇 raisins.

5. Roll into ⚪⚪⚪ balls.

6. Roll in 🍪 graham cracker crumbs.

7. Look 👁️ 👁️ smell 👃 taste 👄 .

Note: You can make your own graham cracker crumbs. Just put crackers in a plastic bag and have children use a rolling pin to make the crumbs.

This is an individual recipe for each child.

Corn Muffins

1 cup yellow cornmeal
1 cup flour
1/4 cup sugar
4 teaspoons baking powder
1/2 teaspoon salt
1 cup milk
1 egg
1/4 cup melted butter, margarine or vegetable oil

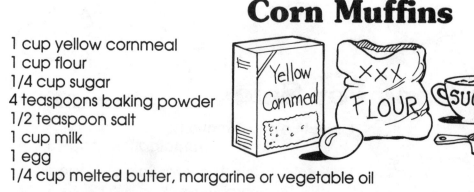

Mix dry ingredients. Add liquid ingredients and mix for one minute until fairly smooth.
Put in cupcake papers in muffin tins. Bake at 425 degrees for 20 to 25 minutes.

Carrot Salad

Grate carrots. Add crushed, canned
pineapple to taste. Add raisins and
some vanilla yogurt to moisten.

Cocoa

Add cocoa to hot tap water
and mix with sugar.

Carrot and Cabbage Cole Slaw

Grate carrots and cabbage. Add Italian or French dressing or cole slaw dressing.

C Pictures for Miscellaneous Activities

Enlarge the cards to make flash cards throughout the study of the "C" sound.

Book List

Bridwell, N. *Clifford.* (series) New York: Scholastic.

Carle, E. (1973). *Have You Seen My Cat?* New York: Franklin Watts.

Carle, E. (1988). *The Mixed-Up Chameleon.* New York: Harper and Row.

Carle, E. (1976). *The Very Hungry Caterpillar.* Cleveland, OH: Collins + World.

de Paola, T. (1975). *The Cloud Book.* New York: Holiday House.

Freeman, D. (1982). *Corduroy.* Somers, New York: Live Oak Media.

Gag, W. (1928). *Millions of Cats.* New York: Coward McCann.

Gray, W. (1976). *Camping Adventure.* Washington, D.C.: National Geographic Society - series.

Green, C. (1983). *Hi, Clouds.* Chicago, IL: Childrens Press.

Krauss, R. (1945). *The Carrot Seed.* New York: Harper and Brothers.

Numeroff, L.J. (1985). *If You Give a Mouse a Cookie.* New York: Harper and Row.

Rey, H.A. (1973). *Curious George.* Boston, Massachusetts: Houghton Mifflin.

Seuss, Dr. (1985). *The Cat in the Hat.* New York: Random House.

Slobodkina, E. (1947). *Caps for Sale.* New York: Scholastic.

Dd

Table of Contents

*Remember to check **B Chapter Table of Contents** (page 4) for additional activities.

Dandy Dog

Art

Materials: construction paper, crayons, scissors, two paper fasteners per student, stapler, staples

Directions: 1. Give the children two large pre-cut triangles for the body. Staple them together down the center. Fold the back triangle so the body will stand.

2. Have the children draw and cut an oval for the face. Staple the face to the front part of the body.

3. The children will then draw and cut out one floppy ear on folded paper. This will create two ears that are identical. Then, they attach the ears to the face with paper fasteners so they can move.

4. On folded paper, have the children draw two tops of a "tree" for paws and cut them out. This will create four paws. Staple two of the paws to the bottom of the triangle and fold them up to help the dog stand up.

5. Attach the other two paws below the head with paper fasteners.

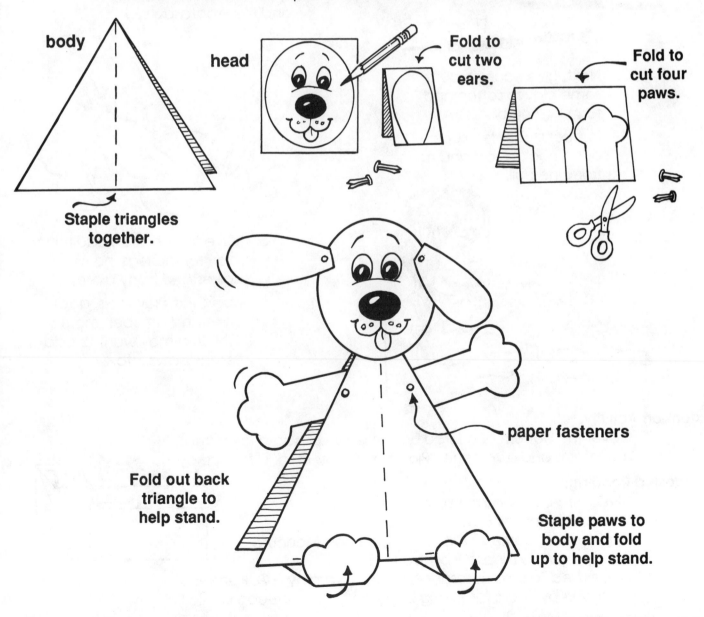

body

Staple triangles together.

head

Fold to cut two ears.

Fold to cut four paws.

paper fasteners

Fold out back triangle to help stand.

Staple paws to body and fold up to help stand.

Dinosaurs

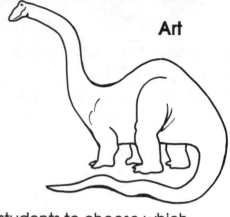

Art

Materials: clay (assorted colors), clay tools or toothpicks, plastic dinosaur models or pictures

Directions: 1. After reading and discussing dinosaur books, explain to students that they will create their own dinosaur from clay. Display the plastic models or pictures.

2. Ask students to choose which dinosaur they would like to create. (Distinctive dinosaurs that turn out well are the Stegosaurus, Tyrannosaurus Rex, Anklyosaurus and the Apatasaurus.)

3. Next, give each student some clay to soften and form into a ball.

4. Instruct students to pinch out a neck, head and tail from the ball.

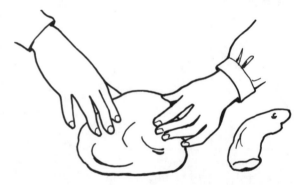

5. Give the children additional clay for the legs, horns, spikes and bony plates.

6. Using the clay tools, add eyes and an open mouth. Children may want to add teeth, claws, etc.

Extension Activity:
Cover the bottom of a large box with sand. Add a lake, trees, mountains and a volcano. Place dinosaurs in sand for display.

Suggested Reading:
My Visit to the Dinosaurs by Aliki
Dinosaur Mania by Edward Radlauer
If a Dinosaur Came to Dinner by Jane Belk Moncure
Danny and the Dinosaur by Syd Hoff
There Used To Be a Dinosaur in My Backyard by B.G. Hennessy
Dinosaurs by Books for Young Explorers National Geographic Society

Design

Art

Objective: To create an abstract design

Materials: construction paper, crayons or markers, white paper

Directions: Tell students that they are going to create a design using curved lines. Each design will be very different and distinct - an original creation - although all will start out with the same directions.

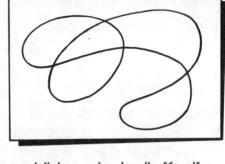

To have children physically "feel" a curved line, have the class line up single file and follow you around the tables and around the desks and chairs. Be sure to curve the line of children as you lead - no sharp corners or angles! Next, have one volunteer walk his/her own curved design by himself. Then, have another child also take a turn walking in curves. Point out that although both children are following the same type of directions, their design paths are different.

Have the class watch as you model a curved design. Using crayon or marker, draw a continuous curved line on the paper allowing the line to intersect and overlap to form a design. (See illustration.)

When finished, connect the end of the design to the beginning. This will close your design. Now the fun of coloring begins! The only rule is that no two connecting shapes may be colored the same color.

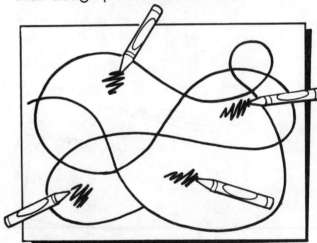

Encourage the children to use many different colors and to place them in a way that is pleasing to themselves. Some children may want to close their eyes when drawing their designs. They may even surprise themselves!

This is a nice activity for the beginning of the year. Mounted on black construction paper and displayed in the classroom, these designs help the children feel a great sense of pride and accomplishment.

51

Dictionaries

Objective: To create personal and/or class dictionaries

Materials: Personal dictionaries - 26 sheets of paper for each student, 2 sheets of construction paper for each student, book rings or bindery

Class dictionary - 40 sheets of paper, 2 sheets of construction paper, book rings or bindery

Directions: Introduce a dictionary to the students. Explain that a dictionary helps us spell. Have students discover how words are organized alphabetically. Next, give each student 26 sheets of paper. Instruct students to write each letter of the alphabet at the top of each page and organize the pages into alphabetical order. Then, supply students with construction paper. Have them write "My Dictionary" on the paper, and illustrate if desired. Bind or staple each book.

As students ask you to spell words for them (for example, during writing assignments, spelling assignments, etc.) you can:

1. Have the students bring their book to you already open to the letter page their word begins with. You then write the word on the page.

2. Supply the students with the spelling and have the students write it in their books.

3. Have the students look up the word in a dictionary and then add the word to their personal dictionary.

A class dictionary can be created the same way the personal dictionaries were made. Words can be added that are frequently used. New sight words, or words pertaining to a particular theme unit you are focusing on, can also be added.

Note: A notebook could replace the student-made book.

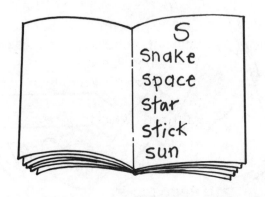

Author Study - Tomie de Paola

Objective and Directions: Refer to **Biography** page 11.

Materials: books written by Tomie de Paola

Background: Tomie de Paola has written over 200 books. Every year, he writes a Christmas book because he loves Christmas so much! He has always wanted to be an artist. He lives in New Hampshire.

Helga's Dowry   *The Art Lesson*   *Big Anthony and the Magic Ring*
Strega Nona   *Charlie Needs a Cloak*

Dinosaur Big Book

Materials: large sheets of construction paper, markers, notebook rings, dinosaur names on cards, container

Directions: Pair each child with a partner. Have each pair select a card with a dinosaur name from a container. This will be their very own dinosaur to describe and illustrate. Working together, the pairs will blend their talents and skills to design at least one page of the book. When completed, bind the big book with notebook rings.

You could also use this method to create a class book about dogs.

Tyrannosaurus Rex

Triceratops

Suggested Reading:
Refer to **Dinosaurs** page 50.

Science

Decompose

Objective: To expose children to some materials that decompose, and to create an awareness that some materials do not decompose

Materials: plastic objects (straw, utensil), vegetable or fruit (Lettuce leaf works well.), rock, a paper item (plate, napkin), soil, paper, pen or pencil, potting containers (optional)

Directions: In potting containers, or outdoors, bury all four types of items separately. Allow two (or more) weeks to pass*, then dig up all four items. Discuss what you have found. Make a chart listing the biodegradable materials. To extend the lesson, before lunch or snack time, have the children remove the biodegradable materials from their lunch boxes and place them in front of them. Add the materials to your list.

Does It Decompose?	
YES	NO
lettuce	rock
apple	wash cloth
banana peel	plastic straw
bread	ribbon
pickle	button
leaf	shoe string
tissue	plastic bag
	eraser

*To incorporate math, mark the "dig-up" day on your calendar. Keep a daily tally of the number of days before "dig-up" day.

Suggested Reading:
It Was Just a Dream by Chris Van Allsburg

Dot-to-Dot

Math

Objective: To design a cover for a book using the dot-to-dot technique

Materials: white construction paper, crayons

Directions: Have children place ten dots in a random fashion on the paper. Have children number their dots and then connect the dots in numerical order. If the design is open, close it. A design will appear. Have the children color the individual sections of the design with different crayons.

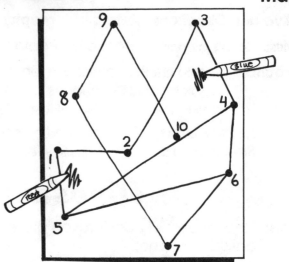

Daisy Counting Chart

Objective: To show "one more" and illustrate numerical order

Materials: graph paper with large boxes, crayons

Directions: Have children draw the center of one daisy with one petal in the upper left hand box. Next, have children draw the center of two daisies in the second row. Each daisy in the second row should have two petals. Continue with three daisy centers with three petals each in the third row, etc. Emphasize the concept of "one more" as the children complete the graphs.

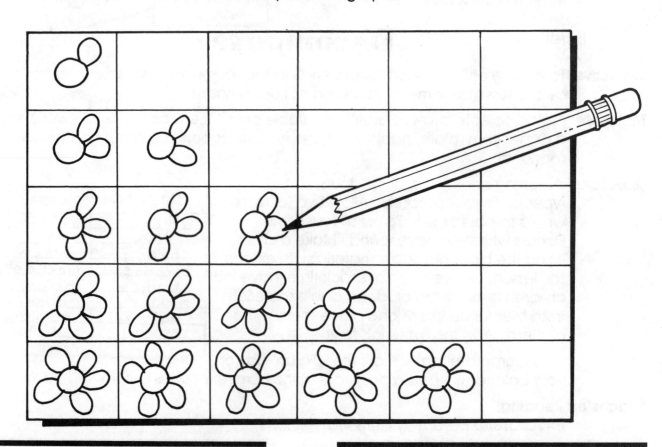

54

Dial 911

Social Studies

Objective: To become familiar with how to use the phone to obtain help

Materials: 2 toy phones, construction paper, red markers, pencils

Directions: Discuss what an emergency is and how the students can obtain help by dialing 911. Using the phones, role-play an emergency phone call several times with a student acting as the individual in need of help and you acting as the dispatcher. Request the necessary information from the student (i.e. name, address, problem). Cut out the phone pattern below and trace around it on construction paper for each student. With the red marker, have each student write "911." On the back of the phone, have each student write or dictate his/her full name and address. Instruct the children to take the paper phone home and hang it near their own phone in case of an emergency.

Doctor/Dentist

Social Studies

Objective: To become familiar with the roles of the doctor and the dentist

Materials: copies of the chart below

Directions: Discuss the roles of the doctor and/or dentist - what they do, why people go to them and how they help people. This is also a good opportunity to stress good health habits and the care of teeth. Involve parents by sending home a "tooth brushing chart" at the beginning of each month (with an accompanying explanatory letter). At the end of the month, if all the children have brought their charts back to school properly checked, you might want to have a special class celebration for "D" Day - (Dental Health Day). Invite a doctor and a dentist or a dental hygienist to visit the class. Have the dental hygienist demonstrate proper brushing techniques.

Suggested Reading:

Dr. DeSoto by William Steig
I Can Be a Doctor by Rebecca Hankin
I Can Be a Dentist by Ray Broekel
Curious George Goes to the Hospital by H.A. Rey

I brushed my teeth today!

S	M	T	W	Th	F	S

Dominoes

Use dominoes to match and count numbers.

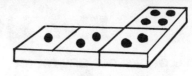

Games

Duck, Duck, Goose

Variations of this game can be played by asking children to think of other animals that begin with the sound for "D."

dog, dog, CAT!

    i.e. dog, dog, cat
           donkey, donkey, horse
           deer, deer, goat
           dromedary, dromedary, camel
           dinosaur, dinosaur, elephant
           dormouse, dormouse, chipmunk
           Dalmation, Dalmation, poodle

The child who is tapped with the animal name that does not begin with the sound for "D" is the one who must get up and chase the "tapper" around the circle.

Dinner at the Diner

This is a game of progression and memory. One child starts and says, "I had dinner at the diner, and I had a hot dog." (Each child selects his/her own food.) The next child continues, "I had dinner at the diner, and I had a hot dog and string beans." The game continues as long as someone remembers the entire progression.

A Delicious, Delightful Dessert

Cooking

Melt semi-sweet chocolate chips. Dip slices of banana and whole strawberries into the melted chocolate. Put them on waxed paper to cool and solidify. Enjoy!

Doughnuts

Materials: tube of biscuits, oil, sugar, cinnamon, electric fry pan, paper towels

Directions: Separate the biscuits. Roll and reshape each one into a circle. Fry in oil in an electric fry pan until brown. Drain on paper towels. Sprinkle with either confectioners sugar or a sugar and cinnamon mixture.

Poetry

Five Little Ducks

There were five little ducks, not any more.
One swam away, and then there were four.

There were four little ducks nesting near the tree.
One swam away, and then there were three.

The three little ducks looked at the sky so blue.
One swam away, and then there were two.

Those two little ducks were looking for some fun.
One swam away, and then there was one.

That one little duck who was swimming all alone,
He looked up and said, "Where have all the others gone?"

by Ada Frischer

If a Dinosaur Came to Dinner

Dramatization

Objective and Directions:
Refer to **Dramatizations** page 30.

Materials: book - *If a Dinosaur Came to Dinner* by Jane Belk Moncure, bowl and spoon, dandelions, plastic/paper yellow flowers, doughnuts, plastic/paper rings, dinosaur figures, toy boat

Music

Drum Activities

1. Play a march such as "Yankee Doodle" on a piano or use a tape to record. Have one or two children beat the rhythm on a drum. The rest of the class can clap or march to the rhythm.

2. Say each child's name in a syllable pattern. Have each child beat the rhythm of his/her name on the drum.

   i.e. Steph a nie   Rich ard son

Suggested Trips

• Have a doctor and/or dentist visit the classroom or arrange for your class to visit them.

• Dinosaur exhibit (if available)

• Dairy farm

Museum of Natural History

D Pictures for Miscellaneous Activities

Enlarge the cards to make flash cards throughout the study of the "D" sound.

Book List

Aliki. (1981). *Digging Up Dinosaurs.* New York: Harper and Row.

Berenstain, S. and Berenstain, J. (1987). *The Berenstain Bears Go to the Doctor.* New York: Random House.

Berenstain, S. and Berenstain, J. (1981). *The Berenstain Bears Visit the Dentist.* New York: Random House.

Freeman, D. (1977). *Dandelions.* Penguin Books.

Hankin, R. (1985). *I Can Be a Doctor.* Chicago, Illinois: Childrens Press.

Hoban, T. (1977). *Dig, Drill, Dump, Fill.* New York: Greenwillow Books.

Hoff, S. (1978). *Danny and the Dinosaur.* New York: Harper and Row.

Mayer, M. (1977). *Just Me and My Dad.* Western Publishing.

McCloskey, R. (1976). *Make Way for Ducklings.* New York: Penguin Books.

Most, B. (1984). *What Ever Happened to the Dinosaurs?* New York: Harcourt Brace Jovanovich.

Wildsmith, B. (1984). *Daisy.* New York: Pantheon Books.

Zion, G. (1956). *Harry the Dirty Dog .* New York: Harper and Row.

Table of Contents

*Remember to check **B Chapter Table of Contents** (page 4) for additional activities.

Fall Trees

Art

Objective: To create fall trees and colors using fingerprints and paint

Materials: smocks, cray-pas or crayons, light-colored construction paper, five shallow cups of paint (red, orange, yellow, brown and green)

Directions: 1. Using brown cray-pas or brown crayons, have children draw and color a deciduous tree, trunk and branches without leaves.

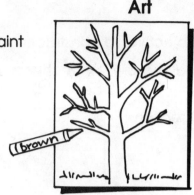

2. Set up a table with the five cups of paint. Working with five children at a time, have each child stand in front of one color of paint. Starting with the pinky finger, have each child dip his/her finger into the paint in front of him/her and "paint" leaves on and around his/her tree.

3. When enough leaves of this color have been painted, help the child pick up his/her paper with his/her clean hand and move to the next color in line.

4. Using his/her ring finger, the child now paints leaves in a second color.

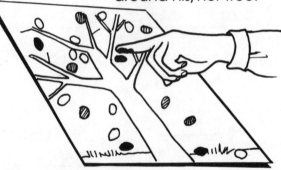

5. When this color is finished, move the child to the third paint cup and switch to the middle finger.

6. Continue in this manner until all five colors and all fingers have been used.

Some "leaves" may already have "fallen" to the ground. Others are still attached to the branches, and still others appear to be blowing in the wind. This is a good time to discuss fall, including the leaves and fall colors.

61

Fire Trucks

Art

Objective: To construct a fire truck in connection with lessons about fire safety

Materials: 12" x 18" sheets of red construction paper, black pre-cut circles for wheels (2 per child), crayons, paper fasteners (3 per child), scissors

Directions:

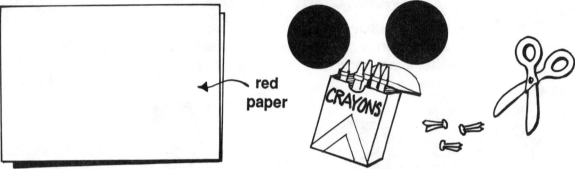

red paper

1. Fold large, red construction paper in half the long way to form a 6" x 18" rectangle.

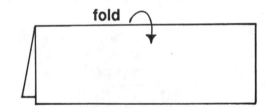

fold

2. Cut a rectangle from the folded side to form a ladder.

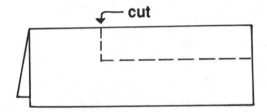

cut

3. The remainder of the paper becomes the truck.

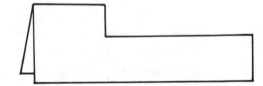

4. Slip the two circles in between the open end of the truck and attach them with paper fasteners.

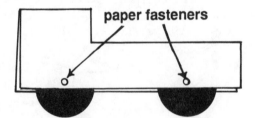

paper fasteners

5. Draw lines on the small, cut rectangle to resemble a ladder. Attach the ladder to the back of the cab with a paper fastener so that it will move.

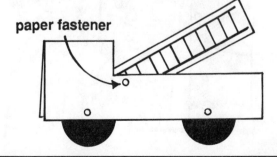

paper fastener

6. Add windows, doors, a bell, an axe and some letters (F.D.).

62

Free Form Flowers

Art

Objective: To design flowers

Materials: green construction paper, construction paper scraps (all colors), scissors, pencils, paste

Directions: Using the green construction paper, model for the children how to cut out a stem and draw and cut out leaves. Paste the leaves onto the stem.

Using the colored construction paper scraps, have the children design their own flowers.

Have students:

- Cut a circle for the center.
- Cut separate petals and paste them onto the flower center.
- Cut a shape like a tulip.
- Design other flower shapes.

Paper Plate Fish

Objective: To create a fish from a paper plate and to become familiar with characteristics of a fish (gills, fins, scales, etc.)

Materials: a paper plate for each student, scissors, pencils, three 2" x 1" strips of paper for each student, glue, hole punch, yarn, crayons

Directions: Give each child a paper plate and instruct him/her to:

1. Create the mouth of the fish by drawing two lines to create a "piece of pie." Next, they will cut the "pie piece" out and glue it to the opposite side of the plate to create a tail.

2. With their crayons, the students can add scales by drawing rows of upside-down "V's".

3. Give each student three strips of paper. They will glue them on the body of the fish to create gills.

4. Next, students can add an eye, fins and color their fish.

5. If desired, punch a hole and thread yarn through it so the fish can be hung.

Note: It is helpful to model these steps for the students.

Suggested Reading:

The Biggest Fish in the Sea by Dahlov Ipcar   *Swimmy* by Leo Lionni
A Fish Out of Water by P.D. Eastman   *Fish Is Fish* by Leo Lionni

My Feelings Book

Writing/ Reading

Objective: To write and illustrate a book about feelings

Materials: 5 sheets of white paper for each child, crayons or markers, a copy of the sentence strips below for each student

Directions: After reading and discussing books that relate to particular feelings (See Suggested Reading below.), have students complete the sentence strips at the bottom of the page. Then, have the students cut out the strips and glue each one on a separate piece of paper.

Next, have each student illustrate his/her feelings. For an attractive cover, divide a sheet of paper into four sections. Draw a circle in each box to represent a face. Students can draw and label expressive faces in each section (sad, happy, etc.).

Suggested Reading:

Books that deal with happy emotions:
The Happy Day by Ruth Krauss
Happiness is Smiling by Katharine Gehm

Books that deal with sad emotions:
The Cow Who Said Oink by Bernard Most
Little Blue and Little Yellow by Leo Lionni
Sylvester and the Magic Pebble
by William Steig

Books that deal with frightening emotions:
What Mary Jo Shared by Janice May Udry
Lost in a Museum by Miriam Cohen
What Was I Scared Of? by Dr. Seuss

Books that deal with angry emotions:
I Was So Mad! by Norma Simon
Nobody Listens to Andrew by Eli Guilfoile
Alexander and the Terrible Horrible No Good Very Bad Day by Judith Viorst

I am happy when _____ .

I am sad when _____ .

I am frightened when _____ .

I am angry when _____ .

My Family Book

Objective : To write and illustrate a book about families

Materials: seven 9" x 12" sheets of white paper for each student, crayons, glue, copy of sentence strips below for each student, book rings, bindery or stapler

Directions: Discuss families and the various make-up of families. (See **Families** page 76.) Ask volunteers to discuss the members and make-up of their families. Next, tell students they will make a family book. Make copies of the family book sentence strips below. Cut them apart. Have students fill in, or take dictation, to complete the first strip. Students then glue the strip to the bottom of the white sheet of paper.

Students will then illustrate their families. Proceed with the second, third, fourth and fifth strips in the same manner. Have students design a front cover. Add a sheet for a back cover. Bind, staple or use book rings to fasten pages.

Family Book Sentence Strips

There are _____ people in my house.

This is our house.

When we're together, we like to _____
_____ .

I help my family when I _____ .

My family helps me when _____ .

I Like My Friend Because . . .

Materials: paper, crayons/markers

Directions: Discuss what "friend" means with the class. Why do you like your friend? What does your best friend do that you like? Why do you think your friend likes you? Get several different responses from the children. Give each child a paper that says, "I like my friend because . . ."

At this point, get a secret response from each child. Take the dictation from the children and have them illustrate their responses. When everyone has completed the task, celebrate each child's work.

Follow the same procedure with "My friend likes me because . . ."

The discussion can be expanded to include "How to be a good friend."

Forms of Literature

Objective: To introduce children to several forms of literature: fiction, non-fiction, fables, fairy tales

Materials: large chart paper, markers

Directions: Line the chart paper leaving a large space for the title of a book, and four boxes after the title space. Label each column: fiction, non-fiction, fables, fairy tales.

Title	fiction	non-fiction	fable	fairy tale
Snow White				√

Discuss each of these forms of writing. Select several books that represent each area. After reading a book, help the children decide in which category to record the type of book. Keep a running list of all books shared and complete the chart as books are read to the class.

Some stories will belong to more than one category.

Fall Season

Science

Objective: To help children become aware of the change of the summer season to fall

Materials: crayons, 9" x 12" sheets of oaktag, green construction paper, stapler

Directions: Discuss the change of the season to fall as it relates to the leaves. Explain how leaves change color. Because the weather is colder, the trees no longer need the leaves to produce food. When the chlorophyll disappears, the beautiful colors of the sugars and starches appear.

1. To make a model of this occurrence, give the children a piece of oaktag. Have them color it with the beautiful colors of fall: orange, red, yellow and brown. They should blend in these colors and cover the entire sheet.

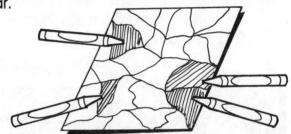

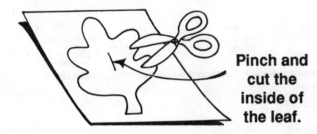

Pinch and cut the inside of the leaf.

2. Next, have children cut a leaf outline from a worksheet of a large leaf. (You can either make this worksheet or use a pattern on page 130.)

3. Have the children pinch the leaf in the middle and make a snip big enough for the scissors to fit in.

4. Cut around the inside of the leaf outline, being sure never to cut through the edge of the paper.

5. Discard the cutout center and staple the sheet with the leaf outline to the colored oaktag, leaving the stem side open. The leaf will appear to have beautiful fall colors. Refer to these colors as the sugars and the starches.

6. Cut the green construction paper so that it fits inside and behind the leaf outline. Refer to this green paper as the chlorophyll.

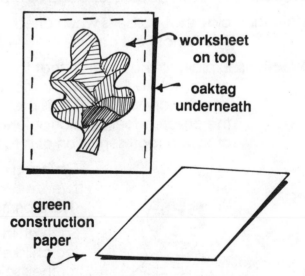

worksheet on top

oaktag underneath

green construction paper

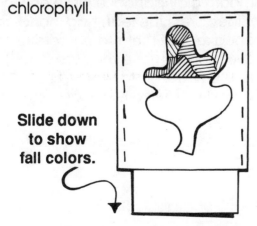

Slide down to show fall colors.

7. Have the children slowly slide their chlorophyll (green paper) as you repeat the story of how leaves change color and trees get ready for winter. Refer to the beautiful colors of fall as the sugars and starches that were there all along. It's as if the leaf were wearing a mask of chlorophyll all summer long, waiting for the cooler temperatures of fall to show its beautiful colors!

Forests

Objective: To become aware of how animals need forests and the effects on these animals when forests are cut down

Materials: mural paper, assorted paints, brushes, smocks, black marker

Directions: • Discuss what animals live in a forest. Divide the mural paper in half by drawing a thick black vertical line down the center. On the first half of the paper, have students paint a forest. (Be sure students include birds, insects, rabbits, deer, beavers, bears, fox, snakes, etc.)

• On the second half of the mural paper, instruct students to paint tree stumps. Discuss what would happen to all the living creatures included in the first half.

Fossils

Objective: To learn about fossils and to create a "fossil"

Materials: clay that hardens when dried, leaves, twigs, ferns, bones, shells, tweezers (Plaster of Paris can be used in place of clay.)

Directions: Explain to the children that fossils are relics of the past. They are remains of plant or animal life that have hardened and are preserved in rock. Introduce vocabulary words such as prehistoric, archaeologist and paleontologist. When the children feel comfortable with these terms, explain that you are going to create a representation of a fossil. Discuss why you cannot create a real one.

Gather a collection of things that you want to use. Include tweezers, various leaf varieties, ferns, twigs, shells, bones, etc. (Handprints and footprints can also be used.)

Each child will select an item to make into a fossil. Instruct the children to form a smooth clay pancake large enough for their selection. Then, they press the leaf, twig, hand or foot, etc. on the clay pancake. Tell them to be careful not to leave fingerprints. Have them remove the item from the clay. (You might want to use tweezers to remove the object from the clay.) Let the clay dry or bake it in a kiln. Paint if desired.

You could display the fossils in conjunction with a theme unit on dinosaurs.

Suggested Reading:
Dinosaurs by Books for Young Explorers National Geographic Society

Farm Animals

Science

Objective: To help children recognize common farm animals and make farm animal sounds

Materials: opaque projector, oaktag, markers, scissors, cards below

Directions: To make farm animal flashcards, cut out the animal pictures below on the dotted lines. Use an overhead projector to enlarge them on oaktag. Color them with markers.

Hold each card up and ask the children to name the animal. Then have the children make the appropriate animal sounds. Sing "Old MacDonald Had a Farm" and read *On the Farm* by Richard Scarry.

Baby Farm Animals
Science

Objective: To help children recognize baby farm animals and their names
To help children recognize farm products

Materials: colored index cards, crayons, pictures of adult farm animals, pictures of baby farm animals, pictures of farm animal products, paste

Directions: Make a concentration game for the children by pasting pictures of baby farm animals and their matching words on the back of index cards. Several different games may be designed. (Use different-colored index cards for each game.)

1. identical baby farm animal matched to identical baby farm animal
2. adult farm animal matched to offspring (Use the pictures from page 69.)
3. baby farm animal picture matched to baby farm animal word
4. adult farm animal matched to product

Other suggestions: duck - duckling - eggs; hen - chick - eggs; cow - calf - milk; sheep - lamb - wool; goat - kid - milk, cheese; goose - gosling - down; pig - piglet - pork; horse - foal - love; dog - puppy - love

Favorite Fruit Graph

Math

Objective: To create a bar graph

Materials: fruits, crayons, graph paper (Make your own using 1/2 inch squares.)

Directions: Have each child bring one favorite fruit to school. List all the fruits that have been brought to school on the graph paper and have each child record his/her own choice by coloring in a square next to his/her fruit choice. Tally the children's choices.

🍎 apple	▨								1
🍌 banana	▨	▨	▨						3
🍐 pear	▨	▨							2
🍊 orange	▨								1

Write a math story such as:

We brought our favorite fruits to school. We recorded our fruits on a graph, and this is what we found out. Most of the children liked bananas the best. The same number of children like apples and oranges. Three children liked bananas. Two children like pears.

After the graph is completed, use the fruit to make a fruit salad (See Cooking, page 73.) and to discuss good nutrition. (See **Nutrition Category Game** page 161.)

Fold into Fourths

Objective: To learn the concept of fourths

Materials: 8 1/2" x 11" drawing paper, crayons

Directions: Show the children the proper way to fold. Remind them to match the corners and then use their hands to crease the folds.

First they fold into halves, then into fourths. Direct them to draw one "F" object in each fourth.

Extension Activity: Give children another piece of paper to fold into fourths. Have them draw a food that begins with "F" in each fourth.

71

Fish in the Net

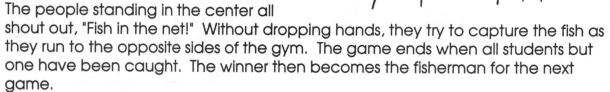

Materials: gym or large area

Directions: Line the class up at one end of the gym. Tell the students that they are now fish. You stand in the middle of the gym. You are the fisherman. To play the game, the fisherman calls out, "Fish in the net!" The students must then run across the gym to the other side without being tagged by you (fisherman). Any students tagged join hands with you and become part of the fisherman's net. The people standing in the center all shout out, "Fish in the net!" Without dropping hands, they try to capture the fish as they run to the opposite sides of the gym. The game ends when all students but one have been caught. The winner then becomes the fisherman for the next game.

Follow the Leader

Materials: gym or large area

Directions: Talk about the importance of feet. Talk about the different ways people can move their feet. Let children take turns showing different ways to move their feet. Then, play "Follow the Leader." Have children take turns being the leader.

As a rest time afterward to quiet the children, read *The Foot Book* by Dr. Seuss.

Find What's Missing!

Objective: To practice observation skills

Materials: tray, a variety of "F" objects, newsprint, pencil

Directions: Place a variety of "F" objects on a tray or cookie sheet. Show the children the tray of objects. Walk around the room with them so the children have plenty of opportunity to see the objects. Tell them to look very closely to try to remember what they see. Then, remove the tray of objects from their view. Have them draw pictures of as many objects as they can remember.

Fruit Salad

Make a fruit salad using the fruits that were brought in for the **Favorite Fruit Graph**, page 71.

Cooking

Fudge

Melt one large bag of chocolate bits in a double boiler.

Add - 1 can condensed milk - sweetened
      1 teaspoon vanilla
      chopped nuts

Pour into a pan over waxed paper and let cool. Cut into squares.

Fun Fish Food

If possible, take your class to visit the seafood counter in your local grocery store. Arrange with the person in charge to have him/her talk to the children about the various kinds of fish and show them examples of freshwater fish, saltwater fish, shellfish, etc. Perhaps there will even be a live lobster tank.

Have the store steam some fish so the children can try a sample.

If you cannot walk to a store, bring a can of tuna, some raw shrimp and some cooked shrimp to class. Show the children how the shrimp changes colors after it is cooked.

Let them sample the tuna using plastic forks, always bringing their attention to the "F" words. Give the students three plastic forks each so they can form the letter "F".

As an extension activity, let them try to make other letters of the alphabet.

is for fork.

73

American Flag

Social Studies

Objective: To introduce the children to the significance of the American flag and to create one

Materials: paste, white crayons and for each child the following:

1 sheet of 9" x 12" white construction paper - Put an X in the top left quadrant.
3 strips of red paper 12" x 3/4", 4 strips of red paper 6" x 3/4"
1 piece of blue paper 6" x 5", tongue depressors, ice cream sticks,
paper towel tube or construction paper

Directions: This can be tied in with Flag Day and the Fourth of July.

Discuss the flag and what it stands for. Show them the flag. Let some children hold it out. Explain that our first American flag had 13 stars. Why do they think this. Ask students how many stars they think there are on the flag now. Then, count the stars. Count the stripes and explain that the 13 stripes represent the 13 original colonies.

1. Have the children paste the blue paper in the left top corner of the white paper where the X is.

2. Paste one long red strip across the bottom of the white paper.

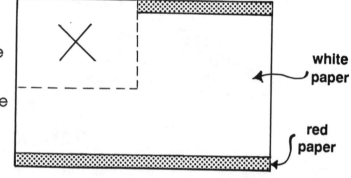

white paper

red paper

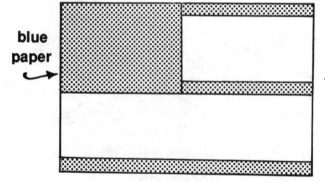

blue paper

3. Paste one short red strip across the top of the white paper.

4. Paste another short red strip extending out from the bottom corner of the blue paper.

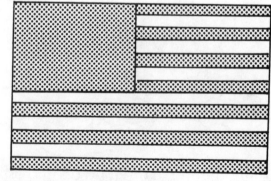

5. Now fit in the two remaining long and short strips in the appropriate places.

6. Have the children draw stars with a white crayon. Crossed lines are easy to make.

7. Attach the flag to ice cream sticks or tongue depressors that have been taped together. It can also be attached to a paper towel tube or a piece of rolled up construction paper.

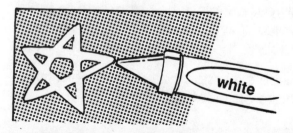

white

74

Fire Safety

Social Studies

Objective: To learn how to react in case of fire in school or at home

Directions: Hold a discussion on what may cause a house or building to catch fire. Next, tell the students that they need to know what to do in case of a fire. First discuss, and then role-play, the following:

Fire Emergency Procedure	Reason
1. Always stay close to the ground by crawling on your hands and knees.	There is less smoke near the floor because smoke rises.
2. Cover your mouth with a cloth, shirt, etc.	This will help prevent smoke from being inhaled.
3. Never open a door without first touching it to feel if it is hot.	A hot door would indicate fire on the other side.
4. You should know at least two ways out of any room.	If one exit is blocked by fire, you will have an alternative.
5. If your clothes should catch fire, you should stop, drop and roll.	This will cut oxygen to help extinguish the flames.
6. You should have a meeting place outside your home/school after exiting a burning building.	Family members and firefighters will know you are safe.

Suggested Reading:

I Can Be a Firefighter by Ray Broekel
Curious George at the Fire Station by Margaret Rey

Remember . . .

DON'T PLAY WITH MATCHES!

Families

Social Studies

Objective: To create a family mobile

Materials: a paper plate for each student, yarn, hole punch, 9" x 4" sheets of white paper, construction paper (assorted colors), crayons, paste or glue, scissors

Directions: Discuss what a family is. (See Suggested Reading below for springboard to discussion.) Ask several volunteer students to name the individuals who make up their families. Next, explain to students that they will create a family mobile.

1. On the sheets of white paper, instruct students to draw and color each member of their family (one person per sheet).

colored paper

2. Have students cut out each picture and paste it on construction paper. They should cut the construction paper to frame the individual portraits.

Punch holes.

3. Hole punch the frame and hole punch a spot on the rim of the paper plate.

4. Attach the frame to the plate with yarn. Repeat the same for each family member.

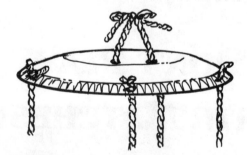

5. Next, punch two holes near the center of the plate. String one piece of yarn through the two holes so that the mobile can be hung.

Suggested Reading:
  Peter's Chair by Ezra Jack Keats
  Just Like Daddy by Frank Asch

Five Funny Fish

Poetry and
Finger Plays

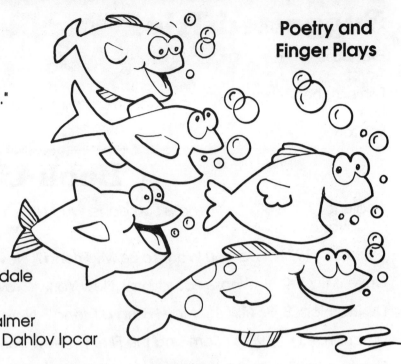

Five funny fish swimming in the ocean.
The first one said, "I have a notion."
The second one said, "The water is deep."
The third one said, "Don't fall asleep."
The fourth one said, "Let's swim away."
The fifth one said, "But not today."
Along came a man with a line and bait.
The fish swam away. They didn't wait.

by Ada Frischer

Suggested Poetry:

"Fog" by Carl Sandberg
"The Falling Star" by Sara Teasdale

Suggested Reading:

Fish Out of Water by Helen Palmer
The Biggest Fish in the Sea by Dahlov Ipcar

Five Funny Fish

Dramatization

Objective and Directions:

Refer to **Dramatizations** page 30 .

Have the children stand in front of the group representing fish 1, 2, 3, 4, 5 in the poem above. The rest of the class recites the poem except for the roles of each fish which are recited by the appropriate child. At the end, all five "fish" swim away.

The Farmer in the Dell
Music

Using this tune, have the children suggest other verses about the farmer such as the farmer plows his field, the farmer plants his seeds, the farmer builds a fence, etc.

"Frère Jacques"

Using the tune of "Frère Jacques", make up a song that the children can repeat as a response chant. After singing it several times, sing it as a round. (An example is shown.)

I see piglets
I see piglets
On the farm,
On the farm,
Playing, rolling, oinking,
Playing rolling oinking,
In the mud,
In the mud.

I see piglets
I see piglets.

I see piglets
on the farm,
on the farm.

Suggested Trips

Firehouse
Florist
Fish hatchery - aquarium
Farm
Factory

Book List

Anglund, J. (1958). *A Friend Is Someone Who Likes You.* New York: Harcourt Brace Jovanovich.

Carle, E. (1971). *Do You Want To Be My Friend?* New York: Crowell.

Coxe, M. (1990). *Whose Footprints?* New York: Crowell.

De Regniers, B. S. (1964). *May I Bring a Friend?* New York: Atheneum.

Eastman, P.D. (1986). *Sam and the Firefly*. New York: Beginner Books.

Elkin, B. (1957). *Six Foolish Fishermen.* New York: Macmillan.

Heine, H. (1986). *Friends.* New York: Macmillan.

Ipcar, D. (1972). *The Biggest Fish in the Sea*. New York: Viking Press.

Lionni, L. (1970). *Fish Is Fish.* New York: Pantheon Books.

Lionni, L. (1967). *Frederick.* New York: Pantheon Books.

Lobel, A. (1976). *Frog and Toad, All Year.* New York: Harper and Row.

Lobel, A. (1972). *Frog and Toad Together.* New York: Harper and Row.

McPhail, D. (1985). *Farm Morning.* San Diego, CA: Harcourt Brace Jovanovich.

Miller, J. (1992). *Farm Counting Book.* New York: Simon and Schuster Trade.

Palmer, H. (1967). *Fish Out of Water*. New York: Beginner Books.

Provensen, A. and Provensen, M. (1992). *Our Animal Friends at Maple Hill Farm.* New York: Random.

Rey, M. (1985). *Curious George at the Fire Station.* New York: Houghton Mifflin.

Rojankowsky, F. (1967). *Animals on the Farm.* New York: Knopf.

Ryder, J. (1977). *Fireflies.* New York: Harper and Row.

Seuss, Dr. (1960). *One Fish, Two Fish.* New York: Beginner Books.

Seuss, Dr. (1968). *The Foot Book.* New York: Random House.

Travis, E. (1990). *Finders Keepers.* New York: St. Martin's Press.

Zolotow, C. (1971). *A Father Like That.* New York: Harper and Row.

Table of Contents

*Remember to check **B Chapter Table of Contents** (page 4) for additional activities.

Glue a Goose!

Art

Objective: To learn about parts of a bird and make a realistic rendition of a goose

Materials: newsprint, waxed paper, white glue, black crayons or markers, string

Directions: Have the children draw a goose flying. (See example.) Put a sheet of waxed paper over each drawing. Instruct the children to put glue on their paper outlining their goose pattern. Then, fill in the outline with glue.

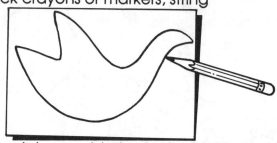

Cover with wax paper.

Set the pictures aside to dry for 2 to 3 days. They must dry completely. Carefully peel the goose away from the paper. Thread a string through an opening and hang the geese from the ceiling or display them on windows.

The geese will dry a cloudy white, much the color of real geese!

Extension Activities:

Discuss parts of the bird (wings, feet, feathers, beaks, etc.). If pictures are available, compare beaks and feet.

Suggested Reading:

Are You My Mother? by P.D. Eastman
Bird Talk by Roma Gans

Glue and Glitter

Objective: To reinforce letter and numeral recognition using glue and glitter

Materials: construction paper, white glue, glitter

Directions: Using white glue, have children write their names, numerals, capital and lower case letter partners, or draw pictures on construction paper. After using the glue, have students sprinkle glitter over the glue. Allow the glue and glitter to dry for a few minutes before shaking off the excess. The extra glitter may be saved by pouring it back into the original container. The only rule to this activity is to work quickly to apply the glitter before the glue dries, or else the glitter will not stick! Try having the children practice the capital and lower case "G."

Grandparents Book

Writing/ Reading

Objective: To create a book about grandparents

Materials: 4 sheets of newsprint per child, crayons, pencils, stapler

Directions: Use the books below as an introduction to a discussion about grandparents. Have the children talk about things they do with grandparents, why they like to visit them, etc.

Fold and staple.

Grandmother and I by Helen E. Buckley
Grandfather and I by Helen E. Buckley
Grandparents Around the World by Dorka Raynor

Each child will "publish" his/her own book. Give each child 4 pieces of newsprint. Have children fold them in half to make an 8-page book. Prepare 8 pages for each book as follows:

1. **Cover** - Discuss appropriate titles with the children. Write the title as selected by each child. Have the children design the cover.

2. **Dedication Page** - This book is dedicated to . . . - Take dictation from each child. Add a publication date to the page.

3. **These are my grandparents.** (Children will draw their grandparents.)

4. **My grandparents like . . .**

5. **I love my grandparents because . . .**

6. **My grandparents love me because . . .**

7. **This is what I like to do with my grandparents:**

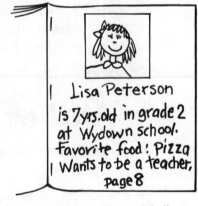

For pages 4, 5, 6 and 7, take dictation from each child and have the children illustrate the text.

8. **Author's Page** - Each child can draw a picture of himself/herself or paste in a photograph on the page and write his/her name. Help students write a brief biography (age, grade, favorite food, school attending, what author would like to be, etc.).

Variation: Instead of pages 4, 5, 6 and 7, have each child dictate a story about his/her grandparents. Put two or three sentences on a page and have the child illustrate them.

In the event that a child does not have a grandparent, this book could be about "My Favorite Person" (friend, aunt, uncle, parent, etc.).

Coordinate this activity with Grandparents Day. (See Social Studies page 85.)

Giggle Book

Objective: To create a page of a book full of nonsense situations to make students giggle

Materials: a sheet of white paper for each student, crayons, pencils, book rings or bindery

Directions: Ask the students, "Can you imagine a dog that said meow?" "Can you imagine a chair with ears?" "Can you imagine me with purple hair?" "All of these things would make me giggle!" Next, ask the students to imagine some things that would make them giggle. Discuss the students' responses. Give each student a sheet of white paper. Explain to students that they are to write and illustrate something that they think would make them giggle. Have students complete the sentence, "When I imagine _____ , I giggle." (For young students, run the partial statement off on a copy machine so that you or a volunteer may fill in the sentence as it is dictated by the child.) Have students illustrate their sentences. Create a cover, collect work and bind with book rings or bindery.

Suggested Reading: *Emma Giggled* by Lou Alpert

"Go Get the Green" Book

Objective: To provide alliteration with the hard sound for "G" and to emphasize the color green

Materials: white construction paper, crayons

Directions: Have each child complete the sentence, "Go get the green _____ ." Children may copy the sentence, or you may want to run off the sentence starter for them.

Children illustrate their sentences using lots of green in their pictures. Collect and assemble them into a book. The cover can be a design using blue and yellow paint mixed together - perhaps finger paint.

Suggested Reading: *Little Blue and Little Yellow* by Leo Lionni

Author Study - Gail Gibbons

Objective and Directions: Refer to **Biography** page 11.

Background:

Gail Gibbons was making books even before she knew how to write! She was born in Oak Park, Illinois. She now lives in Corinth, Vermont, in a home she and her family built themselves. She has two children, Becky and Eric. Her book, *The Seasons of Arnold's Apple Tree* was inspired by a real tree near her home.

Suggested Reading:

Paper, Paper Everywhere　　　　　*Sun Up, Sun Down*
The Seasons of Arnold's Apple Tree

Watching Grass Grow

Science

Objective: To show children how to grow grass in small containers

Materials: grass seed, soil, egg cartons, markers, trays

Directions: Carefully poke two small holes in the bottom of each section of the egg carton. Separate each cup from the carton and have the children decorate them by drawing a face on two sides. For "growth insurance," you may want to provide two or three cups per child. Fill each cup with soil and sprinkle some grass seed on top. Press lightly into the soil, water gently, place in a sunny spot and wait for hair to grow!

Keep a record of how many days pass before the first "hair" is noticed.

Garbage

Objective: To become aware of the excessive amount of garbage individuals create and how students can help reduce that amount

Materials: garbage from students' snack or lunch (non-food items), scale, paper bag, chart paper, marker

Directions: Instruct students to save all of their paper, foil, juice boxes, etc. from their snack or lunch. When they have finished eating, collect the garbage. Discuss the quantity and weigh it. Next, make a list of ways the students can decrease the amount of garbage in their snacks/lunches (i.e. use a thermos instead of a juice carton, a lunch box instead of a paper bag, etc.).

Extension Activity:

Ask students to try to cut down on the amount of garbage in their snack or lunch for one day. Then, collect and weigh the garbage and compare the two days' results.

Background Information:

Each American creates approximately four pounds of garbage per day. Most of it ends up in landfills. Scientists are studying garbage to try to help the U.S. garbage problem.

Suggested Reading:

It Was Just a Dream by Chris Van Allsburg
Trash by Charlotte Wilcox

Grocery Graph

Math

Objective: To make a graph using grocery boxes

Materials: large graph paper, markers, food boxes brought from home

Directions: Have each child bring one empty food box to school. Label the graph paper with general terms, such as cereal, rice, soup, cookies, crackers, etc. As each child presents his/her box, have him/her mark the graph in the appropriate place.

	Cereal	Rice	Soup	Crackers	Cookies
7					
6					
5					
4					
3					
2					
1					
0					

Read the graph with the class. Which category had the most items? the least items? Were there any ties?

Write a math story about the grocery graph as described under F - **Favorite Fruit Graph**, page 71.

Use the food boxes to set up a grocery store (See Dramatization page 88.) in the classroom or glue them together to make a gigantic creation.

Let's Guess!

Objective: To practice guessing (estimation)

Materials: containers, "G" items (gumballs, Goobers, giraffes, groceries, etc.)

Directions: Put a bunch of like items in a container (perhaps feature one each day). Have students write down how many of the item they believe are in the container.

Count the items together. Emphasize to students that no answer is wrong when estimating. Point out that it is good, however, to get as close to the actual number as possible.

Compare various containers of items. Ask questions like, "Why are there less items in this container than the other? How many of this item do you think will fit in this container?" Put items in and count together.

84

Grandparents Day or Special Guest Day

Objective: To celebrate Grandparents Day or Special Guest Day   **Social Studies**

Directions: Send grandparents (or special guest) a note from the children. (See below.)

Plan a program for the special guests. Have the children show their guests around the room. Entertainment might consist of songs and a reading of *Grandmother and I* and *Grandfather and I.*

Prepare refreshments with the children for the guests. The children can make doughnuts (See Cooking D page 57.), corn muffins (See Cooking C page 46.), peanut butter (See Cooking P page 184.) and granola mix (See Cooking G page 88.).

The children can also teach their grandparents a skill they have learned such as weaving.

Children will present their grandparents with the gift (**Grandparents Book**) that they have published. (See Writing/Reading page 81.)

Suggested Reading:

Grandmother and I by Helen E. Buckley
Grandfather and I by Helen E. Buckley

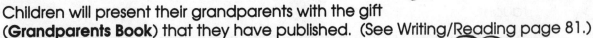

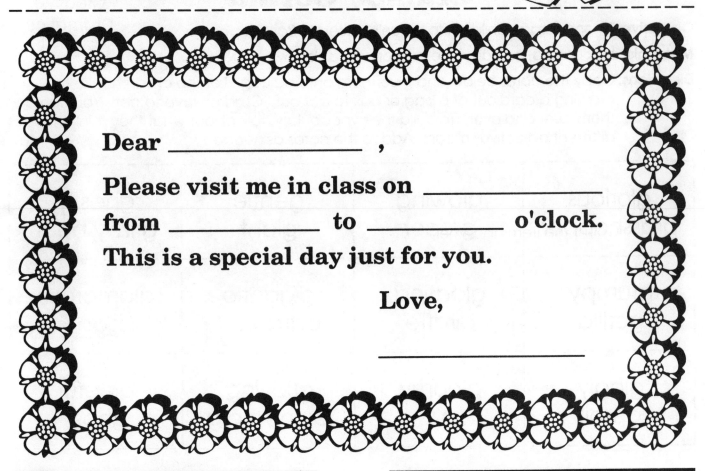

Dear _____ ,

Please visit me in class on _____

from _____ to _____ o'clock.

This is a special day just for you.

                    Love,

                    _____

Globe Game

Social Studies

Objective: To identify and locate places on the globe (countries, oceans, poles, equator, etc.)

Materials: globe, box, index cards, markers

Directions: Depending on the age and ability of the children, teach them to identify and locate places on the globe.

Write the names of the places you have taught the children on index cards. Put the cards in a box. Each child selects a card and takes a turn finding the place on the globe. If the child is unable to read the card, the teacher should read the word for him/her.

Continue to add more index cards to the box as more places on the globe are taught.

You may want to start this activity early in the year. Add one or two new cards and places each week. The game provides a constant review!

Grumpy Gorilla

Creative Dramatics

Objective: To encourage children to be uninhibited in front of people

Materials: box or bag, oaktag, glue, scissors, cards below

Directions: Copy the cards below and glue them onto oaktag. Let the children take turns drawing a card out of a bag or box to act out. Children love to act! You can do them over and over. To build their vocabulary, talk about what they think the different adjectives mean. Add to the cards as needed.

glorious grasshopper	glowing grocer	gentle giant	ghastly grizzly bear
grumpy gorilla	gloating giraffe	gigantic gardener	glamorous goat
giggly gerbil	gloomy girl	grieving Guinea pig	gleeful ghost

Ground-Hog Day

Social Studies

Objective: To become familiar with Ground-Hog Day and the term "predictions"

Materials: 9" x 12" sheets of paper with the outline of a ground hog on it and the word "predicts" above it, crayons

Directions: Start to discuss Ground-Hog Day with the children a day or two before February 2. Introduce the words "legend" and "prediction" and discuss the "accuracy" of the ground hog's "prediction."

If the ground hog sees its shadow, it runs back into its hole, and there are six more weeks of winter. If it does not see its shadow, spring will be here soon.

Discuss and illustrate how shadows are made and the need for sun or light to create a shadow. Talk about the "fun" aspect of Ground-Hog Day.

The children are now ready to make their own predictions. Give each child a piece of 9" x 12" paper with a ground hog's outline in the middle and the word "predicts" above it.

Predicts

_____ name _____ yes or no

Have each child make his/her own prediction. The children will write their names in the appropriate place and then predict "yes" or "no". Since a "yes" prediction means that the ground hog will see his shadow, the child will also draw a sun and a shadow along with a tree, a ground hog's hole, grass, etc.

If a child predicts "no", he/she will not include a sun or shadow on the page.

Tally the predictions and graph the results.

Will the ground hog see his shadow?												
Yes												total
No												total

On the eve of Ground-Hog Day, give the children a homework assignment to find out what the ground hog did on that Ground-Hog Day.

See Poetry - **The Ground Hog's Prediction** page 88.

Granola Mix

Using a granola cereal as a base, discuss with the children what healthy foods can be added to granola to make a good snack (i.e. raisins, sunflower seeds, cut-up dried fruits or fresh fruits).

Make selections using a voting system and then prepare the mix.

The Ground Hog's Prediction

Poetry

I saw a ground hog on Ground-Hog Day.
He looked for his shadow but he wanted to play.
He saw his shadow.
It scared him so.
He ran back in his hole and he said, "Oh no!"
  "It's not spring yet!
  Six more weeks of winter, I bet."
                                    by Ada Frischer

(See Social Studies page 87.)

Grocery Store

Dramatization

Objective: To act out a trip to the grocery store and to act as a grocer

Materials: toy cash register, play money, wallets or purses, empty cereal boxes, milk cartons, cans, egg cartons, plastic foods, toy grocery cart or shopping basket

Directions: Ask parents to help you collect the materials needed. Set up the grocery store in a corner of your room by placing items on shelves or tables. Set the cash register on a table near an imaginary door. Supply the register and purses/wallets with play money. Place basket or cart near the "Door." Your store is now ready for use!

Extension Activity:
    Refer to **Grocery Graph** page 84.

Suggested Trips

Greenhouse
Grocery store

Book List

Buckley, H.E. (1961). *Grandmother and I.* New York: Lothrop, Lee and Shepard.

Buckley, H.E. (1959). *Grandfather and I.* New York: Lothrop, Lee and Shepard.

Carle, E. (1977). *The Grouchy Ladybug.* New York: T.Y. Crowell.

Krauss, R. (1947). *Growing Story.* New York: Harper and Row.

Seuss, Dr. (1957). *How the Grinch Stole Christmas.* New York: Random House.

Showers, P. (1974). *Where Does the Garbage Go?* New York: Harper and Row.

G Pictures for Miscellaneous Activities

Enlarge the cards to make flashcards throughout the study of the "G" sound.

Hh

Table of Contents

*Remember to check **B Chapter Table of Contents** (page 4) for additional activities.

House (I Know My Address) Art

Objective: To help children remember their addresses and to create a house

Materials: 9" x 12" construction paper, scissors, crayons/markers, glue

Directions: Discuss "half." (Refer to Math page 101.)

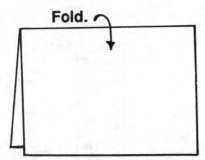

Fold.

1. Have children fold the paper in half.

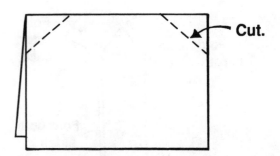

Cut.

2. They should then cut off the corners to resemble the shape of a house.

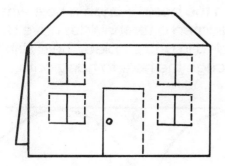

3. Then students cut open a door and windows (on solid line) and fold back (on dotted line).

4. Have children draw and color their family to fit inside the house in the doors and windows.

5. They cut the family out and glue them behind the doors and windows, just gluing around the edges.

Note: Use this as an opportunity to have the children learn their addresses. As soon as each child can remember his/her address, write it on the house and send it home.

Suggested Reading:
> *The Little House* by Virginia Lee Burton
> *A House for Hermit Crab* by Eric Carle

Helicopter

Art

Objective: To create a helicopter that twirls

Materials: 9" x 12" construction paper, scissors, string, hole punch, stapler, pattern

Directions: Use the pattern at the bottom of the page to make copies for your class.

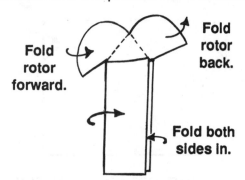

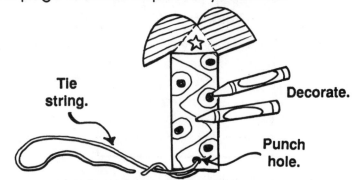

1. Cut on the solid lines and fold on the dotted lines. When folding the "rotors," be sure to fold one forward and one back. The bottom section folds in thirds toward the center.

2. Have the children decorate the rotors and the base. Punch a hole where indicated after the sides have been folded in and stapled. Tie a string through the hole to hang onto.

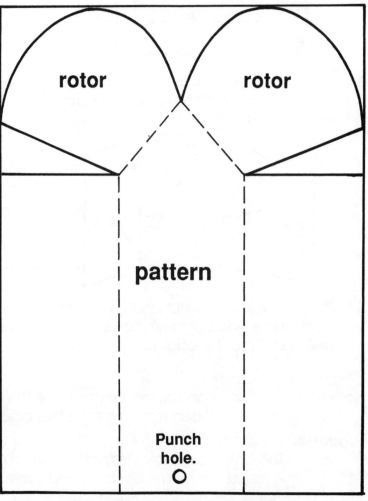

rotor   rotor

pattern

Punch hole.

3. Take the helicopter out to the playground. Run with it and watch the rotors spin.

Hats

Art

Objective: To design a hat

Materials: paper plates, white glue, assorted materials such as crêpe paper, streamers, ribbons, buttons, beads, construction paper, tissue paper, shells, pasta shapes, glitter, gummed stars, feathers, artificial flowers, etc.

Directions: Tell the children that they are going to be hat designers and model for them some outlandish things they can do with the above materials. Make sure the materials are glued to the bottom side of the plate. Attach ribbon, yarn or cord to the sides so the hat can be tied under the chin. Have a "fashion" parade in school.

Suggested Reading:

Jennie's Hat by Ezra Jack Keats

Extension Activity:

Read the original poem on page 103, **All the Hats**. Make copies of it for the whole class. Mount them on light colored construction paper and let the children draw all kinds of hats all the way around the poem.

Hearts

Art

Objective: To create hearts from construction paper without using a pattern

Materials: 4" x 5" sheets of newsprint, 4" x 5" sheets of construction paper of various colors, scissors, hole punch, posterboard, optional - paste

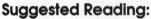

Fold.

Directions: Fold the sheet of newsprint in half. (Newsprint is an inexpensive material to practice with, and it is easy to cut.) With the folded side on the left, make a two. (See illustration.)

Next, cut on the "2." Open and you have a heart!

When students have had the opportunity to practice with the newsprint, supply them with different sizes of construction paper. Make a heart collage by pasting hearts to posterboard, or create heart necklaces by punching holes and stringing them on yarn.

What Do You See in a Hole?

Writing/ Reading

Objective: To encourage creative thinking and writing

Materials: paper, crayons, paste or stapler

Suggested Reading:

Look Again! by Tana Hoban
Take Another Look by Tana Hoban
A Hole Is to Dig by Ruth Krauss
What Does Word Bird See? by Jane Belk Moncure

Directions: Use these books to lead a discussion about different kinds of holes and what you might see in them.

i.e. hole in a tree - squirrel
hole in grass - rabbit
hole in a house - mouse
hole in a hive - bees
hole in a doghouse - dog
hole in a sock - toe
hole in a glove - finger
hole in a leaf - ladybug, aphid, caterpillar
hole in an apple - worm

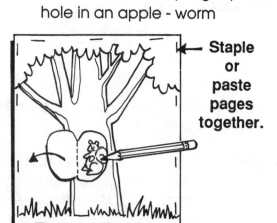

← **Staple or paste pages together.**

Give children the sentence, "I looked into a hole, and this is what I saw." On a piece of paper, each child will draw an object that has a hole in it, such as a tree. Help students cut or tear a hole in their object, leaving the torn piece connected to the paper to become a flap. Paste or staple this paper on another blank piece of paper. Then, under the flap, the students can draw what they see in the hole.

Extension Activity:

Take dictation using, "I looked into a hole, and I saw . . . " as a start. Encourage the children to describe what they saw instead of just naming it.

You could also use the sentence, "I looked into a hole, and what do you think I saw?" Then, have each child describe, but not name, what he/she saw. The rest of the class can guess and then lift the flap to see if they were correct.

I looked into a hole, and I saw . . .

94

I Can Help With My Helping Hands

Objective: To write and illustrate how students can help and to trace their own helping hands

Writing/ Reading

Materials: 12" x 18" sheets of white paper, crayons or markers, pencils, glue, scissors, paint (optional)

Directions: Discuss with students how they can help family and friends. On the bottom of their paper, have students trace both their right and left hands. (If preferred, you may have students trace and cut out hands on construction paper, then glue them to their paper, or make handprints using paint.) At the top of the paper, have students complete the sentence, "I can help _____ ." Last, students can illustrate their sentences.

Author Study - Tana Hoban

Objective and Directions: Refer to **Biography** page 11.

Background:

Tana Hoban lives in Philadelphia with her husband and daughter. Tana Hoban not only illustrates some of her books, but she also takes pictures with her camera for some of them. Her pictures are displayed at the Museum of Modern Art, as well as several other galleries around the world. She has won several prizes and gold medals for her work.

Suggested Reading:

A, B, and See!
Round & Round & Round
Take Another Look
One Little Kitten
I Read Symbols
26 Letters and 99 Cents
Look Again!

Health Habits

Social Studies

Objective: To reinforce good health habits such as, "Cover your sneeze, please."

Materials: poem on page 97, one 9" x 12" sheet or 12" x 18" sheet of construction paper (for the face), one 9" x 12" sheet of construction paper (for the hand), crayons, paste, scissors, tissues, stapler, staples

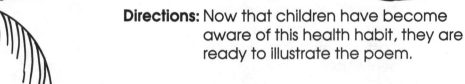

Preparation:

Discuss good health habits with the children. Talk about why it is important to cover your sneeze. Keep a tissue box handy in the classroom and indicate its location to the children. Tissues should be thrown away after each use. If you have a sink in your classroom, hands should be washed. Read the poem on page 97.

Directions: Now that children have become aware of this health habit, they are ready to illustrate the poem.

Using 9" x 12" or 12" x 18" construction paper, have them draw a large oval or circle for their face. Have them add eyes, nose, mouth and hair. Cut out the face.

Each child will trace and cut out one hand. (They may need help cutting. Or, you could provide a hand previously prepared.) Paste or staple tissue over the nose and mouth and paste or staple the hand over the tissue. (See illustration.)

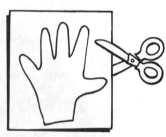

Read the letter on page 97 with the children. Have each child sign his/her name and send it home with the poem and the art activity to help reinforce this good health habit at home.

Suggested Reading:
Stand Back Said the Elephant, I'm Going to Sneeze

Dear Parents,

We are learning about good health habits in school. I learned this poem, and I made a picture of myself covering my sneeze. Please help me remember this at home.

Love,

_____

Ahhhhh...

Cover Your Sneeze, Please

Please, please cover your sneeze
Not your toes,
Not even your knees.
When you have a cold,
And maybe you wheeze,
Please, please cover your sneeze.

Please, please cover your sneeze.
We don't want your germs.
We want none of these.
Not us, not the bees,
Not the birds in the trees.
So, please, please cover your sneeze.

by Ada Frischer

TISSUE

Hearing - Match the Sounds

Science

Objective: To introduce the children to the sense of hearing

Materials: 10 toilet paper rolls, 20 squares of paper to cover the open ends of the rolls, 20 rubber bands, 10 paper clips, 10 staples, 2 erasers, 4 jingle bells, 12 identical wooden beads

Directions: Explain to the children that hearing is one of the five senses and that we hear through our ears. This is a good time to introduce some good hygiene habits.

- Don't scream in someone's ears.
- Don't play music or TV too loud.
- Don't stick things in your ears.
- Keep your ears clean.

After some discussion about hearing, explain to the children that you are going to play a game, and that the sense of hearing is very important to the game.

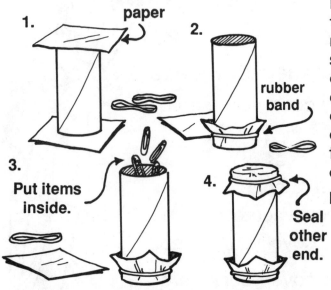

1. paper
2. rubber band
3. Put items inside.
4. Seal other end.

Place one square of construction paper over the end of a paper roll and secure it with a rubber band. Put 5 paper clips in the roll and seal the other end with another square of construction paper. Shake it, so the children can hear the sound. Prepare another one, exactly the same. Now, shake this one alternately with the first one. Ask the children if they can tell you about the two sounds. (They are the same.)

Now, prepare the remaining sets as follows:

5 staples in each of two rolls
1 eraser in each of two rolls
2 jingle bells in each of two rolls
6 identical wooden beads in each of two rolls

As you prepare each set with the children, demonstrate several times how each one sounds. Be sure the children are aware that two have the same sound.

Now, we are ready for the game. Mix up all the shakers and set them up as for a game of concentration.

Invite one child to come up and try two shakers. If they match, take them out of the game. See if the child can guess what is in them. If they do not match, the child puts them back in their original places. Continue the game until all five pairs are matched.

Hearing

Science

Objective: To utilize the sense of hearing by trying to discriminate between sounds

Materials: shoe box, small objects (marbles, rocks, M & M's, rulers) tape recording of household sounds (a door closing, water dripping, individual climbing stairs, etc.)

Directions: Discuss the sense of hearing with students. How do we hear? What do we hear with? Why do we have two ears?, etc. Next, have students close their eyes. Place one of the small objects you have collected in the shoe box. Have one student shake the box and allow him/her to guess the content. Repeat until all materials have been utilized. A second approach to this activity is to pre-record household sounds and then play each sound, allowing students to guess the source of the sound.

Habitat

Objective: To become familiar with the word "habitat" and which animals live above, on and below the ground, and those that live in water

Materials: mural paper, magazines, scissors, crayons, glue

Directions: On mural paper, make four equal sections by drawing three vertical lines. Label each section "Trees - Above the Ground," "Land - On the Ground," "In the Dirt - Underground" and "Water." Have students illustrate each section leaving out any animals. Next, over a period of days, have students cut out pictures of mammals, fish, insects, reptiles, etc., and glue them on the mural in the appropriate box. If the animal has a habitat of two categories, glue the picture on the line dividing the categories. (For example, a frog lives on the ground as well as in the water.)

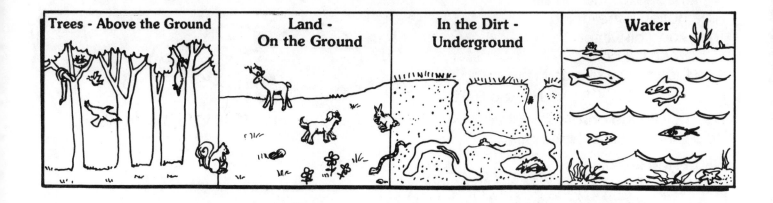

Hot and Cold

Science

Objective: To use a thermometer to distinguish between the temperatures of hot and cold

Materials: one thermometer per child, one container of hot water and one container of cold water per child

Directions: Show a thermometer to the children. Tell them that this is the instrument used to determine temperature. Discuss the many ways thermometers are used; for example: outside and inside temperatures, oven temperatures, body temperatures. Be sure the children understand that the higher a temperature is, the higher the numbers will be. Encourage the children to experiment with the water containers and the thermometers, reading the temperatures in degrees and watching the thermometer readings rise and fall.

HOT   COLD

Hibernation

The sheep's wool grows thick in the winter.
The hair on the dog does too.
You can see many animals all year-round
When you visit them in the zoo.

But the bear sleeps all winter.
Into his cave he goes too.
A snake curls up in a hole in the ground
And sleeps all winter through.

The frog swims down into mud
And sleeps the winter away.
The ground hog tunnels into the ground
And comes out on Ground-Hog Day.

The frog and the ground hog
    The snake and the bear
Hibernation is their thing.
They sleep all winter
    when it is cold
And then they wake up in the spring.
             by Ada Frischer

Discuss with the children what various animals do in the winter and how nature prepares for cold winters. Stress hibernation.

Suggested Reading:
    The Happy Day by Ruth Krauss
    Buzzy Bear Goes South by Dorothy Marino

Half

Math

Objective: To identify half and visualize a half as two equal pieces of a whole

Materials: white squares or rectangles, crayons

Directions: Present a situation to your students in which they are asked to share something evenly with a brother or sister (a candy bar perhaps). Hold up a set of unifix cubes, or draw a rectangle on the board to represent the candy bar. Ask them how much they would get? How much would their brother/sister get? After showing the students half of several objects, distribute paper squares or rectangles. Show the students how to fold their shape in half. Next, have students color half.

Hundred

Objective: To count orally to 100
To practice recognizing numerals 1 to 100

Materials: flashcards depicting the numbers 1 to 100

Directions: Young children enjoy showing their counting ability. Count to 100 beginning with one child and changing "counters" every five numbers.

Find a set of flashcards with the numbers 1 to 100 on them. Mix them up. "Flash" them one at a time and let different children identify the number.

Horizontal

Objective: To help students understand the meaning of horizontal

Materials: 8 1/2" x 11" sheet of newsprint for each student, pencils

Directions: Give each student a piece of newsprint. Tell students to turn their paper horizontally. Demonstrate what that means. Have them draw a horizontal line to divide the paper in half.

Use this opportunity to explain vertical to students. Have them turn their paper so it is vertical. Have students draw a vertical line to divide their paper in half.

Hexagon

Objective: To recognize the hexagon shape

Directions: Explain that some shapes have a certain number of sides and that the number of sides determines the shape's name. Tell them that a hexagon has six sides. If you want, you could explain that "hex" is Latin for *six*.

Draw this hexagon shape on the chalkboard.

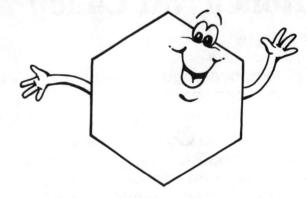

Hand Signal - Hot and Cold

Games

Objective: To find an object that has been hidden

Materials: one small object (For letter "H", you may want to use a plastic horse, a toy helicopter, a hat, etc.)

Directions: A student is chosen to be "the hunter," while another student hides an object in the room. (The remaining students should be aware of the object's location.) When the object has been hidden, the class helps "the hunter" find the object using hand signals. "The hunter" walks around the room in search of the object.

If the student is not close to the object, the students place their hands on their knees. As "the hunter" gets closer to the hidden object, the students move their hands to their shoulders. If "the hunter" is "hot," or very close to the hidden object, the students would indicate so by shaking their hands above their heads. The game ends when the object has been found.

You're getting "hotter!"

Cooking

Honey Fruit Bits

Peel and cut apples and bananas into chunks. Dip in honey and then in graham cracker crumbs. Serve with toothpicks.

Honey Nut Candy

4 oz. honey
1/8 cup sugar
1/2 teaspoon ginger
1 cup chopped walnuts
1 cup dry cereal

Boil honey and sugar - add cereal, nuts and ginger and stir. Spread the mixture on waxed paper - about 1/2 inch thick. When cool, cut in pieces.

Poetry

All the Hats

There are big hats and little hats,
    Blues ones and red.
But the best hats are hats
    That fit on your head.
There are top hats and police hats
    And fire hats too.
And animal hats to wear
    At the zoo.
There are green hats and black hats,
    Pink ones and red.
But the best hats are hats
    That fit on your head.

             by Ada Frischer

My Hat

I wear a hat upon my head
It keeps me warm and it's all red.
My sister's hat has ribbons and bows.
It keeps her ears warm
And not her nose.
        by Ada Frischer

The Hokey Pokey   **Music**

Directions: Gather students in a circle. Review the concept of right and left by asking
students to hold up their left hand, their right foot, etc. Next, demonstrate how to
place body parts "in" the circle and "out." Next, demonstrate the "Hokey Pokey"
following the song below. Now, you are ready to play!

The Hokey Pokey

You put your right arm in
You take your right arm out
You put your right arm in and you shake it all
    about.
You do the Hokey Pokey (Shake arms in air.)
And you turn yourself around.
That's what it's all about. (Clap 2 times.)

Repeat the above using:

    your left arm
    your right leg
    your left leg
    your right hip
    Your left hip
    Your backside
    your whole self

You do the Hokey Pokey...

Harold and the Purple Crayon

Objective and Directions:
Refer to **Dramatizations** page 30.

Dramatization

Materials: book - *Harold and the Purple Crayon*
by Crockett Johnson
white mural paper, purple crayons

Allow children to become "Harold" by drawing on the mural paper! They can tell a story as they draw.

Suggested Trips

Horse farm

Book List

Aliki. (1962). *My Hands.* New York: Harper and Row.

Anno, M. (1985). *Anno's Hat Tricks.* New York: Philomel Books.

Asch, F. (1982). *Happy Birthday, Moon.* Englewood Cliffs, N.J.: Prentice Hall.

Burton, V. (1942). *The Little House.* New York: Houghton Mifflin.

Carle, E. (1987). *A House for a Hermit Crab.* Saxonville, MA: Picture Book Studio.

Castle, C. (1985). *The Hare and the Tortoise.* New York: Dial Books for Young Readers.

Cutts, D. (1979). *The House that Jack Built.* Mahwah, NJ: Troll Associates.

Galdone, P. (1968). *Henny Penny.* New York: Ticknor and Fields.

Galdone, P. (1985). *The Little Red Hen.* New York: Houghton Mifflin.

Geringer, L. (1985). *A Three Hat Day.* New York: Harper and Row.

Grimm, J. (1975). *Hansel & Gretel.* New York: Scribner.

Hurd, E. (1960). *Hurry, Hurry.* New York: Harper and Row.

Johnson, C. (1955). *Harold and the Purple Crayon.* New York: Harper and Row.

Keats, E.J. (1966). *Jenny's Hat.* New York: Harper and Row.

Krauss, R. (1949). *The Happy Day.* New York: Harper and Row.

Morris, A. (1989). *Hats, Hats, Hats.* New York: Lothrop, Lee and Shepard Books.

Seuss, Dr. (1963). *Hop on Pop.* New York: Beginner Books.

Seuss, Dr. (1940). *Horton Hatches the Egg.* New York: Random House.

Seuss, Dr. (1954). *Horton Hears a Who!* New York: Random House.

Zion, G. (1956). *Harry the Dirty Dog.* New York: Harper.

Zolotow, C. (1987). *The Hating Book.* New York: Harper and Row.

Table of Contents

*Remember to check **B Chapter Table of Contents** (page 4) for additional activities.

Jungle Scene

Art

Objective: To create a jungle scene using crayon resistance

Materials: construction paper, crayons, green paint, white paint, water, paintbrushes

Directions: Using white paper, have the children draw a jungle scene with crayons. It is important that they press down heavily as they draw.

Mix a little water, white paint and green paint to thin it to make a light green "wash."

Quickly, with light sweeping strokes, paint over the entire drawing with the green "wash." Like magic, the drawing will reappear.

Explain to the children that the paint rolls off the waxy crayon surface.

Suggested Reading:

The Trek by Ann Jonas
Sitting in My Box by Dee Lillegard
A Wise Monkey Tale by Betsy and Giulio Maestro

(See Poetry page 114.)

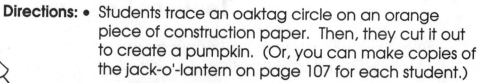

Jack-O'-Lanterns

Objective: To practice eye-hand coordination by cutting out and matching letters

Materials: oaktag circles with an 8" diameter (for tracing), 9" x 12" sheets of orange construction paper, assorted colors and sizes of construction paper (Scraps from other projects work well.), markers, jack-o'-lantern worksheet (page 107), scissors, pencils, paper plates, paste or glue

Directions:
- Students trace an oaktag circle on an orange piece of construction paper. Then, they cut it out to create a pumpkin. (Or, you can make copies of the jack-o'-lantern on page 107 for each student.)

- They are to write the words "Jack-O'-Lantern" across the space where the mouth of the jack-o'-lantern should be.

- Give each student a copy of the worksheet and a paper plate. Have them cut out the letters and place them on the paper plate.

- Next, have students glue the letters from the plate onto their pumpkins to spell Jack-O'-Lantern.

Lay out assorted colors of construction paper on a table. Demonstrate how students can use this paper to create eyes, nose, stems, etc. Encourage creativity. The eyes do not have to match. More than one shape can be used for each feature. Students can add ears, hair, cheeks and eyelashes.

Jack-O'-Lantern Worksheet

Art

L	J	E	N	A	T
A	-O'-	C	K	R	N

Journals

Objective: To encourage journal writing

Journal writing is an activity that can start in September and continue through June. This activity is stressed during "J" week.

Directions: To prepare journals, pick a shape for the month. Use construction paper for the front and back covers and insert approximately five pages for each month. Write "My Journal" on the cover. An apple pattern you might use for September is given at the bottom of the page. Enlarge it before copying if you desire a larger size.

Suggested Journal Shapes:

September - apple   October - pumpkin   November - Pilgrim hat
December - bell   January - snowman   February - heart
March - kite   April - umbrella   May - flower
June - sun

To introduce journal writing, provide motivation by telling the children two or three exciting events that you were involved in, such as a vacation, special guests, a funny experience, etc. Select one idea and draw a picture on the chalkboard to illustrate the experience while you are relating it. After you have finished the illustration, write two or three sentences to help relate your story.

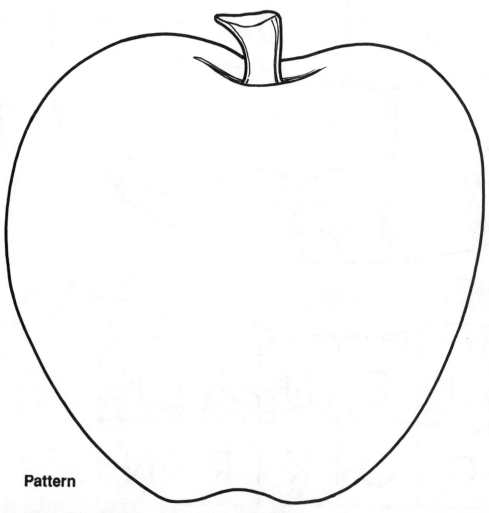

Invite the children to relate an experience and then discuss how they can illustrate it. When they have completed the illustration, help them write about it on the same journal page.

When the journal stories are completed, celebrate by reading them to the class with the "help" of the author.

As the year progresses, and the children are introduced to more letter sounds, encourage them to write their own words and/or sentences by sounding out the words and writing the sounds they hear (inventive spelling).

Pattern

The Jungle Jogging Book

Writing/ Reading

Objective: To create a class book about the jungle

Materials: construction paper, crayons

Directions: Have the children complete this sentence and illustrate it:

"In the jungle jogged a _____ . Jog, jog, jog."

Each page will be different, but each one will have the same repetitive refrain making it fun and easy for even the youngest child to read this book!

Suggested Reading:

Jungle Sounds by Rebecca Emberly
Wonders of the Jungle by National Wildlife Federation
Lost in the Amazon by Robert Quackenbush

Jumbled Book

Objective: To create a jumbled word book

Materials: stapler, copy machine, paper, pencils, crayons or markers, magnetic letters, chalk and chalkboard

Directions: • Using magnetic letters, form the word "cat." Ask the students to read the word.

• Next, change the order of the letters in "cat" to create a word jumble. Now, ask the students if they can figure out what the word could read if the letters were in the right order.

• Next, using the board and chalk, draw a simple picture of a pig's face. Again, using the magnetic letters, place the letters p-g-i under the picture. Ask the students to solve the jumble.

• Repeat the process using simple pictures and small words (dog, sun, cup, etc.).

• Now, have students create their own jumble by first illustrating the word and writing the letters of the word below it in a jumble fashion. Under the scrambled letters, have them create a short line to write the word correctly.

So that each student can work in his/her own book, run off a copy of each jumbled page. Staple or bind them .

Author Study - Ann Jonas

Objective and Directions: Refer to **Biography** page 11.

Background:

Ann Jonas grew up in New York. She now lives in Brooklyn with her husband and two daughters. Her husband, Donald Crews, is an author and illustrator. Ms. Jonas worked with him for many years as a graphic designer. Her book, *Round Trip*, was chosen one of the *New York Times* Best Illustrated Book of the Year in 1983.

Suggested Reading:

The Trek	*Two Bear Cubs*	*Round Trip*
When You Were a Baby	*Holes and Peeks*	

Jungle Environment

Science

Objective: To make a large classroom diorama depicting a jungle environment

Materials: large box, construction paper, scissors, glue, tape, markers, paint, paintbrushes

Directions: Paint or cover box with construction paper. Stand box on one end, leaving a large side open. Have children draw and cut background elements for a jungle scene including trees, plants, mountains, vines. Next, have children draw and cut out jungle animals. Tape or glue the animals in place.

You may want to label the main parts of the jungle environment using small pieces of index cards folded in half or taped to the scene.

Suggested Reading: See **Jungle Scene** page 106.

Junk

Objective: To talk about the meaning of the word junk (i.e. junk food and junk objects)

Materials: pictures of food, junk objects.from food, sheets of construction paper, glue

Healthy Food	Junk Food

Directions: Activity #1: Cut out pictures of all kinds of food - healthy food and junk food. Make certain there are enough pictures for each child to have several from each category. Give each child a sheet of construction paper. Write the categories of food on the chalkboard. Have the children fold their papers in half and write the two categories. They then paste their pictures in the proper column. Let them share their papers and tell why they think some food is healthy and other food is called junk food.

Activity #2: Have each child bring a piece of junk from home, something that needs to be disposed of. Share the items and talk about how to get rid of them, i.e. what is recyclable and what isn't. Make a pile of the junk. Discuss the fact that if everyone in America had that much junk, think how tall the pile would be! They will probably come up with quite humorous comparisons.

A Jar of Jellybeans

Math

Objective: To teach estimation, counting and graphing

Materials: 50 jellybeans, jar, projector, copies of the graph below

Directions: Fill a jar with jellybeans using 4 different colors.

1. Have the children guess how many jellybeans they think are in the jar and record their estimates.

2. Count each color jellybean and record the amounts.

3. Count all the jellybeans and record.

4. Use an opaque projector to enlarge the graph below. Hang it at eye level for the children. Let each one have a turn filling in the graph to show the number of each color of jellybean.

5. Give each child a copy of the graph below. Fill it in as a group.

6. Write a math story recording such things as:

   a. How many more red than black jellybeans?
   b. How many less . . . ?
   c. Which color is greatest in number?
   d. Which color is least in number?
   e. How many of each color?

7. Celebrate the child whose estimation was the closest with a Jolly Jellybean Jell-O Party. See Poetry - **Jellybeans** page 114, Cooking - **Jolly Jellybean Jell-O** page 114.

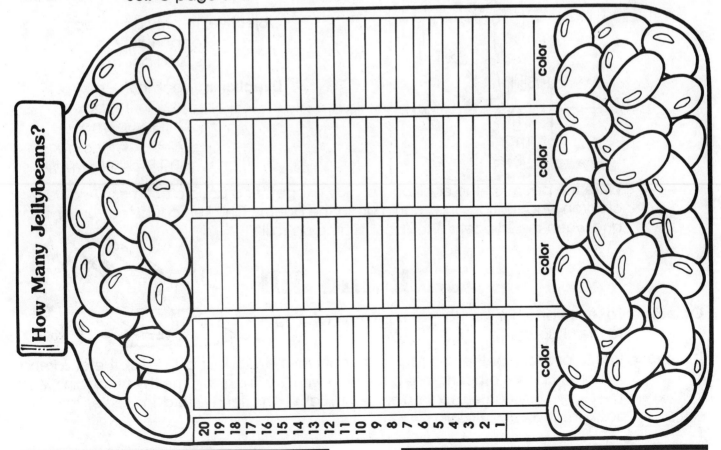

How Many Jellybeans?

color

color

color

color

20 19 18 17 16 15 14 13 12 11 10 9 8 7 6 5 4 3 2 1

111

Jumping - Jack Be Nimble

Objective: To learn a nursery rhyme and practice repeating it

Games

Materials: cylinder block or unbreakable candlestick

Directions: Have the children sit in a circle. Place a cylinder block or candlestick in the center to represent a candlestick. Review the nursery rhyme below.

> Jack be nimble.
> Jack be quick.
> Jack jump over
> the candlestick.

Replace the name "Jack" with the children's names to indicate when it is their turn to jump over the block in the center of the circle.

> i.e. Mary be nimble
> Mary be quick.
> Mary jump over
> the candlestick.

For a variation, each "jumper" can repeat the rhyme inviting the next jumper to take his/her turn. To help the children listen for the "J" sound, tell them to jump up each time the name of the child whose turn it is begins with the "J" sound.

Jack in the Box

Objective: To provide an additional opportunity to learn a "J" sound poem

Directions: Jack in the box
> Jack in the box
> Curled up small
> Open the lid
> And he jumps up tall.

Write the poem on the chalkboard. Say it together a couple of times. Ask the children what actions they could do to the poem. Children could "curl up small" and when the lid opens, they could "jump up tall!"

Jack and Jill

Objective: To recite another familiar nursery rhyme relating to the "J" sound

Directions: Recite or sing together the familiar nursery rhyme "Jack and Jill." Ask the children to come up with other names beginning with "J". Then, say the rhyme again with the suggested names. Examples: John, Jane, Jim, Jenny, Jordan, Jessie, Jerry, Jacklyn, Judy, Joy, Jason

Jolly Jogger in the Neighborhood

Objective: To create a neighborhood and a character to jog through the neighborhood

Materials: clay, felt, yarn, markers, materials listed under **Community** (See page 42.)

Social Studies

Directions:
- To create a neighborhood, see **Community** page 42.
- To create a jolly jogger, take a piece of clay and pinch out a neck and a head.
- Add arms, legs and face. Add hair with yarn.
- Using felt, create a cape. Write the letter "J" on the jogger's cape.
- Students give him/her a name beginning with the letter "J." During activity times, allow students to help your jolly figure jog through the neighborhood!

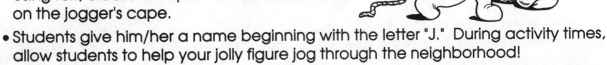

Extension Activity:
Create a class story or book on your "Jolly Jogger's" adventures.

Suggested Reading:
Willie's Walk by Margaret Wise Brown
And To Think I Saw It On Mulberry Street by Dr. Seuss

Jobs and Jigsaws

The Adventures of Jolly Jogger

Objective: To discuss what a job is and why people have them

Materials: copies of the J pattern, envelopes, crayons, scissors

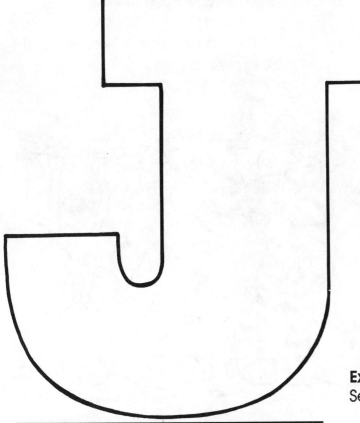

Directions: Immediately after play period, and before cleaning up, have students sit in a circle. Discuss what the best way would be to get the room cleaned up. Discuss the word "job." Next, have students volunteer for specific jobs to get the work done!

Using an easel, brainstorm all the different kinds of jobs the children can think of. In a separate list, write only the jobs that begin with "J". Enlarge the J shown. Make copies for the class. Have the students divide their J into 4 puzzle sections. In each section, they should illustrate a job that would interest them. They cut their puzzles apart and put them in envelopes with their names on them. Allow them time to exchange their puzzle with a neighbor.

Extension Activity:
See **I Can Help With My Helping Hands** page 95.

113

Cooking

Juice

Discuss the importance of oranges (Vitamin C) in the diet. Ask the children how they think orange juice, from a container, is made. Use several oranges to make enough juice to have a juice-tasting party.

Talk about other kinds of juices. Together, make a graph of the children's favorite juices.

Jolly Jellybean Jell-O

Follow the directions on the Jell-O box. Pour into individual serving "dishes," such as foil cupcake-size baking cups. Top with a jolly jellybean face. Celebrate "J" week with a Jell-O Jellybean and Juice Party.

(See Math page 111 and Poetry **Jellybeans** below.)

Poetry

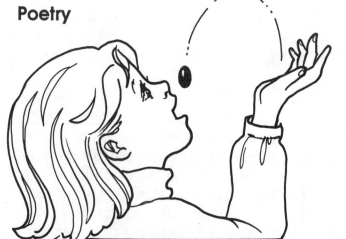

Jellybeans

There are jellybeans in the closet.
There are jellybeans on the floor.
There are jellybeans in my pocket.
There are jellybeans near the door.

I like jellybeans in the north.
I like jellybeans in the south.
But the place I like jellybeans best
Is in my mouth!

by Ada Frischer

The Jungle

I went to the jungle
And what did I see?
All the animals were roaming free.
The lions and tigers and monkeys too.
Living in the jungle - not in the zoo.

The lions roared
They are the kings.
The parrots talked
And flapped their wings.
The monkeys climbed up in the tree.
I think the animals like being free.

by Ada Frischer

114

Just Me

Dramatization

Objective: Refer to **Dramatization** page 11.

Materials: book - *Just Me* by Marie Hall Etts

Directions: Read the story to the children, perhaps more than once. Record the story on tape. Play the tape for the class. Students can act out the animal movements just as the little boy does in the story.

Music/ Physical Education

Jumping Jacks and Jumping Rope

Teach the children to do jumping jacks. Then, teach them to jump to the rhythm and tempo of music. Using a piano or guitar, vary the rhythm and tempo. You could have the children say 1 J, 2 J's, 3 J's, 4 J's, etc. as they jump.

Children love to jump rope. Find some fun jump rope jingles and do them outside during recess. Encourage the children to teach the class jumping jingles that they know.

Book List

Aliki. (1986). *Jack and Jake.* New York: Greenwillow Books.

Berenstain, S. and Berenstain, J. (1985). *The Berenstain Bears and Too Much Junk Food.* New York: Random House.

Galdone, P. (1982). *Jack and the Beanstalk.* Ticknor and Fields.

Hoban, R. (1964). *Bread for Jam and Frances.* New York: Harper and Row.

Keats, E.J. (1966). *Jenny's Hat.* New York: Harper and Row.

Schulman, J. (1977). *Jack the Bum and Haunted House.* Greenwillow Books.

Tresselt, A. (1948). *Johnny Maple Leaf.* New York: Lothrop, Lee and Shepard.

Van Allsburg, C. (1981). *Jumanji.* New York: Houghton Mifflin.

Table of Contents

*Remember to check **B Chapter Table of Contents** (page 4) for additional activities.

Kite

Art

Objective: To create and design a kite using a ruler and to listen and follow directions

Materials: 9" x 12" sheets of construction paper (one per student), 12" x 3/4" strips of paper (one per student), tongue depressor or ice cream stick, scraps of colored paper or assorted fabric scraps, ruler, string, scissors, glue

Directions:

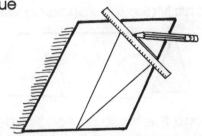

1. Give children a piece of construction paper folded in half the long way with a dot 1/3 of the way down on the open side.

2. Show children how to use a ruler to draw a line from the dot to the top corner on the fold, and from the dot to the bottom corner on the fold.

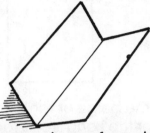

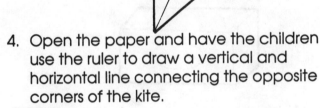

3. Children will draw the lines with the ruler, then cut on the lines with the paper folded.

4. Open the paper and have the children use the ruler to draw a vertical and horizontal line connecting the opposite corners of the kite.

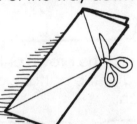

5. Have the children decorate each quadrant of the kite.

6. Attach a 12" x 3/4" strip for the tail. Paste scraps of paper or fabric on the tail.

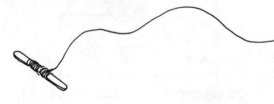

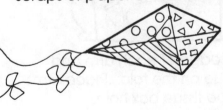

7. Attach a string to the other end and wrap it around a tongue depressor or ice cream stick.

8. Take a walk to the playground to fly the kites.

Suggested Singing:

"Let's Go Fly a Kite" from Mary Poppins - music and lyrics by Richard M. Sherman and Robert B. Sherman

Kangaroo

Art

Objective: To create a kangaroo with a pouch to use in a phonics activity

Materials: an empty tissue box for each student, beige or tan paper, brown or tan paint, paintbrushes, glue, crayons, scissors

Directions: Make the kangaroo with the class, step-by-step.

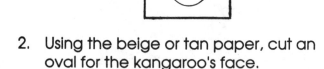

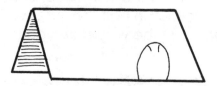

1. Place the tissue box on its side with the hole facing you. Paint it brown or tan.

2. Using the beige or tan paper, cut an oval for the kangaroo's face.

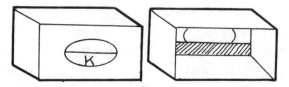

3. Draw a face with crayons.

4. Draw, cut and glue on ears.

5. For arms, fold the brown or tan paper in half, and at the bottom, draw and cut an arch.

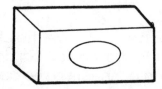

6. Using the same piece of paper, draw a leg in the corner approximately half the height of your tissue box.

7. Next, cut a piece of brown or tan paper the length of your box and half the height to create a pouch.

8. Glue it across the opening to your tissue box. Draw a "K" on the pouch.

9. Fold the edge of each arm and place glue on the fold. Place arms above the tissue box hole.

10. Glue the legs to the sides of the box.

11. Place glue on the outer edge of the pouch, and place it at the bottom of the box.

Extension Activity:

See **K Is for Kangaroo** under Writing/Reading page 119.
The kangaroo the children made will be used in this activity.

Suggested Reading:

Katy No-Pocket by Emmy Payne

K Is for Kangaroo

Writing/ Reading

Objective: To determine which picture cards begin with the sound for "K" as in "Kangaroo"

Materials: the kangaroo from page 118 or a child-size apron and a large piece of felt, white paper, marker, oaktag

Note: Instead of the kangaroo made on page 118, you could make an apron with a pouch on it. Just cut a piece of felt and glue it to the apron to represent a kangaroo's pouch. With a marker, write the letter "K" on the pouch.

Directions: Enlarge and cut out the pictures below. Some begin with the "K" sound and some do not. Glue them on oaktag to create cards. Place the apron on a student who is now a kangaroo! Seat students in a circle with the "kangaroo" standing in the front. Place the cards in a pile. Ask individuals to come up, pick a card and place it in the pouch if it begins with "K." (If you are using the tissue-box kangaroo, students place cards in the box/pouch.)

Suggested Reading:

Katy No-Pocket by Emmy Payne
What Do You Do With a Kangaroo? by Mercer Mayer
A First Look at Kangaroos by Millicent Selsam

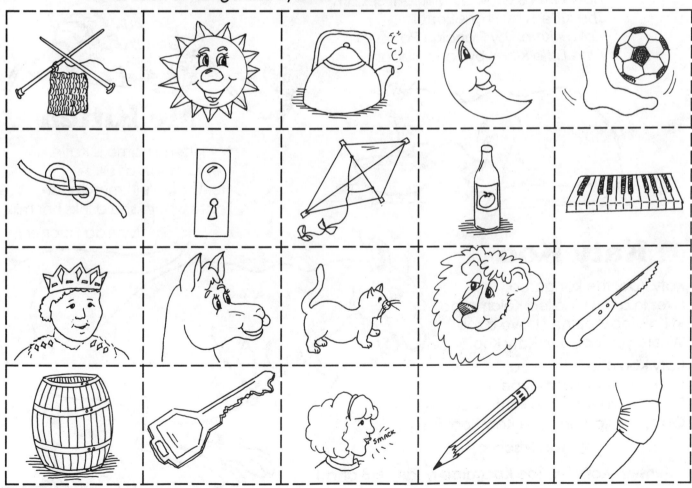

119   ©MCMXCIII Instructional Fair, Inc.

If We Had a Kitten in Kindergarten . . .

Writing/ Reading

Objective: To have students imagine that they have a kitten in their classroom and to encourage them to write about what they would do with this little critter (This can be made into a class book.)

Materials: paper, crayons, pencils

Directions: Ask the students to imagine that there is another student in kindergarten, except that this student is soft and fluffy, has four legs and a quiet voice that only says, "Meow." Ask the class these questions: What would you do if there was a kitten in kindergarten? Would you put it in the doll carriage? Would you build it a house of blocks? Would you let it sit on your lap?

After several responses have been generated, provide students with paper and crayons and let them illustrate their ideas. You or a volunteer could take dictation at the bottom of each page. If desired, create a cover and bind/staple the pages together to create a class book.

Extension Activity:

Have students "read" their ideas to another kindergarten class.

Suggested Reading:

How Kittens Grow by Millicent Selsam
The Kittens by Phyllis Bartell
Koko's Kitten by Francine Patterson
One Little Kitten by Tana Hoban

My Kitten

My kitten's name is Katie.
Her fur is soft as silk.
Her basket's in my kitchen.
That's where she drinks her milk.

by Ada Frischer

Katy Koo

Katy Koo, the kangaroo,
Lives in a town called Kalamazoo.
In Kalamazoo, they have a zoo
Where you can visit Katy Koo.

Katy Koo, the kangaroo,
Needs a friend or maybe two.
So when you go to Kalamazoo,
Go to the zoo and see Katy Koo.

by Ada Frischer

Extension Activity: See **Kangaroo** pages 118 and 119.

Key Words

Writing/ Reading

Objective: To make a list of "key" words on a paper key

Materials: a copy of the key below, marker, tape, projector

Directions: Enlarge the key below using an opaque projector. On the copy of the key, create a class list of words. Your key words could be a list of words beginning with "K", a list of words needed for a writing assignment in this "K" chapter, or an ongoing list of new sight words. Hang and label the key in your classroom.

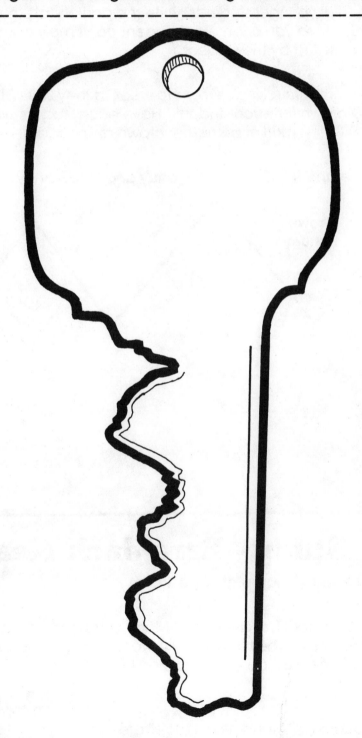

If I Were a Kind King

Writing/ Reading

Objective: To write about and illustrate how students would rule their kingdom if they were a kind king

Materials: white paper and crayons, pencils, marker

Directions: Discuss what kindness is. (See Social Studies page 123.) Read the story suggested below. Next, ask the students what kind of rules they would make if they were a kind king. When the discussion is over, allow each student to write and illustrate his/her thoughts. (For younger students, write the partial statement, "If I were a kind king, I would . . . " so you or an older student can simply complete the sentence as it is dictated by the student.)

Extension Activity:

Provide each student with a king's crown to wear as they write. Use the pattern below to make a crown for each student. Have each student write or trace the words, "Kind King" with a marker on his/her crown and decorate it.

Suggested Reading:

The King, The Mice and The Cheese by Nancy and Eric Gurney

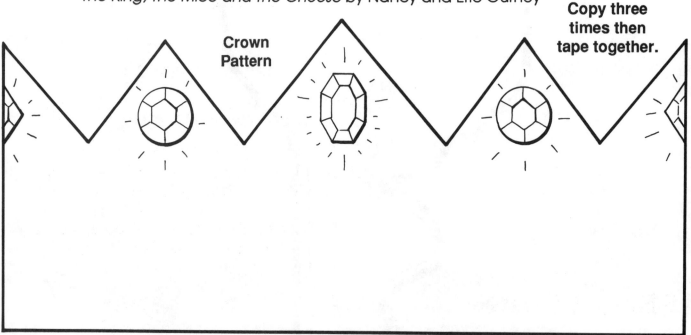

Crown Pattern

Copy three times then tape together.

Author Study - Ezra Jack Keats

Objective and Directions: Refer to **Biography** page 11.

Background:

Mr. Keats was born in Brooklyn, New York. Many of his stories take place in a city. He has loved to draw since he was four. He was in the U.S. Air Corps during World War II as a camouflage expert. Mr. Keats died in 1983.

Suggested Reading:

Peter's Chair	*The Snowy Day*	*Whistle for Willie*
Jennie's Hat	*Maggie and the Pirate*	

Kaleidoscope

Science

Materials: three identical rectangular mirrors, an inexpensive kaleidoscope

Directions: Arrange the three mirrors so that a triangle is formed with the mirrors inside. See illustration.

Carefully, tape the sides of the mirrors together so that they form a triangular tunnel. As you hold the mirrors, invite the children to take turns looking into the "tunnel." This demonstration may help the children understand the way a kaleidoscope works.

Show the inexpensive kaleidoscope to the children and invite them to enjoy the beautiful shapes and designs for themselves.

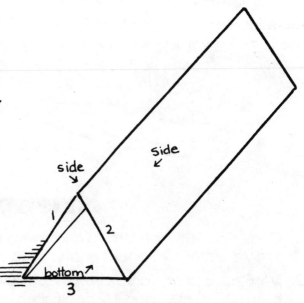

Social Studies

Kindness

Objective: To create a definition for kindness and create a list of ways they can be kind

Materials: large chart paper, markers

Directions: Ask students what it means when someone is kind. Write the word "kindness" on the chart paper. Next, write the students' definitions. Make a list of ways students feel they can be kind to each other.

Martin Luther King, Jr.

In conjunction with "kindness," now may be a good time to discuss Martin Luther King, Jr.'s life, and his struggle for equality, fairness, and kindness among all people.

Suggested Reading:

Meet Martin Luther King, Jr. by James T. de Kay

The Picture Life of Martin Luther King, Jr. by Margaret B. Young

Martin Luther King Day by Linda Lowry

123

Katy No-Pocket

Dramatization

Objective and Directions:
Refer to **Dramatization** page 30.

Materials: book - *Katy No-Pocket* by Emmy Payne, carpenter's apron or a kitchen apron with several pockets sewn on, small stuffed animals

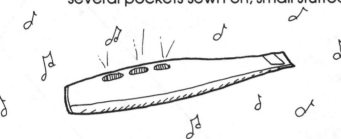

Kazoo   Music

If you can, obtain several kazoos, form a kazoo band and parade around the room, or the playground if it is too noisy!

Krispy Krunchies

Cooking

1. Cook one cup dark brown corn syrup until it forms a firm ball in cold water. Stir occasionally. Add one teaspoon vinegar.

2. Mix 5 cups of dry, crisp cereal such as rice crisps, corn flakes, bran flakes, etc., and 1/2 cup salted peanuts in a greased bowl.

Pour mixture 1 over mixture 2 and stir until coated.

Pack into a greased pan. Cool and break into pieces.

A Kitchen Korner

Objective: To identify various kitchen items

Materials: various kitchen items, pictures of kitchen items, oaktag, glue, scissors

Directions: 1. Gather old magazines that will most likely have kitchen pictures in them.
2. Let children go through and cut out kitchen pictures they like.
3. Give children 2 pieces of oaktag to paste kitchen items on.
4. Make a large kitchen collage with the remainder of the pictures on a big piece of butcher paper. Let each child paste his/hers where he/she wants.

Suggested Trips

Fly a kite in the playground. Share stories with another kindergarten class.

Book List

Keats, E. (1974). *Kitten for a Day.* New York: Macmillan.

Mayer, M. (1987). *What Do You Do With a Kangaroo?* New York: Scholastic.

Patterson, F. *Koko's Kitten.* New York: Scholastic.

Payne, E. (1985). *Katy No-Pocket.* New York: Houghton Mifflin.

Selsam, M. (1975). *How Kittens Grow.* New York: Four Winds Press.

Sendak, M. (1973). *In the Night Kitchen.* New York: Harper and Row.

Table of Contents

*Remember to check **B Chapter Table of Contents** (page 4) for additional activities.

Lion Puppet

Art

Objective: To reinforce the "L" sound and to learn about the expression "March comes in like a lion."

Materials: lunch-size paper bags, 9" x 12" sheets of yellow and brown construction paper, crayons, markers, scissors, glue

Directions: Tell the children the expression, "March comes in like a lion . . ." Ask them how they think a lion would come in (i.e. with a roar, loudly, fiercely). Ask them how that might apply to weather. Ask them to give examples of lionlike weather. Then, make the lion below with them. Have each student bring in a lunch-size paper bag. Give each student a piece of brown and yellow construction paper. Then, work through each step with the class.

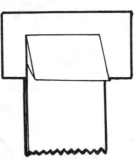

1. With the bag folded flat, glue 9" x 12" yellow construction paper to top back of paper bag. Be sure to center the paper and line it up with the flap of the bag. (See illustration.)

2. Draw a "mane" around the paper bag. Cut out the "mane" with the paper bag attached. Draw eyes, a nose and whiskers with a black crayon or marker. (Another way to create a mane would be to glue strips of yellow and brown paper to bag. Wrap paper strips around a pencil and curl strips toward front.)

3. Next, fold a 9" x 12" sheet of brown paper in half. To make paws, have children draw two "trees," one larger than the other. When the trees are cut, the children will have two sets of paws. (See illustration.)

4. Open the brown paper and find space to draw a "broom." This will become the tail! Have the children cut fringe for the tail hair.

5. Turn the paper bag and mane over and glue the paws and the tail on from the back. (See illustration.)

Lamb Puppet

Art

Objective: To complete the old saying with the phrase, "March goes out like a lamb."
To help children be aware of how our language uses metaphors to compare things

Materials: lunch-size paper bags, cotton balls, purple or pink 9" x 12" construction paper, crayons, markers, scissors, glue

Directions: See if the children can remember the phrase that went with making their lion puppets. Say it together. Then, tell them the rest of the saying, "March goes out like a lamb." Ask the children how a lamb might act (meekly, quietly) and how that might apply to weather.

Follow the same basic instructions for making a lamb puppet as you did when making the lion. All that is different is the woolly hair and the ears. Display the lions and lambs on a bulletin board with the saying, "March comes in like a lion and goes out like a lamb."

Draw ears and woolly hair instead of mane on purple or pink construction paper. Cut around ears and hair. (See illustration.)

Follow same procedure as lion puppet for paws. The tail is a cotton ball glued to the back of the paper bag. Glue cotton balls on the woolly hair. (See illustration.)

Lincoln Log Cabin

Objective: To create a log cabin in conjunction with a Social Studies theme about Abraham Lincoln

Materials: Each child will need the following: 5 tongue depressors, 2 ice cream sticks, white glue, one sheet 9" x 12" construction paper, crayons

Directions: Children will count out the correct number of tongue depressors and ice cream sticks that they need.

They will glue the tongue depressors horizontally starting at the bottom of the construction paper to resemble logs. The ice cream sticks will form a peaked roof.

They will use the crayons to add a door, windows, grass, trees, sky and perhaps Abraham Lincoln in his tall black hat.

Suggested Reading:
The Boy on Lincoln's Lap by Jerrold Beim
Just Like Abraham Lincoln by Bernard Waber

Writing a Letter
Writing/Reading

Objective: To become familiar with the reasons for letter writing and to write a letter

Materials: paper and pencils, book - *The Jolly Postman* by Janet and Allan Ahlberg

Directions: Read *The Jolly Postman.* As you read the book, discuss the reason why each letter has been written. (It would be helpful to make a list of these reasons. For example, to tell, to ask, to sell, to invite, to thank, etc.) Next, students can write letters to individuals with one of the chosen reasons for letter writing. Or, you could write a class letter. Students may write to a friend, a family member, a storybook character, a super hero, etc.

Library

Objective: To begin your classroom lending library

Materials: books students have written, books donated by students' families, library cards and pockets

Directions: In a corner of your room, set up a table or shelves on which to place books. Paste pockets and insert cards inside book covers. Explain to your students what a library is. Set limitations for your library (i.e. for how long a book will be loaned, how to care for books, how they should be transported to and from school, the procedure for borrowing a book).

Listening for L Words

Objective: To increase awareness of "L" words and to listen for specific sounds

Materials: newsprint and markers

Directions: Tell children they are going to practice their listening skills as you read them sentences with "L" words in them.

Have children fold their paper in half, then in half again and then in half one more time. As they open them back up, ask how many sections they have. Have them number the sections 1 through 8. As you read each sentence, they are to draw a picture of the word they hear that begins with the "L" sound.

1. See the soft, woolly lamb.
2. I heard the lion roar.
3. Write on the line.
4. She ate the lollipop.
5. There are two lemons.
6. The clown had red lips.
7. The leaves fell from the trees.
8. Put the logs on the fire.

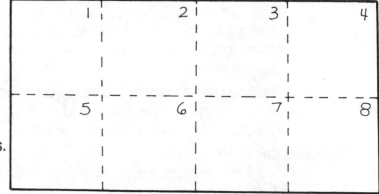

Lists

Objective: To learn what a list is used for and to create one of their own

Materials: paper and pencils

Directions: Ask students if they have ever seen a list. What is a list used for? Next, create a list with the students. You may use of one the following suggestions:

    a list of "L" words
    a homework list
    a list of favorite books
    a class list of names
    a list of class birthdays
    a list of things to do in school today
    a list of jobs
    a list of family members

Letters

Objective: To review the letters (consonant sounds) studied thus far

Materials: paper, pencils and crayons or markers

Directions: Ask students to recite the letters of the alphabet. Then, talk about the sounds that letters make. Write the 8 consonant sounds that have been studied thus far on the chalkboard (B, C, D, F, G, H, J, K). Let children tell words for the different sounds. Then, have the children fold their papers in half three times and write the 8 letters in the sections as shown. They then will draw a picture to illustrate each sound.

Author Study - Leo Lionni

Background:

    Leo Lionni was born in Amsterdam, Holland. His wife's name is Nora. They have two children. The Lionni's live in Porcignano, Italy. Mr. Lionni does not write books for children. Rather, he writes them for the part in everyone that is still a child.

Suggested Reading:

    Little Blue and Little Yellow
    Cornelius
    Frederick
    It's Mine
    Let's Make Rabbits
    Alexander and the Wind-Up Mouse

Leaf Rubbing

Science

Objective: To select a variety of leaves and create a leaf print

Materials: 8" x 11" white construction paper, 9" x 12" colored construction paper, an assortment of small pieces of crayon with the paper covering removed

Directions: Take a class walk around the school grounds. Have each child find 3 different kinds of leaves to bring back to the classroom. If you are in an area where the leaves turn colors and fall off trees in autumn, this is a good time of year for this project.

If leaves are not available to you, use the patterns below to make oaktag cutouts of various leaf shapes.

Tape the leaves, vein side down (or oaktag cutouts) to the paper.

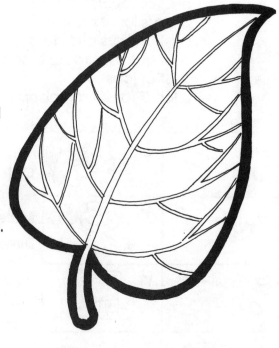

Turn the paper over. Use the crayons on the sides to rub over the leaves. Use several colors over the leaves to create a blended look. (Red, brown, yellow, orange and green make a good autumn mixture.) Remove the leaves (or cutouts) and mount the rubbing on a piece of contrasting colored construction paper to form a frame.

Liquid

Science

Objective: To experiment with water and other liquids, to encourage observation and to introduce the scientific terms "liquid" and "solid"

Materials: paper cup, water, heavy cream, plastic container with lid, Jell-O, bowl, spoon, kettle, burner or stove, measuring cup

Directions: Talk about the characteristics of a liquid. It is something you cannot pick up with your fingers.

Experiment #1
On a cold day, put some water in a paper cup and put it outdoors. Check it regularly. (If you do not have cold days, put it in a freezer.) What happened to it? After it turns into a solid, bring it back into the classroom to check it. What happened now?

Experiment #2
Make butter. Watch the cream change from a liquid to a solid.

Experiment #3
Make Jell-O. Watch the liquid change to a solid.

Experiment #4
Measure one cup of water. Put it in a kettle and boil it. Observe what happens to the liquid. Let the water boil for about 15 minutes. Then, measure the amount of water remaining in the kettle.

Light

Objective: To experiment to find out how light travels, what happens to light when it is blocked and when it is reflected

Materials: flashlight, baby powder, mirror, chalkboard, overhead projector

Directions: Discuss with students what light is and what our light sources are. (See Suggested Reading below.)

Experiment #1:

On the chalkboard, draw a curved line, a straight line and a zig-zag line. Have students predict in which fashion light travels. Turn out the lights. Standing approximately six feet from the students, hold the baby powder in an upright position and squeeze the container allowing a small amount of powder to enter the air. Next, shine the flashlight in the direction of the powder. Students should be able to see the line the light creates.

Experiment #2:

To find out what happens when light is blocked, simply shine the flashlight in the direction of your hand, a student's head or a book. Explain that light cannot pass through your hand as it does through a window. When light is blocked, a shadow is created. Use an overhead projector to let the students take turns making shadows.

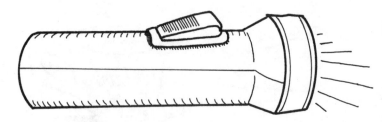

Experiment #3:

To find out what happens when light is reflected, hold a mirror. Ask a student to shine the flashlight on the mirror.

Ask the class:

1. to locate the object the light is shining on
2. to name objects for you to reflect the light upon
3. what happens to light when it is reflected, when it is bent

Suggested Reading:

Light by Donald Crews
Shadows and Reflections by Tana Hoban
Shadows, Here, There and Everywhere by Ron and Nancy Goor
Mother, Mother, I Feel Sick by Remy Charlip

Extension Activity:

See **Silhouette** page 214.

Light Sensitive Paper
Science

Objective: To use light sensitive paper to make handprints

Materials: one square of light sensitive paper for each child (blueprint paper), water

Directions: Go outside on a bright, sunny day. Working with small groups, give each child a piece of light sensitive paper large enough for his/her hand. Tell children to place their hands on the paper but they cannot move their hands once they are on the paper. Wait about five minutes and then have students carefully remove their hands. Bring the papers inside and rinse them with water for about one minute. Blot with paper towels and dry the papers on a flat surface.

When dry, handprints may be mounted, framed and displayed.

Litter

Objective: To create an awareness of litter that surrounds us and to make a "backyard litter bag"

Materials: grocery bag, yarn, stapler, crayons

Directions: After having a class discussion on litter, and perhaps cleaning litter from your own school yard, ask each student to bring in a grocery bag. As you collect each bag, open it up and roll down the sides of the bag twice. Then, fold the bag flat. Students can use crayons to decorate their litter bags appropriately. Create a "No Littering" slogan. Each student can write the slogan on his/her bag. With a stapler, fasten yarn to create a shoulder strap on each bag. Students can take their bags home to clean up their own yards.

Note: Be sure to emphasize safety precautions (i.e. Do not pick up broken glass.).

Suggested Reading:
It Was Just a Dream by Chris Van Allsburg

Listening for Litter

Objective: To create an awareness of sounds of litter and how certain noises "litter" our environment

Materials: a group of listening children

Directions: Talk with the class about littering sounds. These can be sounds of things being tossed to the ground or noisy, unpleasant sounds that litter our environment in a different way. Take a walk with your class around school and the neighborhood to listen. When you return, sit in a circle and let the children share the different sounds they heard and whether or not they considered them "littering sounds."

Living/Non-Living

Science

Objective: To distinguish between living and non-living things

Directions: Ask the children to name things that are living. Lead the discussion to animals, people, insects, fish and plants.

Discuss how living things are different: size, shape, color, covering (skin, hide, fur, feathers), number of legs, wings, horns, paws, feet, hands, tails, how they move, speak, live.

Discuss how living things are the same. They need proper food, shelter and protection. They reproduce their own kind.

A pumpkin seed will grow a pumpkin,
A monkey will have a monkey baby,
A human will have a human baby, etc.

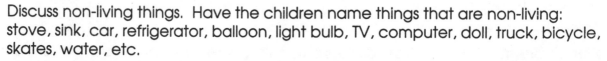

Discuss non-living things. Have the children name things that are non-living: stove, sink, car, refrigerator, balloon, light bulb, TV, computer, doll, truck, bicycle, skates, water, etc.

How do these things differ from living things? (They cannot reproduce. A stove will not have a baby stove, skates will not have baby skates for your little brother or sister, etc.)

Prepare two books with several blank pages in each. Label one book **Living** and one **Non-Living**. Have the children bring pictures to school and share them with the class. The children should be able to tell if their picture is a living or non-living object and why. Have the children paste their pictures in the appropriate book.

An appropriate extension would be to have the children tell what letter sound his/her object begins with. He/she might want to write that corresponding initial consonant letter in the book next to his/her picture.

Lollipop Counting Book
Math

Objective: To create a lollipop counting book

Materials: construction paper, crayons, markers, stapler or notebook rings and hole punch

Directions: Give each child a number (from 1 to the number of students in your class) and a piece of construction paper. Using a marker, have the children write their numeral in the lower right corner of their papers. Then, using crayons, have children draw and color the correct number of lollipops to match their numerals. (See illustration.)

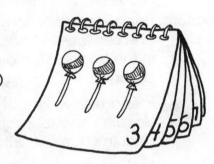

The books may be as long as you and the children want them to be! When finished, have the children put the pages in numerical order for you to staple.

Lollipop Graph

Objective: To help children estimate and graph the flavors of lollipops in a bag

Materials: a bag of lollipops, copies of the graph paper below, markers

Directions: Show the class the bag of lollipops. Ask the children to estimate the number of lollipops in the bag. Ask the children if they think there will be enough for the class to share. Record the children's estimations. Count the lollipops with the class.

Prepare a graph of lollipop flavors. Give each student a copy of the graph below. Students will color each lollipop a different color and then color a square for each lollipop above its flavor.

Count and tabulate the flavors. Write a math story with the class noting which flavor had the most lollipops, the least and if there were any ties.

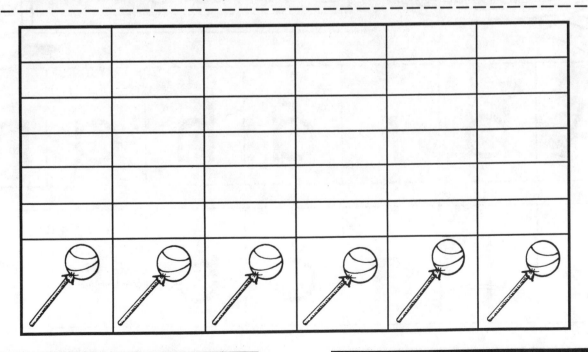

Lincoln Letter Match

Social Studies

Objective: To help children remember the name of Abraham Lincoln and learn that he was our 16th President and to practice matching letters

Materials: several pennies, magnifying glasses, teacher-prepared worksheet, glue, a small paper plate for each child

Directions: Using a magnifying glass, help the children locate Lincoln sitting in a chair in the Lincoln Memorial on the back of a penny.

Prepare a worksheet for letter matching Lincoln's name. Each letter of Abraham Lincoln's name should be in a box square. (See Illustration below.)

Make enough copies of this worksheet for each child to have two sheets, each one in a different color. For example, run a set in red and a set in blue.

Have the children identify the letters by name. The letters are cut from one colored sheet and matched and glued to the other sheet. Use the paper plates as storage trays for the cut letters. Have the children cut all the letters from one sheet of paper before pasting them on the other paper.

Have the children check to be sure the letters are not glued on upside-down!

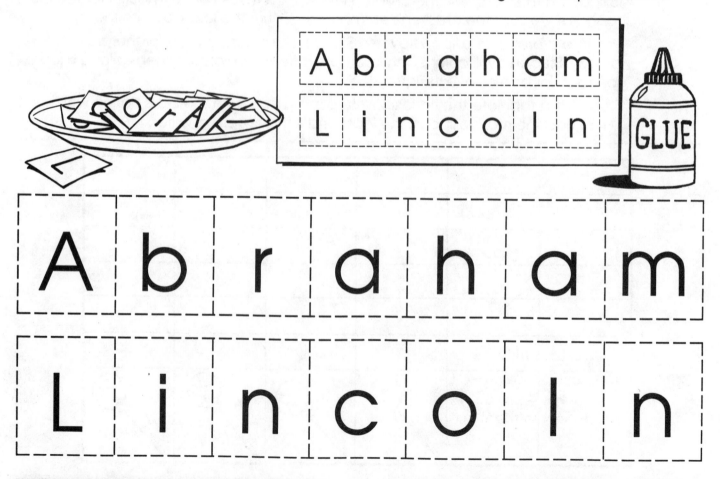

Conversation With a Lion

I talked to a little lion
He was living at the zoo.
He roared and roared and roared again
So I answered, "How do you do?"

He answered with another roar.
And I am happy to say,
We had a polite conversation
In the zoo that lovely day.

by Ada Frischer

Things I Like

I like to laugh
I like to play
Laughing makes a happy day.
I like to learn
I learn in school
In school I learn the Golden Rule.

by Ada Frischer

Lollipop

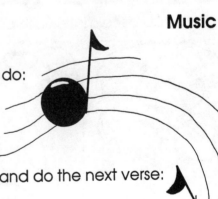

Lucy had a lollipop
She gave it to her sister
Her sister ate the lollipop
Then Lucy kissed her.

Lucy had a lollipop
She gave it to her brother
Her brother ate the lollipop
So Lucy got another.

Lucy had a lollipop
She didn't give it away
Lucy ate the lollipop
On another day.

by Ada Frischer

Extension Activity:
See **Lollipop Graph** page 135.

Looby Loo

Children stand in a circle. Holding hands, they walk or skip in the circle singing the chorus:

Here we go Looby Loo
Here we go Looby Light
Here we go Looby Loo
All on a Saturday night.

Music

Everyone stands in the circle. All drop hands and sing and do:

I put my right hand in
I put my right hand out
I give my right hand a shake, shake, shake
And turn myself about.

Repeat chorus walking or skipping in the circle. Then, sing and do the next verse:

I put my left hand in, etc.

Continue song using the following verses:

I put my right foot in.
I put my left foot in.
I put my whole self in.

End with the chorus.

Suggested Trips

Your local library

Book List

Beim, J. (1955). *The Boy on Lincoln's Lap.* New York: Morrow.

Burton, V. (1942). *The Little House.* New York: Houghton Mifflin.

Giff, P.R. (1987). *Lazy Lions, Lucky Lambs.* Delacorte.

Guarino, D. (1989). *Is Your Mama a Llama?.* New York: Scholastic.

Hoban, T. (1981). *Take Another Look.* New York: Greenwillow Books.

Kay, H. (1956). *One Mitten Lewis.* New York: Lothrop, Lee and Shepard.

Keats, E.J. (1968). *A Letter to Amy.* New York: Harper and Row.

Kraus, R. (1971). *Leo the Late Bloomer.* New York: Windmill Books.

Lionni, L. (1959). *Little Blue and Little Yellow.* McDowell, Obolensky.

Lobel, A. (1964). *Lucille.* New York: Harper and Row.

McCloskey, R. (1914). *Lentil.* New York: Viking Press.

Moncure, J.B. (1981). *Love.* Chicago, IL: Childrens Press.

Piper, W. (1976). *The Little Engine That Could.* New York: Platt and Munk.

Rice, E. (1987). *Oh, Lewis!* New York: Macmillan.

Rockwell, A. (1977). *I Like the Library.* E.P. Dutton.

Skorpen, L.M. (1970). *All the Lassies.* New York: Dial Press.

Waber, B. (1965). *Lyle Lyle Crocodile.* Boston, MA: Houghton Mifflin.

Waber, B. (1969). *Lovable Lyle.* Boston, MA: Houghton Mifflin.

Zemach, M. (1983). *The Little Red Hen.* Farrar.

L Pictures for Miscellaneous Activities

Enlarge the cards to make flash cards throughout the study of the "L" sound.

Mm

Table of Contents

*Remember to check **B Chapter Table of Contents** (page 4) for additional activities.

Mosaic

Art

Objective: To introduce mosaics as an art form

Materials: small squares of construction paper in many colors, large sheet of white construction paper per child, black markers, paste

Directions: With a black marker, have children draw a free form closed design. (See illustration.)

Using a pattern or randomly selected colors, children fill in the design by pasting the small colored squares inside the design. All squares must be inside the design and should not overlap each other. The result is a marvelous expression of color!

Extension Activity:

Brainstorm adjectives to describe their mosaics that begin with the "M" sound. Examples: marvelous, magical, multi-colored

Marble Painting

Materials: several marbles, assorted colors of paint in shallow containers, several spoons, white paper, gift boxes or cartons no deeper than 4", tape

Directions: Tape paper to the bottom of various boxes or cartons. Using a spoon, let each student dip a marble in a container of paint and then place the marble on the paper. The student holds the box or carton with both hands, tilting it to make the marble roll from side to side over the paper, leaving a track, or design, on the paper. Continue the procedure, using several marbles and colors until every student has had an opportunity to paint.

Suggested Reading:
Playing Marbles by Julie Brinckloe

Extension Activity:
See **Marbles** page 153.

Mittens

Art

Materials: white construction paper, yarn, pencils, water colors, paintbrushes, scissors, a mitten, a glove, newspaper

Directions: Recite the nursery rhyme, "Three Little Kittens" below. Enlarge the mitten and the poem below and display it so you can read the poem with the class. Discuss the similarities and differences between a glove and a mitten. Show students one of each. Next, tell students that they will create mittens on paper. Have students place their hand on a white sheet of paper with their fingers together and their thumb away from their fingers. Have them draw around their hand to create a mitten. Repeat using the opposite hand. (Young students can trace the same hand twice. When it is cut, flip it over to create the opposite mitten.) Students cut out the mittens and place them on newspaper with the thumbs together. Decorate mittens by painting them using water colors. Attach mittens by punching a hole and tying them with yarn. If desired, display mittens in your classroom by hanging them over a piece of yarn strung across the room.

Suggested Reading:
Runaway Mittens by Jean Rogers

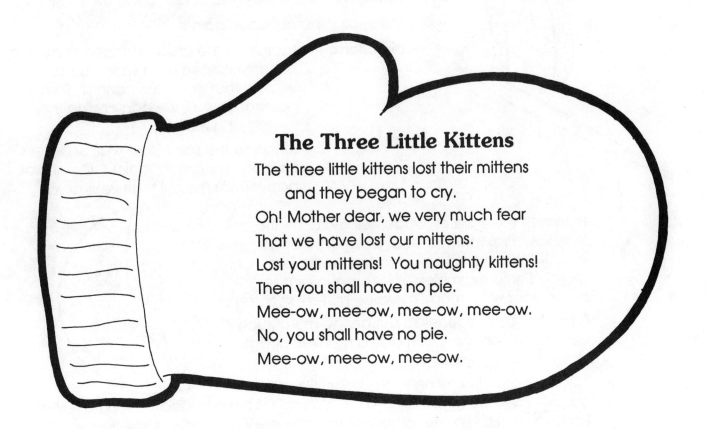

The Three Little Kittens

The three little kittens lost their mittens
and they began to cry.
Oh! Mother dear, we very much fear
That we have lost our mittens.
Lost your mittens! You naughty kittens!
Then you shall have no pie.
Mee-ow, mee-ow, mee-ow, mee-ow.
No, you shall have no pie.
Mee-ow, mee-ow, mee-ow.

Masks

Art

Objective: To create a "safe" mask using a paper plate and a tongue depressor

Materials: paper plate, crayons, scissors, yarn, construction paper, tongue depressors

Directions: Discuss with the children how different kinds of masks can look funny, silly, scary, happy, sad, excited, etc. Each child should decide what "look" his/her mask will have. Then, distribute the paper plates and have each child draw a face on the plate. You may cut out the eyes if you wish, but it is not necessary because this mask will not be worn on the face covering the eyes. It will be attached to a tongue depressor and held up to the face so that it can be easily moved.

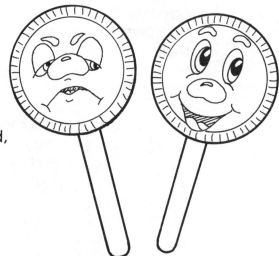

Use the yarn to make hair - long, short, braided, etc. Have each child design a hat to attach to the mask. Earrings can also be added.

Attach the paper plate mask to a tongue depressor and hold it up to, but not against, the face.

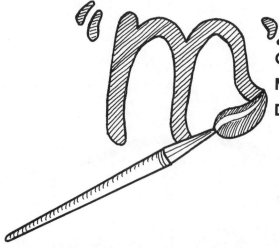

Mural

Objective: To create a mural consisting of "M" objects

Materials: mural paper, paints

Directions:

1. Explain to the children that a mural is a picture painted on a wall. Further explain that since we cannot always paint on a wall, we can create the feeling of a mural.

2. Measure the size of the wall or bulletin board you want to "paint." Cut mural paper from the roll to fit your area.

3. Plan with the children what their mural might look like. Brainstorm a list of words that begin with "M" that would be good to include in a mural. Some examples: mice, mountains, music, monkeys, maps, marbles, mitten, monster

4. Discuss specific scenes to put on the mural such as a mouse on the moon and a monkey skiing down the mountain.

5. Tape the mural painting to the floor. Recruit volunteers to paint specific things. You might have a moon, mountain and ground "crew." The remainder of the things will be added individually.

6. Let the mural dry and staple it to the bulletin board or tape it on the wall.

Monster Book

Objective: To stimulate imagination using creative thinking and creative drawing and to create a class book

Materials: construction paper, crayons, paper punch, yarn
books: *Millicent the Monster* by Mary Lystad
Where the Wild Things Are by Maurice Sendak
The Fourteenth Dragon by James E. Seidelman

Directions: Read the above books and discuss the fun and fiction aspects of monsters. Since monsters are not real, there is no special way a monster should look. Monsters can be happy or sad, funny or scary, big or little, fat or thin, etc. Everyone can create his or her own monster.

Discuss with the children how they want to create their monsters (i.e. an umbrella tail, doughnut eyes, banana nose, etc.).

Give each child a piece of construction paper and crayons and encourage each child to "create" a monster.

Have each child dictate something about his/her monster such as how it looks, what it likes, what it does, where it lives, etc., and write it on the page.

Assemble the book. Design a cover. Include a dedication page and have each child sign the author page. The author page can consist of the signatures of all the students who contributed to the book.

Author Study - Robert McCloskey

Objective: Refer to **Biography** page 11.

Materials: books written by Robert McCloskey

Background:

Mr. McCloskey's birthday is September 15. He was born and grew up in Hamilton, Ohio. To help him illustrate his Caldecott Award winning book, *Make Way for Ducklings*, Robert McCloskey purchased ducks which lived with him in his New York City apartment bathtub. This helped him to draw the ducks, as he wasn't satisfied with the illustrations he created using stuffed or wild ducks. Robert McCloskey is married and has two daughters, Sally and Jane.

Suggested Reading:
Make Way for Ducklings
One Morning in Maine

Blueberries for Sal
Lentil

My Mom Book

Writing/ Reading

This is a good activity and project for Mother's Day.

Objective: To write a book about Mom as a personal Mother's Day gift
(This activity should take a week or so to complete.)

Materials: copies of the pages below and on page 145, construction paper, crayons, pencils, stapler or notebook rings

Directions: 1. Read *Are You My Mother?* by P.D. Eastman. Discuss the ways in which offsprings resemble their parents. Follow up with questions such as:

How are you like your mom?
How is your mom different from you?
What are some things your mom does?

2. Copy the boxes below and on page 145 for your class. Give students construction paper to make their covers. Have the children print "My Mom" (emphasize the M) and then draw a picture of their mother on the cover.

3. Discuss each page as you present it. Do one every day until the book is complete. Take dictation from the children to complete the sentences and then have the children illustrate the pages.

4. Assemble all pages. Staple, bind or put them together with notebook rings.

My Mom is _____ .

My Mom likes _____ .

My Mom likes to _____
_____ .

My Mom's favorite food is ___
_____ .

My Mom loves me because
_____ .

I love my mom because ___
_____ .

My Month Book

Objective: To create a book of months

Materials: fourteen sheets of 4 1/2" x 9" white construction paper for each student, crayons or markers

Directions: To create a "month book," have students copy the name of each month at the top of a different sheet of paper. Next, students can illustrate an activity that could occur in that month, whether it be their birthday party, a snow scene, a special event in your school, or a first-of-the-year celebration. Teachers can take dictation or students can write a sentence describing the activity. (Some suggestions are given below.) Each student can design his/her own cover.

Note: This activity should be spread out over several days. When completed, have individual students share their book with the class.

Suggestions for My Month Book

January - Martin Luther King, Jr.'s birthday
snow scene
first-of-the-year

February - Presidents' Day
Valentines Day
Ground-Hog Day

March - windy weather - kite flying
St. Patrick's Day
first day of spring

April - rainy weather

May - spring flowers
Memorial Day
circus

June - first day of summer
Flag Day
end of school year

July - Independence Day

August - summer fun

September - new school year
Labor Day
first day of fall

October - Halloween
Columbus Day

November - Thanksgiving
Election Day

December - Holiday time
first day of winter

The Moon

Science

Objective: To create a moon log to record the phases of the moon as they occur

Materials: 9" x 6" black paper - several sheets for each student, several white circles for each student (approximately 4" in diameter), white crayons, stapler, scissors, glue, gold stars (optional)

Directions: Staple several sheets of black paper together to form a book. Using a white crayon, have students label the cover of the books, "Moon Log." Under the title, they can glue a full moon and decorate with stars. Once or twice a week, ask students to check the shape of the moon that night. In school the next day, give each student a full moon. (To reinforce the fact that the moon is always round, have the students cut the circle to resemble what they saw the night before.) Next, glue the moon shape to the page. (Older students can also date it.) As the month progresses, introduce the appropriate vocabulary. For your information, the different phases of the moon are illustrated below (i.e. new moon, waxing crescent, first quarter, waxing gibbous, full moon, waning gibbous, last quarter, waning crescent).

Suggestion:

Begin the log with a new moon. January is a good month for this project since it gets dark early.

Suggested Reading:

The Moon Seems To Change by Franklyn Branley
The Birthday Moon by Lois Duncan
Moon Glows by Bethea VerDorn
The Moon by Andrew Langley
poem - "Old Man Moon" by Arleen Fisher from *Sing a Song of Popcorn*

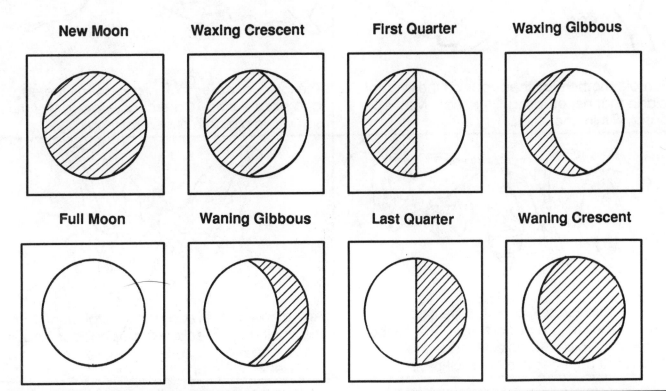

New Moon	Waxing Crescent	First Quarter	Waxing Gibbous

Full Moon	Waning Gibbous	Last Quarter	Waning Crescent

Metamorphosis of Moths

Science

Objective: To introduce the word "metamorphosis," meaning change, and relate it to the life cycle of moths and butterflies

Materials: metamorphosis worksheet, crayons and scissors for each child, stapler, white construction paper for cover

Directions: Discuss the term "metamorphosis" with the class. Remind the children that although the moth and the butterfly undergo a similar metamorphosis, the adult bodies are different. This is a good time to read *The Very Hungry Caterpillar* by Eric Carle or other books about moths or butterflies as they develop from eggs. Your children would also find it fascinating to watch the caterpillars emerge from the egg, spin their cocoons, and then become moths or butterflies. Perhaps you could try this in your classroom.

Distribute copies of the metamorphosis worksheet on page 149. Have children color the different life stages of the moth. Have children cut the worksheet into four pieces and then reassemble them in correct sequence into book form for you to staple together. Add a cover sheet from construction paper. Cut to fit. Let the children decorate their covers.

Review the concept of metamorphosis: from egg to caterpillar to cocoon to adult. Below is an explanation of the metamorphosis of a moth.

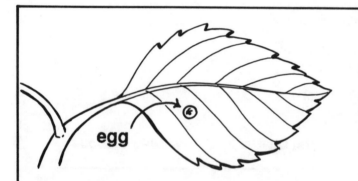

Female mothers lay their eggs on the kinds of plants that her offspring like to eat. Most eggs hatch within one week.

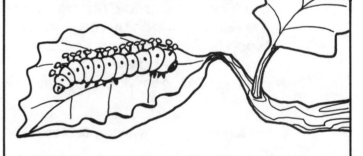

The larva, or caterpillar, crawls out of the egg and starts eating. Caterpillars grow to their full size within a month or several months.

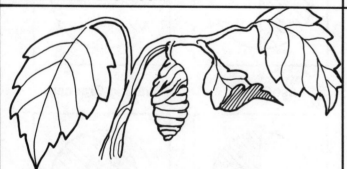

Most caterpillars spin a protective cocoon around itself for the pupal stage. The cocoon is fastened to a solid object. Inside the cocoon, it changes into an adult moth.

At the end of a few days or several months, the adult moth breaks out of its cocoon. Adult moths can live anywhere from a few days to a few weeks to 6 months or more.

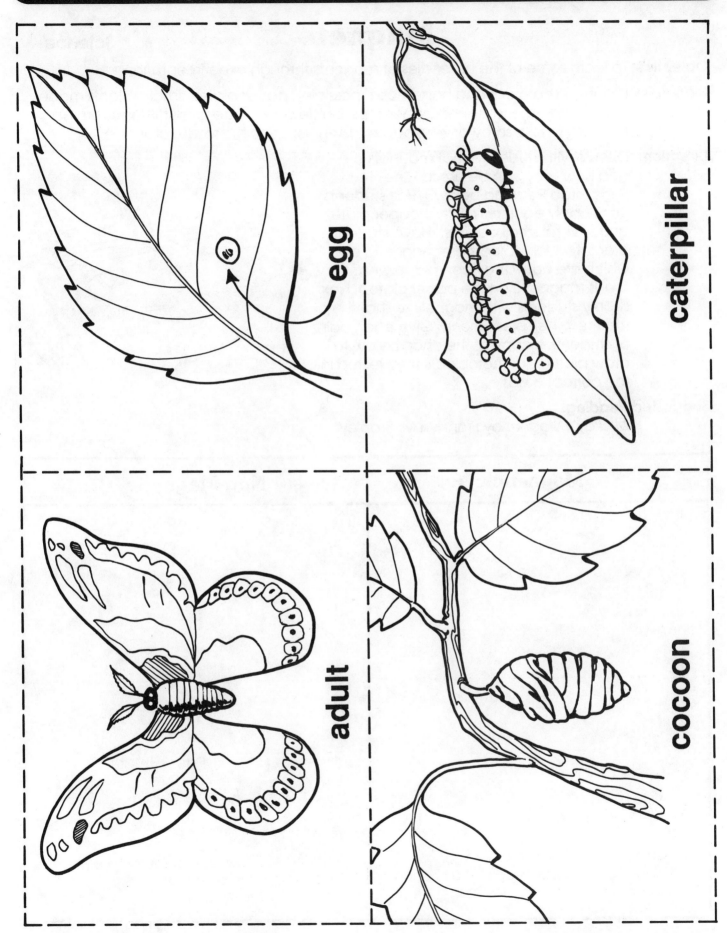

egg

caterpillar

adult

cocoon

Magnets

Science

Objective: To learn some of the properties of magnets through experimentation

Materials: magnets (both bar and horseshoe if possible), paper plates, small objects made of iron, plastic and paper (paper clips, bottle caps, spoons, bottle openers, egg beaters, whisks, screwdrivers, paper fasteners, pencils, erasers, crayons)

Directions: Discuss with students what magnets are and how they can be used. (See Suggested Reading below.) Pair students up. Supply each pair with a paper plate and several small objects. Have students predict which objects are magnetic and which are not. (They can place what they feel is magnetic on the paper plate.) Next, supply students with magnets so that they may test their predictions. Give each pair of students a copy of the chart below to draw pictures of the objects they tested in the correct areas.

Suggested Reading:
Mickey's Magnet by Franklyn M. Branley

Magnetic	Non-Magnetic

M & M Graph

Math

Objective: To use a graph to show the amount of different colored M & M's in a bag

Materials: one small, individual bag of M & M's for each child, one sheet of graph paper for each child, crayons

Directions: Have each child color the first square in each row of the graph a different color according to M & M colors. After they open their bags, they will record their findings by writing an "X" on their graph in the appropriately colored row. The "X" should be written in the same color as the row. (See illustration.) Compare results and write a math graph story.

Color	Number of M & M's					Total
red	X	X				2
brown	X	X	X			3
yellow	X					1
green	X	X				2

Extension Activity:
Combine results of the individual graphs to make a class graph.

Money Game

Objective: To help children learn the value of a penny, a nickel and a dime

Materials: assortment of real coins: pennies, nickels and dimes, container for coins

Directions: Put some coins in the container. Then, gather children on the floor, close to you so that they can see the coins clearly. Review the value of each coin before the game starts. As you hold up a coin, have children indicate by one, five or all ten fingers the correct value. Play the game quietly so you can see quickly which children need more help and practice recognizing the coins.

Another version of this game is to hold up a coin and have one child tell the name and another child tell the value.

Keep your coin container handy so you can play the money game on the spur of the moment whenever you have a few minutes.

Measurement

Math

Objective: To make children aware of measurement and to introduce the use of rulers

Materials: rulers, crayons, pencils, cutout of a foot, tape, *How Big Is a Foot?* by Myller Rolfe

Directions: 1. Read the story, *How Big Is a Foot?* Discuss why the Queen's bed was always a different size and why it is important to have a uniform way to measure things.

2. Give each child the foot cutout to assemble and have them use it to measure things in the room and each other to find out how many "feet" long or tall they are.

3. Give each child a 12-inch ruler. Explain that since everyone's foot is not the same size as the "King's foot," we have a standard unit of measurement. Introduce the word *ruler*. Show the children how to draw lines that are one foot long in a horizontal and vertical fashion to create a plaid pattern. Then, have the children color their pattern. There need not be an equal distance between the lines.

Tab for taping pieces together

Marbles

(For two to four players)

Objective: To increase fine motor control

Materials: several marbles and a container for each player (margarine tubs work well), a paper circle cutout approximately eight inches in diameter, or a circle engraved in a dirt area

Directions: Each player chooses three marbles to place inside the circle. (If using the circle cutout, fasten it to the floor with tape.) Each player then chooses one marble to use as a "shooter." Player #1 places his/her shooter anywhere outside the circle. By using his/her index finger, Player #1 flicks the shooter into the circle to attempt to knock out a marble. If he/she is successful, he/she places the marble in his/her container and shoots again. If unsuccessful, his/her turn is over and Player #2 takes his/her turn. If the shooter marble remains in the circle without knocking any marbles out, the shooter must remain in the circle. The player must choose another marble from his/her container to use as a shooter.

The game is over for a player if he/she should run out of marbles. The game is over for all players when all marbles have been knocked out of the circle. The player with the most marbles wins. To set up for the next game, divide the marbles up equally among the containers/players.

Note: Introduce the game to the class. Next, play or monitor a game with a small group. Then, have these students who have experienced the game help the next group of players.

Macaroni · Cooking

Objective: To observe how cooking alters the volume of objects

Directions: Measure an amount of dry macaroni in a measuring cup. Cook macaroni and observe what changes take place. Measure it again to see if the volume is different.

1) It changes from hard to soft.
2) It "grows."

Have a macaroni snack either as a salad or with sauce.

Milk Shake

1. Milk and chocolate syrup
2. Milk and frozen strawberries
3. Milk and banana

Put one of the above combinations in a blender with 2 or 3 ice cubes and enjoy a special treat.

Memorial Day
Social Studies

Directions: Discuss why and how we celebrate Memorial Day.

Discuss the American flag and make one as described on page 74.

Have a parade in the classroom. (See **March** page 155.)

Mother's Day

Directions and Materials: See **My Mom Book** page 144.

Maps and Models

Objective: To create a map of several land and water forms

Materials: world map, globe, 12" x 8" white paper, crayons

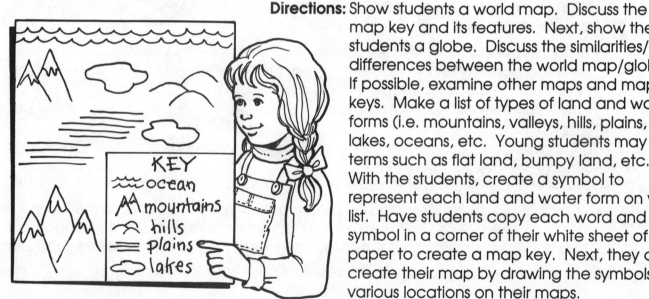

Directions: Show students a world map. Discuss the map key and its features. Next, show the students a globe. Discuss the similarities/differences between the world map/globe. If possible, examine other maps and map keys. Make a list of types of land and water forms (i.e. mountains, valleys, hills, plains, lakes, oceans, etc. Young students may use terms such as flat land, bumpy land, etc.). With the students, create a symbol to represent each land and water form on your list. Have students copy each word and its symbol in a corner of their white sheet of paper to create a map key. Next, they can create their map by drawing the symbols in various locations on their maps.

Extension Activity:

Students can make a model of their map. Use a piece of cardboard for a base. Roll oaktag to create mountains and hills. Cover with papier-mâché if desired and paint. Paint, crayons or markers can be used for plains and water forms.

Divide students into groups. Each group can create a treasure map. (Refer to **X Marks the Spot** page 269.)

Suggested Reading:

Katy and the Big Snow by Virginia Lee Burton
The Secret Birthday Message by Eric Carle

The Mouse on the Moon

Poetry

A mouse is marching to the moon
Making music in every tune.
I hope he gets there very soon
So I can see the mouse on the moon.

      by Ada Frischer

Read "Mice" and "Mary Midling," both by Rose Flyman

Music

March

Using a piano, record or tape, play any of the John Philip Sousa marches to have a parade in the classroom.

Explain to the children that John Philip Sousa is also known as the "March King" because he wrote so many marches, and he conducted a marching band.

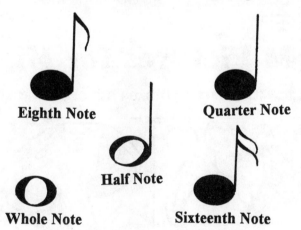

Eighth Note   Quarter Note

Half Note

Whole Note   Sixteenth Note

Musical Chairs

Play the old favorite game of musical chairs. Put enough chairs in a circle for every child less one. Children march around the circle to music. When the music stops, everyone must find a chair. The child who cannot find a chair is out. Continue this until only one chair and two children are left. The final child in the chair is the winner.

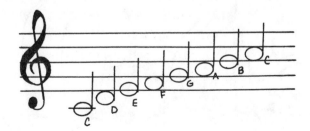

Making Music

Show the children a staff of music. Explain to them about lines, spaces and the letter names. Show them the different kinds of notes (whole note, half note, quarter note, etc.). Explain in a simple way how you count notes.

Book List

Asch. F. (1988). *Mooncake*. New York: Little Simon.

Barrett, J. (1985). *Cloudy With a Chance of Meatballs*. New York: Macmillan.

Bonsall, C. (1973). *Mine's the Best*. New York: Harper and Row.

Branley, F. (1956). *Mickey's Magnet*. New York: Crowell.

Branley, F. (1987). *The Moon Seems to Change*. New York: Crowell.

Brown, M.W. (1947). *Goodnight Moon*. New York: Harper and Row.

Burton, V. (1977). *Mike Mulligan and His Steam Shovel*. New York: Houghton Mifflin.

Duncan, L. *Birthday Moon*. New York: Viking Kestrel.

Eastman, P.D. (1960). *Are You My Mother?* New York: Beginner Books.

Hankin, R. (1984). *I Can Be a Musician*. Chicago, IL: Childrens Press.

Holl, A. (1969). *Moon Mouse*. New York: Random House.

Langley, A. (1987). *The Moon*. New York: Watts.

Lionni, L. (1986). *It's Mine!* New York: Knopf.

Numeroff, L.J. (1985). *If You Give a Mouse a Cookie*. New York: Harper and Row.

Simon, N. (1974). *I Was So Mad!* Chicago, IL: A. Whitman.

Tresselt, A. (1964). *The Mitten*. New York: Lothrop, Lee and Shepard.

VerDorn, B. (1990). *Moon Glows*. New York: Arcade Publications.

Wheat, J.K. (1977). *Let's Go to the Moon*. Books for Young Explorers, National Geographic Society.

M Pictures for Miscellaneous Activities

Enlarge the cards to make flash cards throughout the study of the "M" sound.

Table of Contents

*Remember to check **B Chapter Table of Contents** (page 4) for additional activities.

Night Picture

Art

Objective: To talk freely about night in hopes of making children more comfortable with the dark at night

Materials: heavy yellow construction paper, black crayons, wooden sticks such as Popsicle sticks

Directions: Cover construction paper with a heavy coating of black crayon. Be sure children press down hard and cover the entire paper to make the paper resemble the night sky. When the paper is completely covered with black, have children scratch a drawing using a pointed object, such as a Popsicle stick or their fingernail.

This project works best if the children choose an outdoor scene to draw.

Extension Activity:

Before doing the above activity, read a book about nighttime. Talk about nighttime. Encourage the children to talk about any fears of the night they might have. Talk about why things seem scary at night.

Names

Objective: To talk about names and become aware of the letters and sounds that make up their names

Materials: newsprint, crayons or markers

Directions: Talk with the class about names. Ask them why they like or dislike their names and what other names they might choose for themselves. To encourage them to share freely, talk about your own given name and your feelings about your parents' choice.

Give students sheets of newsprint to create their first name in pictures with a picture for each letter in their name. For example:

Gather up the drawings. Show them to the class one at a time, allowing the class to sound out each picture. Write each letter on the board as the children sound out the pictures.

Newspaper

Writing/
Reading

Objective: To create a class newspaper through interviews,
advertisements and reporting on class/school events

Materials: white sheet of paper for each student, crayons, local newspaper, stapler

Directions: Show the students your local newspaper.
Discuss its contents and purposes. (See
Newspaper page 163.) Tell students that they
will create a class newspaper. Brainstorm
stories or topics that could possibly be
reported. (Students could interview school
personnel, nurse, custodian, report on a school
assembly, fire drill, lunch, rehearsal, after-
school activity or trip.) Have students choose
a topic. Young "reporters" can illustrate their
stories and you or volunteers can take
dictation. Name your paper. Make copies for
each student and bind or staple them.

Note: To make your newspaper look more like a
real newspaper, reduce the size of the
students' work, cut and paste to fit several
stories on each page.

Variation: Instead of reporting on "real" events,
students could report on events that could
have occurred in literature. Possible
headlines could include "Cow Jumps Over
the Moon," "Big Bad Wolf Seen in Forest,"
"Mary's Lamb Goes to School," etc.

Nonsense Stories

"Snow White
and the
Seven Noses!"

Objective: To change a familiar story to
an amusing nonsense story

Materials: familiar short story such as *The Three Billy
Goats Gruff* or *The Little Red Hen*

Directions: Read a familiar story to the students (i.e.
The Three Little Pigs). Next, re-read the
story but leave words out and ask
students to fill in the blanks. For example,
"Once upon a time, there were three little
<u>noodles</u>, who lived together under one
<u>newspaper</u>."

Suggestion:

Before re-reading the story, make a list of
words beginning with "N". Ask students to
use only "N" words to fill in the blanks.

Author Study - John Newberry

Objective and Directions: Refer to **Biography** page 11.

Background:

John Newberry, an Englishman, was the first publisher that deliberately provided books just to amuse children. His first book was published in 1744 entitled, *A Little Pretty Pocket-book*. Because he was the first man to realize that children deserve literature at their level, he is honored with an award given in his name to excellent children's books.

Suggested Reading:

Newberry Award Winners

Name That Name!

Objective: To learn to recognize the names of each student in the class

Materials: strips of oaktag, black marker

Preparation:

Write the names of each child on a strip of oaktag large enough so the class can read it.

Directions: Gather the children in a group on the floor around you. Show a strip to the children and say, "Name this name!" Let the children take turns so the more outgoing ones don't dominate. Give the strip to the child named.

To get the strips back, ask for all the names that begin with the "B" sound, the "L" sound, etc. Ask the class which sound began the most names.

My Name Is...

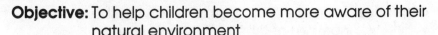

Nature Notebook

Science

Objective: To help children become more aware of their natural environment

Materials: a notebook for each child, crayons, pencil

Directions: Have children record daily observations related to nature in a notebook.

On Friday, have the children enter a date at the top of a page for each day of the following week, one page for each day. Ask the children to record at least one observation per day related to nature - for example: weather, animals, moon phase, seasonal change, temperature, migration, plant life and identification of plants, trees, birds, insects and other wildlife in your area. They can draw a picture in their nature journal or write and illustrate a sentence.

Periodically, have children share some of their special or unusual observations with the class. This activity could take place over a week's period of time or several months, as you see fit.

Illustration caption: MON. JAN. 16 / Today it snowed for 6 hours.

Nutrition Category Game

Objective: To help children learn about the five basic food groups

Materials: 5" x 8" unruled index cards, glue, scissors, 3-minute egg timer

Directions: After a discussion about the five food groups, ask children to bring magazine pictures of food to school. You may want to assign a different food group each night, or divide the class into five groups and assign each group a different area. The basic five food groups are:

1. poultry, fish, meat, beans
2. vegetables
3. bread, cereal, rice, pasta
4. fruit
5. dairy

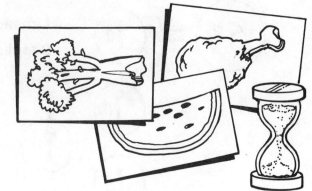

Cut, paste and mount each magazine picture on a separate index card.

On each of five cards, write the name of the category of the food group.

To play the game, five food group cards are spread out on a table. All the picture cards are turned upside-down in a pile. The object of the game is to see if the picture cards can be sorted into the five basic food groups before the three-minute egg timer runs out!

Let children work in pairs and have one child check the other child's accuracy.

Name Graph

Math

Objective: To make a class graph showing the number of "N's" in children's names (Refer to **Graphing** page 21.)

Materials: large, chart-sized graph paper, markers

Directions: Work with the children on this lesson as a class project. Label the graph, "How many "N's" in a name?" Number the squares. Starting at one end of the room, ask each child to tell how many "N's" there are in his/her name. Ask the child to write an "N" in the square next to that number.

When all the children have had a turn, count the "N's" and tally the results.

How Many "N's" in a Name?

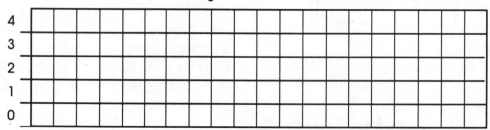

Nickels

Objective: To help children become familiar with a nickel and what it is made up of

Materials: lots of nickels and pennies, newsprint

Directions: Show the children a clear container of pennies and a clear container of nickels. Ask them which they think is worth more, a penny or a nickel. Ask if anyone knows how many pennies it takes to make a nickel.

Give each student a nickel and various numbers of pennies, making certain each one has at least five. Say and count together, "One nickel is equal to five pennies - one, two, three, four, five." Have students write on their papers, "One nickel is equal to five pennies." Write it on the board. Then, have them draw the coins under the sentences.

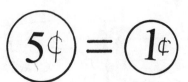

Nurse

Objective: To show appreciation for the school nurse

Materials: Band-Aids, 11" x 18" drawing paper, crayons

Directions: To help young children view the school nurse as a friend and helper, visit the nurse's office as early as possible in the school year. When this is done as a class activity, it often helps alleviate some of the fears young children may have about school nurses.

Have children draw and color large self-portraits in the classroom. While visiting the school nurse's office, ask the school nurse to give a Band-Aid to each child. Have the children place their Band-Aids on their drawings - on "their" arms or knees - as a reminder that the school nurse is a friend and helper.

Extension Activity:

As a class, write an "N" tongue twister describing nurses using as many "N" words as possible. If your class is capable, let them copy the tongue twister and illustrate it.

Examples: Nine nurses named Nancy needed new napkins.
Nice nurses need numerous noodles.
No nurses nap nightly.

Newspaper

Objective: To become familiar with the purposes of a newspaper

Materials: newspaper or newspaper clippings, bulletin board or wall space, scissors

Directions: Ask students to bring in a newspaper. Discuss some of the information that can be obtained from the newspaper (i.e. headlines, weather, television guide, movie schedule, store sales, sports scores, etc.). Have students cut out information from the topics discussed and hang their clippings in a designated area.

Extension Activity:
See **Newspaper** page 159.

Needle and Thread

Games

Objective: To have fun cooperatively

Materials: happy children

Directions: Line students up, side by side, facing you. Tell students that you are a sewing needle and that they are the thread. Ask the students to join hands. The individual at the other end of the line is the knot. The teacher then leads the line toward the last two students. They hold up their arms and the teacher leads all the students under their arms. After everyone has passed under, one student will be forced to turn his/her body in the opposite direction. He/she will be "sewed up" tight!

Lead the line to its original position and then continue, this time ducking under the next two students' arms at the other end. The game is complete when all students have been "sewn up!" You can repeat the game, choosing a student to act as the needle.

As the students are being "sewn," you can chant the following:

> The thread follows the needle
> The thread follows the needle
> Round and round the needle goes
> As we sew the hole in my clothes!

Suggestion:

Have half the class watch and the other half participate when working with large groups.

Before playing the game, emphasize the importance of not dropping hands because that breaks the thread!

164

Number Game

Select a leader. Have him/her think of a number.

The leader says, "I am thinking of a number from 1 to 10." He/she will then select someone to guess the number. If the number guessed is incorrect, the leader has to indicate if his/her number is higher or lower. Then, he/she selects another child to guess. When the correct number is chosen, that child becomes the new leader.

As the children's knowledge of numbers increases, the span of number selection can increase accordingly, i.e. 1 to 15, 1 to 20.

Namely, It Takes Concentration

Materials: two index cards for each student, markers or crayons

Directions: Distribute two index cards to each student. Instruct students to write their first name on each card in large print. Collect the cards. To play the game, lay several sets of the cards name-side down. The first player turns over two cards. If the names match, those cards are out of the game and the player gets another turn. If the cards do not match, the next player receives a turn. The game ends when all the cards have been matched.

Suggestion:

To reinforce the "N" sound and letter "N" recognition, you could print the word "name" on the back of the card.

Number BINGO

Objective: To improve listening skills

Materials: copies of Bingo grids, pieces of construction paper to use as markers

Preparation:

Make Bingo card grids as shown. Randomly write numbers on the Bingo cards so there is one for each student. Use as high a number as you think your students can identify.

Directions: Give a Bingo card to each student along with enough squares of construction paper to cover their cards. Randomly say a number and write it on the chalkboard. The first person to cover his/her card wins.

NUMBER
BINGO

Cooking

Noodle Dessert

Cook 1/2 pound broad noodles according to directions.

Add: 1/2 pint sour cream
1/2 pound cottage cheese
1 teaspoon salt
2 tablespoons sugar
1/2 teaspoon cinnamon
1/2 cup raisins

Noodle Numbers

Macaroni noodles can be softened and dyed. When softened, pasta will stay pliable for a few hours. Dyeing pasta will also cause it to become soft. Soft pasta may be shaped, left to harden and then used at a later time.

Follow the directions below to soften and dye pasta. Then, have the students form the pasta into the shape of the numeral 9 and glue it to a piece of construction paper when it is dry.

To soften pasta:
1. Put pasta in boiling water.
2. Boil until ready for eating. (Time directions are on package.)
3. Pour into strainer to drain.
4. Spread out on tray, cookie sheet or waxed paper to cool. Pieces should not touch one another.

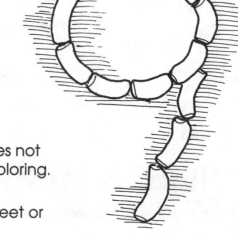

To dye pasta:
1. Put pasta in boiling water.
2. Add a teaspoon of food coloring. If pasta does not take on the color within a minute, add more coloring.
3. Boil 5 minutes and then pour into strainer.
5. When drained, spread out on a tray, cookie sheet or waxed paper so the pieces are not touching.

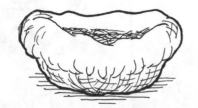

Poetry

Nine Nests

There were nine new nests
sitting in the tree.
There were nine new eggs
all waiting to be
Nine new birds
ready to fly
Out of the nests
and up to the sky.

by Ada Frischer

Nine Nests **Dramatization**

Select nine children to curl up small like an egg.
The rest of the class recites the poem, and the nine
new birds fly out at the appropriate time.

166

Suggested Trips

Nature walk
Nurse's office
Nursery
Neighborhood walk

**WELCOME to
Your Nurse's Office!**

First
Aid

Book List

Brown, M.W. (1939). *Noisy Book.* New York: Harper and Row.

Brown, M.W. (1951). *The Summer Noisy Book.* New York: Harper and Row.

Brown, M.W. (1947). *The Winter Noisy Book.* New York: W.R. Scott.

Guilfoile, E. (1957). *Nobody Listens to Andrew.* Chicago, IL: Follett Publishing Company.

Hughes, S. (1985). *Noisy.* New York: Lothrop, Lee and Shepard.

Kuskin, K. (1962). *All Sizes of Noise.* New York: Harper and Row.

Mayer, M. (1986). *There's a Nightmare in My Closet.* Dial Books.

McGovern, A. (1967). *Too Much Noise.* Boston, MA: Houghton Mifflin.

Raskin, E. (1977). *Nothing Ever Happens on My Block.* New York: Macmillan.

Wood, A. and Wood, D. (1984). *The Napping House.* New York: Harcourt Brace Jovanovich.

Zion, G. (1958). *No Roses for Harry .* New York: Harper and Row.

N Pictures for Miscellaneous Activities

Enlarge the cards to make flash cards throughout the study of the "N" sound.

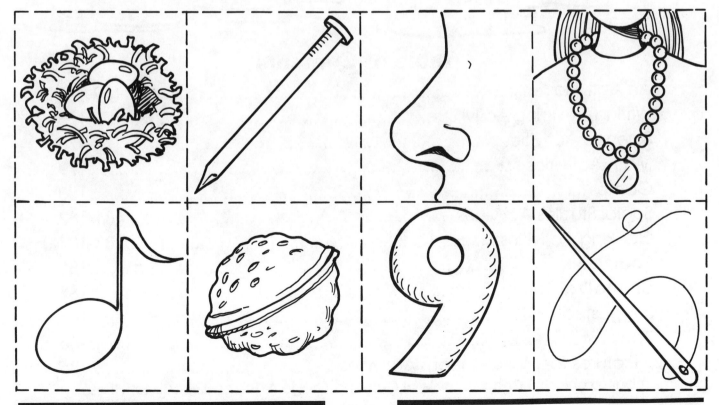

Pp

red

green

blue

yellow

Table of Contents

*Remember to check **B Chapter Table of Contents** (page 4) for additional activities.

Place Mats

Art

Objective: To make place mats to use at a special treat time

Materials: two sheets of 9" x 12" construction paper of contrasting colors (per student), scissors, stapler or tape or glue

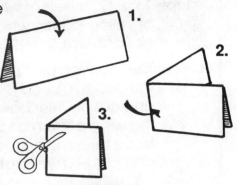

Directions: Fold one sheet of construction paper in half the short way and then in half again the long way.

Cut out small pieces of various shapes on all four sides being sure to leave a space between each cutout. (See illustration.)

Open the paper to a filigree design and staple, tape or paste it to the contrasting color sheet of paper.

This can be made in a 12" x 18" size as well.

Puzzle

Materials: white paper, crayons, glue, scissors, construction paper, ruler, black marker, cup, paintbrush

Directions:

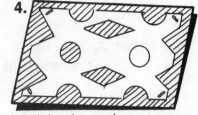

1. Give each student a sheet of white paper on which to create his/her own puzzle design or picture.

2. Pour glue into a cup for each student.

3. With a paintbrush, let students cover the back of each picture with glue.

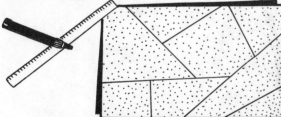

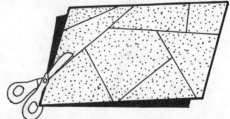

4. Place the "glueside" down onto a piece of construction paper. On the back of the construction paper, have students use a black marker and ruler to draw several straight lines. (For younger students, fewer lines should be drawn.)

5. Then, cut on the lines to create the puzzle pieces.

6. The puzzles are now ready! Provide each student with an envelope in which to store his/her pieces.

Suggestion:

You can tie this activity in with another area of study by directing students to draw or color a ditto of a plant (page 174), a police officer (page 180), a pumpkin, etc.

Penguins

Art

Materials: 18" x 12" sheets of white paper, 9" x 12" sheets of black paper, 4" x 6" sheets of yellow paper, white crayons, patterns, glue, 18" x 12" sheets of oaktag (for pattern), 9" x 12" sheets of oaktag (for pattern), crayons or markers

Directions: The "bowling pin " pattern below becomes the penguin's body. Each student will trace and cut out the "bowling pin." Next, using the wing pattern and white crayon, students trace the wing on the folded black paper and cut two wings at once. On the yellow paper, students can create their own penguin feet and beak. Assemble the pieces.

Extension Activity:

See **Penguins** page 178.

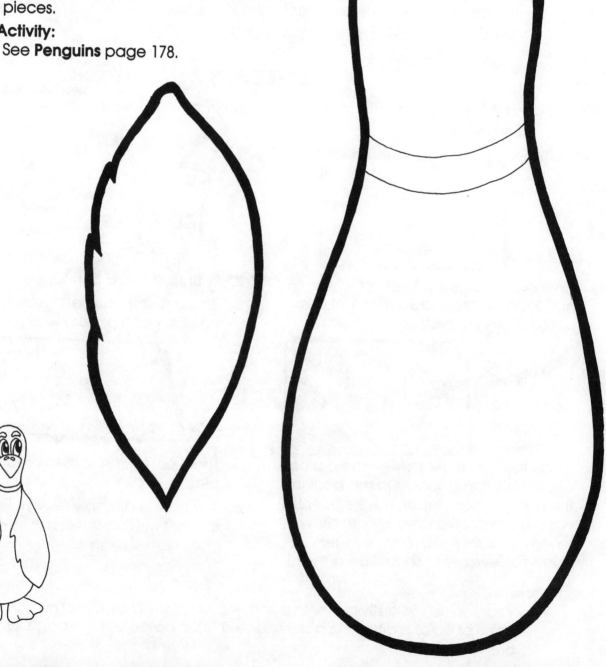

Pussy Willow Scroll

Art

Objective: To celebrate spring, by having children make a pussy willow scroll wall hanging

Materials: 12" x 24" white construction paper, yarn, Chunk o' Crayons or crayons without paper covering, brown paint, paintbrushes, cotton balls, glue, stapler

Directions:

1. Fold back the top 4 inches of the white paper. Have the children color a background for the pussy willow branch by using the side of a large crayon without a paper cover. Encourage them to press lightly and use long, curved strokes, like a rainbow.

Fold.

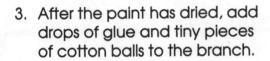

2. Next, have the children paint a branch using the brown paint. (See illustration.)

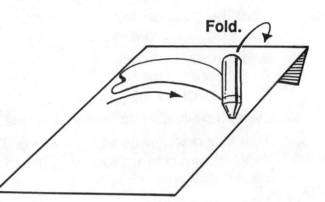

3. After the paint has dried, add drops of glue and tiny pieces of cotton balls to the branch.

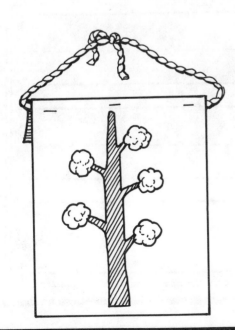

4. Tie a length of yarn in a knot to form a circle. Slip the yarn under the folded flap and staple the flap closed. The scroll is now ready for hanging.

Poetry

Objective: To increase children's awareness of rhyming and poetry

Directions: Discuss with the children words that rhyme.

Recite nursery rhymes and have the children fill in the rhyming word.

When the children are comfortable with the rhyming process, say a word and have the children say a word that rhymes. Write two or three pairs of rhyming words on the chalkboard:

    i.e. cat - hat
        bear - pear
        coat - boat

It would be helpful to sketch a simple picture next to each word.

Then, say a sentence using one word of the pair. Encourage the children to respond with a sentence using the other word of the pair.

    i.e. I went on a boat.
        I wore my coat.

        I saw a bear.
        It ate a pear.

        I have a cat.
        It sat on my hat.

Write the poems the children have created and have them illustrate them. If your class is capable, have them copy their favorite rhyme on copies of the writing paper below and illustrate it.

Assemble several poem pages to create "A Book of Poetry."

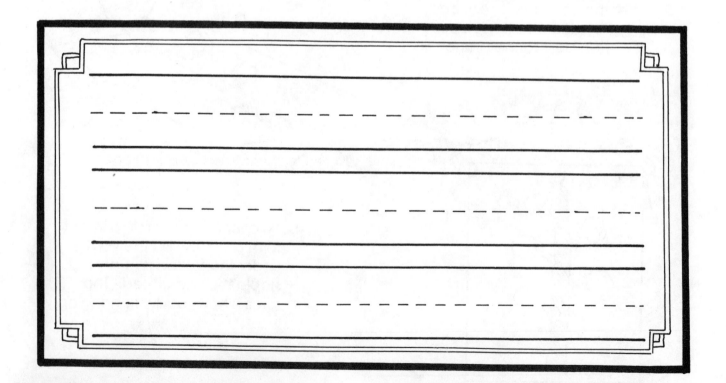

Letter to Peter, Peter, Pumpkin Eater

Writing/ Reading

Objective: To recognize the "P" sound in a familiar nursery rhyme
To critique the nursery rhyme

Materials: 2 large sheets of chart paper, a purple and black marker

Directions: Read the nursery rhyme below to the students:

Peter, Peter, Pumpkin Eater
Had a wife and couldn't keep her
He put her in a pumpkin shell
And there he kept her very well.

Next, copy the nursery rhyme on chart paper, writing all the "p's" in purple. Ask the students what they think of Peter's actions.

Together, on the second sheet of chart paper, write a letter to Peter asking him why he acted the way he did and telling him how you feel about his actions! Perhaps you could provide Peter with an alternate solution.

Author Study - Beatrix Potter

Objective and Directions: Refer to **Biography** page 11.

Background: Beatrix Potter wrote *The Tale of Peter Rabbit* in 1893 in the form of a story written in a letter to the son of her former governess. It was published in 1902, and since then, it has sold over 8 million copies. Beatrix Potter wrote and illustrated about 25 other tales, all illustrated in water colors. She died in 1943.

Suggested Reading:

The Tale of Peter Rabbit	*The Tale of Tom Kitten*
The Tale of Benjamin Bunny	*The Tale of Mrs. Tittlemouse*

P is for Pencil

Objective: To reinforce recognition of words beginning with the "P" sound

Materials: copies of the pencil below, crayons, pencils

Directions: Enlarge the pencil below and give a copy to each student. Have students draw pictures of "P" words on their pencils and then color them. Have students cut them out. Display them on a bulletin board entitled: **P is for Pencil**

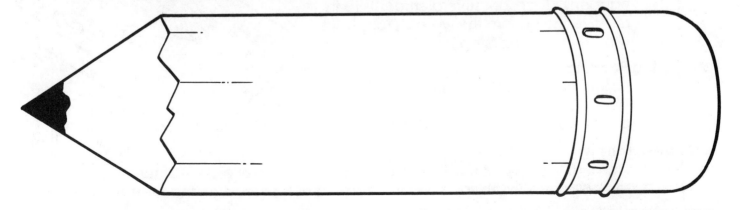

Plants from "Seeds"

Science

Objective: To note shapes of various "seeds" and to observe differences of plants when the seeds grow

Materials: various seeds such as an unroasted peanut, pumpkin and potato "eye", paper cups, soil, tray or dish for draining, sunny windowsill

Directions: Discuss plant needs (soil, sun, water). Tell the children that one of the ways plants reproduce is by producing seeds. Show them the seeds that you have collected: several pumpkin seeds, some peanuts (remove shells), and a potato. Cut a section of the potato containing an "eye." Compare these seeds and plant them in paper cups. Put holes in the bottom of the cups first. Label the cups and place them on a tray or dish for draining. Put them in a sunny window, water them and wait!

Note which seeds grow first and any differences between the plants.

Pollution

Objective: To become aware of water and air pollution

Materials: brownie or lasagna pan, water, cooking oil, sponge, paper towel, a piece of nylon, a coffee filter

Directions: Discuss water and air pollution with the students. (See Suggested Reading below.) So that students can visualize the air pollution present in your classroom, place a coffee filter near a window or in a corner of your room. Observe the dirt that is collected in the filter.

Oil spills have been a source of disaster for our environment. To demonstrate why, fill a brownie or lasagna pan with water. Next, pour a small amount of cooking oil in the water. The cooking oil will act in the same manner as the motor oil. Observe what happens. Then, ask several students to try to remove the oil from the water. (Supply them with the materials listed.)

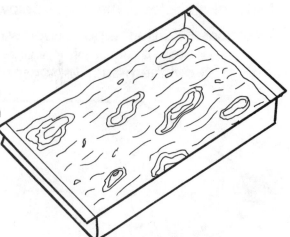

Suggested Reading:

Pollution and Wildlife by Michael Bright
Water Pollution by Darlene Stille
It Was Just a Dream by Chris Van Allsburg

Extension Activity:

Observe the properties of a bird's feather. Pour water on a feather. The feather remains dry. What happens when cooking oil is placed on the feather.

Pulleys

Science

Objective: To construct a single fixed, and a single movable, pulley for each child

Materials: Each child will need: 4' length of string with a loop on one end, two 6" pipe cleaners, weights, (such as a D cell battery), small paper clips bent into "S" hooks, one single pulley

Directions: Single fixed pulley - Attach the pipe cleaner to the back of a chair forming a loop to which the child will attach a single fixed pulley. Wrap the second pipe cleaner around the battery leaving room to attach a paper clip. Put the string over the pulley wheel. Attach the loop of the string to the other end of the paper clip which is attached to the battery. Pull down on the string. The battery will go up.

There is a change in the direction of the way the work is done.

Single movable pulley - Attach a string to the back of a chair. Attach a pipe cleaner with a battery to the bottom hook of the pulley. Thread the string through the bottom opening of the pulley.

Lifting up or down on the string allows the pulley to ride on the string.

These are fun activities to use to introduce children to simple machines and how they help make work easier.

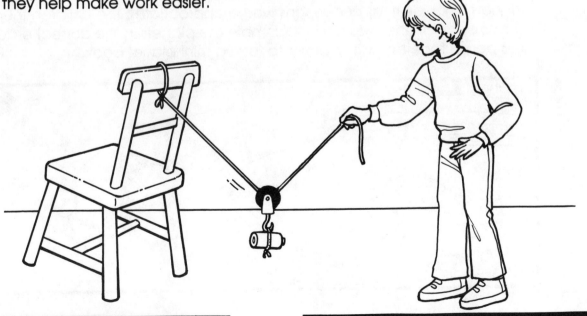

Planet Book

Science

Objective: To learn the order of the planets from the sun and to assemble a planet book in the correct sequence

Materials: a copy of the planet book worksheet (page 177) for each child, crayons, scissors, stapler

Directions: To help the children remember the order of the planets from the sun, teach them the following mnemonic:

Mister	- **M**ercury
Vister	- **V**enus
Eats	- **E**arth
Meat,	- **M**ars
Just	- **J**upiter
Steak,	- **S**aturn
Using	- **U**ranus
Paper	- **P**luto
Napkins	- **N**eptune

Remind them that Mercury is closest to the sun and Neptune is farthest from the sun. Pluto's orbit around the sun takes 248 years. During the years of 1979-1999, Pluto and Neptune have switched their orbital positions with the result that Neptune is the farthest planet from the sun. After 1999, when the orbits are switched again, Pluto will be the farthest from the sun.

Help the children notice and remember the beginning sounds of the names of the planets. Show them the beginning sounds of words in the mnemonic. Help them see and understand the relationship. You may want to present and review this part of the lesson several days before introducing the worksheet. The worksheet will be more effective after the children are familiar with the order of the planets.

Display a chart or list in the classroom depicting the order of the planets from the sun. Allow the children to refer to this list if necessary. Have the children illustrate the boxes on the worksheet with the planets' names by drawing pictures of the planets. Include rings and moons where appropriate. The children then cut the boxes apart on the lines and reassemble the planets in the correct order. Staple the pages together with a cover to form a mini-planet book.

176

Venus

Uranus

Mars

Pluto

Mercury

Jupiter

Earth

Saturn

Neptune

177

Penguins

Objective: To learn about some of the characteristics of penguins

Materials: chart paper and marker

Directions: Ask students to tell you anything they know about penguins. Write or draw the characteristics they come up with on your chart paper. Use the list of information below to help guide your discussion. Keep students active in the discussion by asking them to make predictions, or take a "best guess."

- Penguins are birds that do not fly. They can swim, walk and slide on their bellies across ice.
- Penguins' feathers are less than an inch long.
- The daddy penguin keeps the eggs warm by placing them on top of his feet tucked under his feathers.
- Penguins live only south of the equator.
- Penguins eat fish.

Peanuts

Objective: To learn about the many uses for peanuts and to become familiar with George Washington Carver

Materials: peanuts, peanut butter, pine cones, products containing peanut oil, string

Directions: George Washington Carver made over 300 new products from peanuts including soap, ink and a milk substitute. One of the peanuts most useful forms is peanut butter.

Try some of the peanut activities below.

1. Roll a pine cone in peanut butter and then in birdseed to make a treat for birds. Use string to hang the pine cones from tree branches.

2. Peanut oil is used to fry foods. Many salad oils and dressings, margarine and other vegetable shortenings also contain peanut oil. Bring in some of the products that contain peanut oil. Show students how to locate the name on the product label. Have students bring in products containing peanut oil.

3. There is a lot of fat in peanuts - 47 1/2%! Too much fat is not good for anyone. Discuss fat with students. Study different products and determine their fat content. Teach students how to count fat grams. Have them name foods they think are high/low in fat. Check the labels on these types of products to find the answer.

4. Peanut plants grow in warm climates and can grow up to 2 1/2 feet high and from 3 to 4 feet across. The plants grow best in well-drained, sandy soil and need much sunshine, warm temperatures, little rain and a frost-free period of 4-5 months. Grow some peanut plants in class.

Patterning

Math

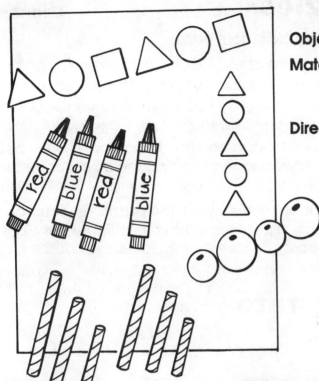

Objective: To identify and create patterns

Materials: colored beads, cubes or markers; shape cutouts - squares, circles, triangles; a package of straws

Directions: Using the colored beads, cubes or markers, demonstrate simple color patterns (i.e. red, blue, red, blue). After modeling several examples, ask students to locate color patterns in the room (i.e. the stripes of the American flag, a student's shirt, etc.). Supply students with beads, cubes or markers to create their own color patterns. Repeat the procedure utilizing the shape cutouts. Patterning with size can be demonstrated and experimented with by cutting straws into three sizes.

Pictograph

Objective: To create a pictograph of their preference - peanuts or popcorn

Materials: large graph or plain white paper, paper cutouts of peanuts, paper cutouts of popcorn, glue, marker

Preparation: Use the patterns below to cut out a stack of peanuts and popcorn.

Directions: To set up the graph, create two sections, one for peanuts and one for popcorn. Label each section. Next, create boxes in each section large enough to fit your popcorn/peanut cutouts. Ask students to state their preference, peanuts or popcorn. As they choose, give each student the corresponding cutout. Next, have each child glue his/her popcorn or peanut cutout on the graph in the appropriate section. Tally and compare the results.

popcorn			peanuts		
🍿	🍿	🍿	🥜	🥜	🥜
🍿	🍿	🍿	🥜		
🍿					

Patterns

Puzzles

Objective: To set up a workable system for sharing classroom puzzles

Materials: puzzles (in as many shapes, sizes and forms as you can find), markers - to color code the backs of all the pieces before you introduce the puzzles to the class

Directions: Have a class discussion about puzzles. Talk about the many different types of puzzles (wooden, floor, shape, double-sided). Be sure your rules for the puzzles are clear to the children. A good rule is to finish one puzzle and put it back before starting another one! Talk about the importance of coding the backs of puzzles. Share your "code system" with the children.

Lastly, give the children some ideas about how to work the puzzle. Encourage children to tell the class how they begin a puzzle and how they figure out clues from the shapes and colors of the pieces. Be sure to talk about the need for cooperation, sharing and responsibility.

Hot Potato

Objective: To play an old, time-honored game

Materials: a potato, timer

Directions: Seat students in a circle. Give one student the potato. Set the timer for a short amount of time (30 to 90 seconds). When the timer is set, students pass the "hot" potato around the circle as quickly as possible. When the timer rings, the student holding the potato is "out." The game ends when there is only one student remaining.

Note: Students who are "out" can still participate by:
1. running a timer.
2. becoming a counter by recording the number of students remaining on the chalkboard.
3. becoming a "judge", judging who had possession of the potato when the timer sounded.
4. becoming a potato "catcher" by retrieving the potato if it is dropped.

Mr./Ms. Police Officer

Objective: To encourage and sharpen observation skills

Directions: Have children sit in a semi-circle. One child is selected as the "Police Officer."

You, the teacher, say, "Mr./Ms. Police Officer, I have a lost boy or girl." Then, you describe something that the child may be wearing such as, "I have a lost boy who is wearing a shirt with short sleeves and 2 buttons." Be sure that there is only one boy/girl that fits this description. Other descriptions could include the letter the child's name begins with or something that the child made. If the police officer cannot find the child, add more clues. When the child is found, that child becomes the new police officer and the game continues.

As a variation, have one of the children give a description of the lost child.

Poll

Objective: To conduct a poll to obtain information

Materials: poll sheet

Directions: Discuss with students how a poll is used to obtain information. With the class, decide what to poll and make a list of questions to include in your poll. Design a poll sheet, using rebus pictures for beginning readers, and make copies for each student. Decide how many people each student will poll, and designate an age group if necessary. Set limitations as to who can take the poll (i.e. a family member, another student, faculty, etc.). Collect and discuss your results.

Suggestion:

Make your poll a popularity poll to find out what is the most popular song, television show, subject, game, etc.

Extension Activity:

Write a general thank-you letter to those who participated and share the results of your poll with them. (Make copies on a copy machine.) Send your results to your school or local newspaper.

Police

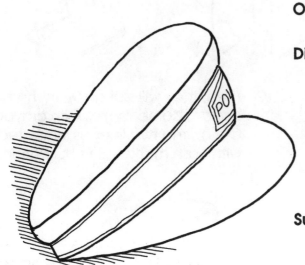

Objective: To become familiar with how police officers can help us

Directions: Discuss with students what they should do if they're lost or need help. Explain how police officers help. Discuss the components and colors of a police officer's uniform.

Refer to **Dial 911** page 55, **House (I Know My Address)** page 91 and **Mr./Ms. Police Officer** page 180.

Suggested Reading:

Let's Find Out About Policemen by Charles and Martha Schapp
I Can Be a Police Officer by Ray Broekel
Police Officers, A to Z by Jean Johnson

Pilgrims

Objective: To make a Pilgrim boy's hat

Materials: Each boy will need: 9" x 12" black construction paper, gray or white rectangular strip for band, small gold foil square for buckle, 2 oaktag strips for headband, glue

Directions: Make a pattern of a hat for children to trace and cut. (See illustration.)

Students will:

1. Glue strip for band and attach above the brim.

2. Cut a small square from the center of the gold foil. Save the outside square for the buckle and glue it on the band.

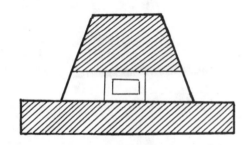

3. Staple two oaktag strips together to make one long strip. Measure and staple each strip to fit their heads.

4. Staple the completed hat to the strip.

Objective: To make a Pilgrim girl's hat

Materials: Each girl will need: 12" x 18" white construction paper, crayons, scissors and yarn

Directions:

1. Students will prepare the girl's hat by folding the 12" x 18" white construction paper into six equal boxes. (See illustration.)

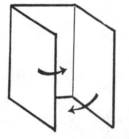

2. Then, they will put an "X" in the two bottom corner boxes with crayons. Cut on the two lines as indicated with slash marks. (See illustration.)

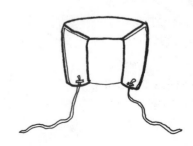

3. Fold both of the boxes with the "X" under and inside the bottom box. Staple to form a bonnet. Attach yarn to each side for the strings.

Popcorn

Cooking

Use this as a science experiment as well as a cooking experiment.

Observe the corn kernel.

How does it feel?
What color is it?
What size is it?

What happens when you add heat?

Observations:

It changes size.
It changes color.
It changes texture.
It becomes edible and chewable.

Gourmet Popcorn

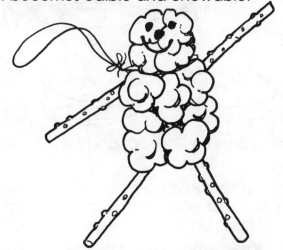

Extension Activity:

Use some of the popcorn to create a "pink and purple popcorn pretzel person."

Use white glue to glue several pieces of popcorn together to form a face. Paint eyes, nose and mouth. Form a body in the same way and paint it pink or purple. Use four thin pretzel sticks for arms and legs.

Hang up the pink and purple popcorn pretzel people to celebrate "P" week.

Potato Puffs

Ingredients: potatoes, one egg, salt, pepper, butter, a little milk, crushed corn flakes

Directions: Peel and boil potatoes. Mash with a little milk, butter, salt and pepper to taste. Roll into little balls.

Beat egg diluted with two tablespoons water.

Dip the potato balls in the egg and then roll in the corn flake crumbs.

Bake on a greased cookie sheet at 375 degrees for about 20 minutes.

It's fun to make your own corn flake crumbs by using a rolling pin and crushing the corn flakes in a plastic bag. However, you can also buy corn flake crumbs.

Peas and Pizza

Cooking

Have a "P" food celebration at the end of "P" Week! In addition to pretzels and popcorn, include the following:

Peas

Ask the children where they think peas come from. Explain to the children that peas do not grow in a box or can. Have them shell peas and taste them raw. Then, cook them in boiling water.

Pizza

Toast English muffin halves, top with pizza sauce or a similar tomato sauce. Add oregano, Parmesan and mozzarella cheese and put them in the oven, or toaster oven, to melt the cheese. Enjoy!

Pudding

Follow the directions on the box.

Peanut Butter

Put roasted shelled peanuts through a food processor and enjoy "pure" peanut butter on crackers.

Punch

Serve all this wonderful food with punch. Invite some guests for "P" foods and punch. Let the children make invitations. Use the P pattern below.

As an extension activity, write the old tongue twister on the chalkboard: Peter Piper picked a peck of pickled peppers. A peck of pickled peppers Peter Piper picked. If Peter Piper picked a peck of pickled peppers, where's the peck of pickled peppers Peter Piper picked?

Say it with the children over and over and faster and faster. They will laugh! Perhaps you can write one together about pizza, popcorn and pretzels.

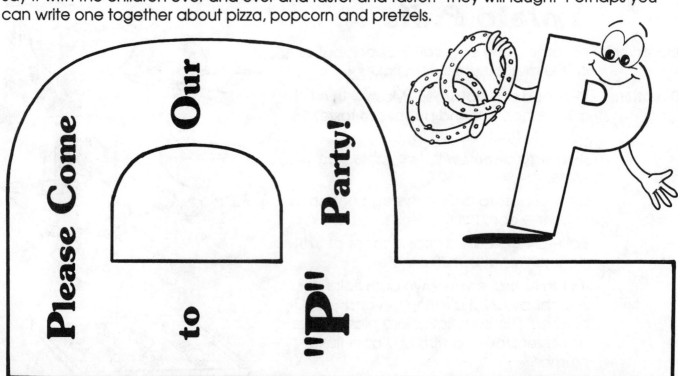

Please Come Our to "P" Party!

Pass the Peas, Please!

Poetry

Please, please, pass the peas.
Not the potatoes, not the cheese.
When I'm hungry, I must have these.
So please, please, pass the peas.

There are no peas?
Well what a squeeze.
I am so hungry, that I may sneeze.
There really are no more peas?
Then, go ahead and pass the pizza, please.

by Ada Frischer

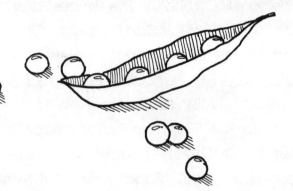

Dramatization

People

Objective: To identify people doing different activities

Materials: magazines, Popsicle sticks, scissors

Directions: Let children cut out people from magazines who are engaged in different activities or careers. Have them mount their people on Popsicle sticks to make puppets. Pair up children and let them develop vignettes to share with the class involving their puppets.

Puppets

Objective and Directions: See **Dramatizations** page 30.

Materials: puppets of any kind

Extension Activity:

Make your own puppets from paper bags (See **Lion/Lamb Puppets** pages 126-127.), pairless socks or paper plates.

Suggested Trips

Post office	Police station
Pizza parlor	A play
Park	A picnic
Planetarium	Pumpkin patch

Book List

Anderson, H.C. (1978). *The Princess and the Pea.* New York: Seabury Press.

Behrens, J. (1985). *I Can Be a Pilot.* Chicago, IL: Childrens Press.

Bond, M. (1973). *Paddington.* New York: Random House.

Carle, E. (1970). *Pancakes, Pancakes!* New York: Knopf.

Collidi, C. (1988). *Pinnochio.* New York: Knopf.

de Paola, T. (1978). *The Popcorn Book.* New York: Holiday House.

Freeman, D. (1978). *A Pocket for Corduroy.* New York: Penguin Books.

Goodall, J. (1980). *Paddy's New Hat.* Atheneum.

Hoban, (1972). *Push Pull Empty Full.* New York: Macmillan.

Keats, E.J. (1967). *Peter's Chair.* New York: Harper and Row.

Matthias, C. (1984). *I Can Be a Police Officer.* Chicago, IL: Childrens Press.

Potter, B. (1955). *Peter Rabbit.* New York: Grosset and Dunlap.

Steig, W. (1980). *Sylvester and the Magic Pebble.* New York: Simon and Schuster.

Van Allsburg, C. (1985). *The Polar Express.* New York: Houghton Mifflin.

P Pictures for Miscellaneous Activities

Enlarge the cards to make flash cards throughout the study of the "P" sound.

Table of Contents

*Remember to check **B Chapter Table of Contents** (page 4) for additional activities.

Quilt

Art

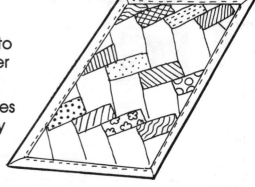

Objective: Turn a bulletin board into a class quilt!

Materials: one 6" x 6" square of white construction paper for each child, markers, enough colored string to cover the perimeter of the quilt to form a border

Directions: The technique of quilting has been used since prehistoric days. Quiltmaking in the United States began during colonial times. Quilters frequently quilted together at social gatherings called quilting bees. Discuss the history of quiltmaking and the many different types of quilts that are made. Some are used as blankets and bed coverings, and some are used as wall hangings. Tell the children that the class will work together to make a "wall hanging" quilt using a classroom bulletin board. You may want to present one theme for the "quilt" beforehand, or you may want to name the "quilt" after the children are finished drawing. Have the children design, draw and sign their squares. Arrange the squares on the bulletin board in a quilt pattern. Some children may have to make two squares to even the sides of the quilt to make a large square or rectangle. Staple a border of colored strips around the perimeter.

Have fun naming the quilt!

Extension Activity:

Read *The Josefina Story Quilt* by Eleanor Coerr. Ask the children to inquire if they have a special quilt at home that was made by a family member or has a story attached to it.

"Q-tip" Painting

Objective: To paint with cotton swabs and paintbrushes

Materials: 9" x 12" sheet of blue or black construction paper, white, brown and green paint, cotton swabs for each child, paintbrushes

Directions: Using brown or green paint, have children paint a deciduous or evergreen tree on the construction paper. When dry, introduce painting with cotton swabs and white paint for snow. Have children dip cotton swabs into the white paint and paint dots to show snow sitting on branches, on the ground or blowing in the wind.

Extension Activity:

This method of painting lends itself to many different themes and creative activities. Children may make their own pictures and designs using a variety of colors.

Introduce students to the work of French artist, Georges Seurat. His style of painting was to paint uniform-sized dots in bright colors side by side rather than using brushstrokes. He called this pointillism.

Q is for Question Mark

Art

Objective: To become familiar with a question mark

Materials: copies of the question mark below, magazines and newspapers, scissors, glue

Directions: Draw a large question mark on the chalkboard. Ask the children if anyone knows what it is and what it is used for. Explain that it is used at the end of a written question. Write several simple questions on the board. Let different children draw a question mark at the end.

Then, give them copies of the question mark below. Let them cut out different question marks from old magazines and glue them on the question marks.

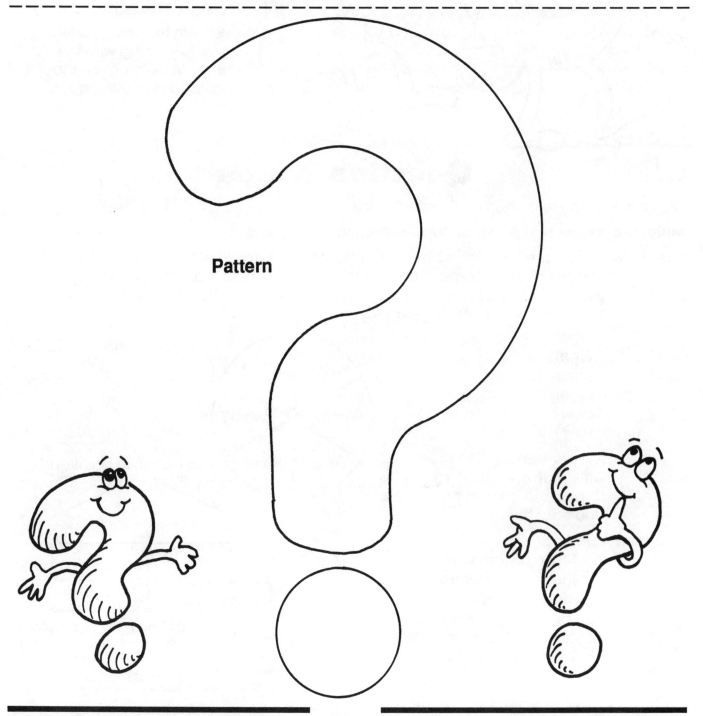

Pattern

**Writing/
Reading**

"Qu" Story

Objective: To introduce the children to the letter "Q" and the spelling "qu"

Directions: Tell the children that "Q" is a queasy letter. When it is used in a word, it always takes along a friend. "Q's" partner is always the letter "U" - it never goes anywhere alone! This little story may help children to remember the silent "U" whenever using "Q."

Ask them to think of different words beginning with the "Q" sound. Write them on the chalkboard, making **qu** bold each time.

Question Words

Objective: To make a chart of question words

Materials: large chart paper or construction paper, markers

Directions: Discuss the difference between questions and statements. Tell the children that you are going to make a chart with the class to help them remember question words. Encourage the children to tell you some question words. You may want to supply a few to get them started.

Who?
What?
Where?
When?
How?
Why?

Review the question mark and write it after each word. Display the chart in the room and refer to it.

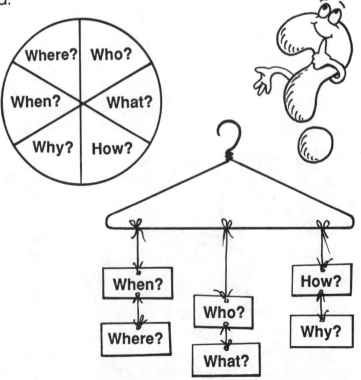

Extension Activities:

1. Make a word wheel with the question words.
2. Make a mobile to hang in the room. Write the question words on both sides of the oaktag cards.

Q Words

Objective: To identify words beginning with the "Q" sound

Materials: copies of the Q below and the pictures on page 192, glue

Directions: Go over each picture with the children and let them identify it. Then, let them cut and paste them on their large Q.

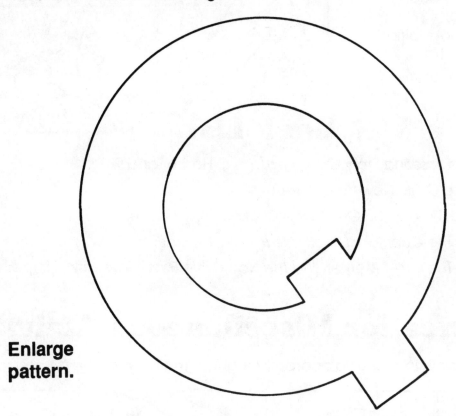

Enlarge pattern.

- -

It's Quarter Time!

Math

Objective: To become familiar with a quarter

Materials: a quarter for every child, crayons, newsprint

Directions: Give every child a quarter. Discuss how a coin is identified by having a "heads" side and a "tails" side. Ask if anyone knows who is on the heads side (George Washington). Talk about the word "Liberty" and ask if anyone knows what it means. Then, read the motto, "In God We Trust." Explain that the year the coin was made is always on the heads side.

Then, turn the quarter over an ask if anyone can identify the bird (the eagle, our national bird). Tell them the name of our country is written there as is the term "QUARTER DOLLAR." Then, give each child a piece of newsprint and show them how to make rubbings of their quarter using different-colored crayons.

Quiet, Quiet

Poetry

There's a new baby in my house.
Shh, Shh, Quiet, Quiet!
I go to school. We're ready to read.
Shh, Shh, Quiet, Quiet!
I'm at home ready for bed.
Shh, Shh, Quiet, Quiet!
I think I'm ready to make a riot!
Shh, Shh, Quiet, Quiet!

by Ada Frischer

Book List

Coerr, E. (1986). *The Josefina Story Quilt.* New York: Harper and Row.

Jonas, A. (1984). *The Quilt.* New York: Greenwillow.

Wood, A. and Wood, D. (1982). *Quick as a Cricket.* Playspaces.

Zolotow, C. (1963). *The Quarreling Book.* New York: Harper and Row.

Zolotow, C. (1989). *The Quiet Mother and the Noisy Little Boy.* New York: Harper and Row.

Q Pictures for Miscellaneous Activities

Enlarge the cards below to make flashcards throughout the study of the "Q" sound.

Table of Contents

*Remember to check **B Chapter Table of Contents** (page 4) for additional activities.

The R Sound

Art

Objective: To become familiar with words that begin with the "R" sound

Materials: copies of the R below for each child, copies of the "R" pictures on page 211, glue

Directions: Brainstorm words that begin with the "R" sound with the children. Then, give them copies of the R below and the pictures on page 211. Identify the pictures together. Have children color, cut them out and paste them on the R. The R's could also be cut out and displayed around the room for "R" week.

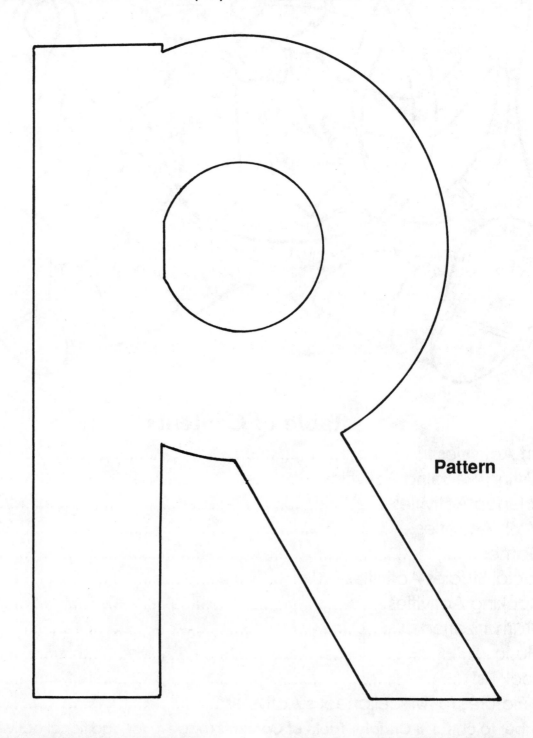

Pattern

Robot

Art

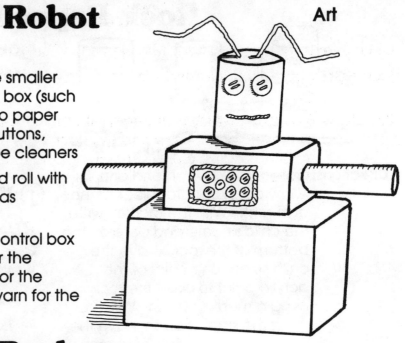

Objective: To create a class robot

Materials: one large box or carton, one smaller carton, one cylinder-shaped box (such as a salt or oatmeal box), two paper towel roll, several assorted buttons, yarn, aluminum foil, glue, pipe cleaners

Directions: Cover the cartons, boxes and roll with aluminum foil and assemble as illustrated.

Glue on yarn to outline the control box and glue buttons in place for the controls. Use pipe cleaners for the antennae and buttons and yarn for the face.

Rocket

Objective: To create rockets

Materials: for each child: 9" x 12" sheet of white construction paper, 6" blue circle, red crêpe paper cut in long strips, crayons, tape, glue

Directions: Have children decorate the 9" x 12" sheet of paper. (See illustration.)

Roll and tape the decorated paper vertically to form a long tube or cylinder. Cut a radius into the blue circle. Overlap the ends and tape to form a cone. Tape this to the top of the cylinder to form the cone of the rocket. Attach red crêpe paper streamers to the bottom of the cylinder to resemble exhaust flames.

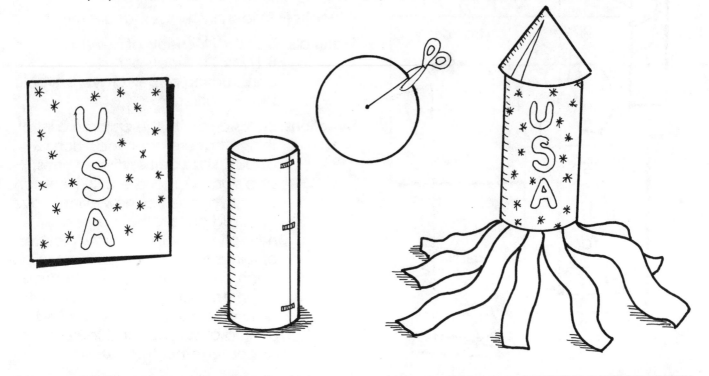

Rock Paper Weight

Art

Objective: To design a rock paper weight

Materials: one small rock for each child, acrylic paints, one can of polyurethane spray, one small and one medium-sized paintbrush per child, marker

Directions: Collect rocks; wash and dry. Allow each child to select his/her own rock. With the marker, write the child's name and date on the bottom of the rock. Have the child select one color of the acrylic paint to paint the rock using a medium brush. When dry, using the smaller brush, have the child paint small dots of one or more colors all over the rock. When dry, spray rock outdoors with the polyurethane. Two or three coats of spray work fine. Allow rocks to dry before touching them.

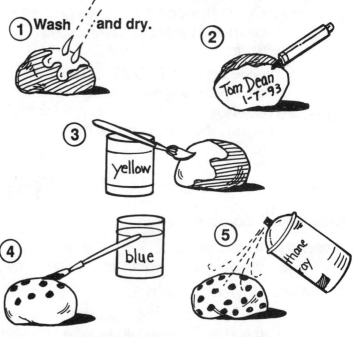

① Wash and dry.
② Tom Dean 1-7-93
③ yellow
④ blue
⑤ thane ay

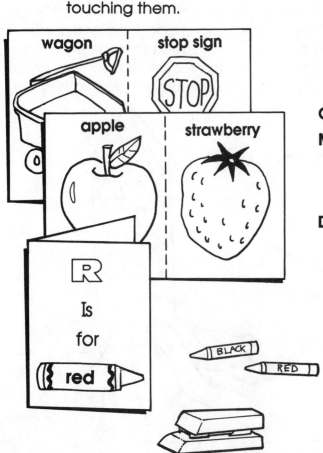

wagon   stop sign
STOP

apple   strawberry

R
Is
for
red

BLACK
RED

R Is for Red!

Objective: To identify things that are red

Materials: 8 1/2" x 11" sheets of newsprint, 8 1/2" x 11" sheets of red construction paper, crayons, stapler, black marker

Directions: Brainstorm with the children a list of things that are often red, such as apples, strawberries, fire engines, stop signs, wagons, etc. Give each child two sheets of newsprint. Have the children fold the sheets of newsprint in half and draw pictures of things that are red on them. Give each child a sheet of construction paper to make the cover. On it, the children should write: **R Is for Red** using a black marker. Staple the pages together to make books.

In the Rain . . .

Writing/ Reading

Objective: To create a class book depicting rain activities or occurrences that take place in the rain

Materials: construction paper, crayons, book rings or bindery

Directions: Discuss with the children what happens when it rains. (The grass becomes wet and slippery, dirt becomes mud, puddles form, people carry umbrellas, birds fly to their nests, etc.) Next, explain to students that they will create a class book about what happens when it rains. Each student will contribute one page to the book by completing the statement, "When it rains . . . " Possible answers may include (When it rains) I jump in the puddles, I drink the raindrops, I make a mud pie, windshield washers swish back and forth. Next, students can illustrate their statements. Create a cover, and bind with book rings or bindery.

Suggested Reading:

Mushroom in the Rain by Mirra Ginsburg
Umbrella by Taro Yashima

Reporters

Objective: To report on a school event, or to report on an event that occurred in literature

Materials and Directions:
Refer to **Newspaper** page 159.

Riddle Book

Objective: To create a class riddle book

Materials and Directions:
Refer to **Riddle Book** page 12.

Rhymes - Complete the Rhyme

Objective: To help children become aware of rhyming

Directions: • Read the poem, "Five Big Rockets," below using voice inflection to stress the rhyming words.

Writing/ Reading

• Then, read the poem having the children fill in the rhyming words.

Five Big Rockets

Five big rockets on launch pads on the floor
One was launched and then there were four.

Four big rockets in launch pads near a tree
Another was launched and then there were three.

Three big rockets on launch pads, oh so few
Another was launched and then there were two.

Two big rockets on launch pads in the sun
Another was launched and then there was one.

One big rocket sent in orbit out in space
It joined the others and all were orbiting in place.

One by one they re-enter and land
On the runway, they look so grand.

The astronauts are welcomed by a Big Brass Band.

by Ada Frischer

• Have the children fill in the missing words in the following rhymes. Read them and write them on chart paper.

Look at the bear.
He's sitting on a _____ . (chair)

We drove far.
We drove in our _____ . (car)

I had some cookies.
I ate four.
They were so good,
I wanted _____ . (more)

It is night.
Turn on the _____ . (light)

I like to run.
It is _____ . (fun)

I have a kitten.
He plays with my _____ . (mitten)

In the fall,
I play foot_____ . (ball)

I ate the fish
On the _____ . (dish)

I look in the mirror.
What do I see?
When I look in the mirror
I see _____ . (me)

Look at my cat.
He is so _____ . (fat)

He is sleeping on the _____ . (mat)

Extension Activity:

Give children the rhyming worksheets on page 199 and page 200. Read the rhymes together on page 200. Have the children find the rhyming words at the bottom of the page and copy them in the appropriate boxes.

Name _____

Rhyme Match

Draw a line to connect the rhyming words.

cat

chair

man

kite

bee

pear

light

hat

tree

pan

Name _____

Rhyme Match

Write the rhyming words in the correct blanks.

1.

Bake, bake,
bake a

_____.

2.

Well, well,
ring the

_____.

3.

Look, look,
read my

_____.

4.

See the bee
in the

_____.

cake

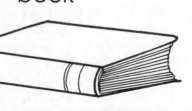

book

bell

tree

Color Rhyme Books

Writing/ Reading

Objective: To create a rhyming color book

Materials: 8 sheets of 6" x 9" white paper, one sheet of 6" x 9" black paper, one sheet of 6" x 9" paper for the cover, notebook rings, crayons, stapler

Directions: This book will have a page for each of the following colors: red, orange, yellow, green, blue, purple, black, brown and white.

Tell the children that on the red page, they will draw a picture in red of something that rhymes with red. For each page, use a different color with the same directions.

Use the black paper with white crayon or white chalk for the color white. Some colors do not rhyme easily, so improvise.

Examples:
  red - red bed, red sled
  orange - orange orange
  yellow - yellow fellow, yellow Jell-O,
        yellow fellow eating Jell-O
  green - green bean, green queen
  blue - blue shoe, blue two
  purple - purple "slurple"
  black - black tack, black snack, black pack
  brown - brown town, brown clown,
        brown clown upside-down
  white - white kite, white light

Write the color and rhyming object at the top of the page. Have the children design a cover. Assemble the book using notebook rings or staple. The children will enjoy being able to read their books.

R is for Reading

Objective: To encourage reading by setting up a reading center

Materials: books, pillow, rug

Directions: Make a comfortable area in which the children can "read" books. Provide a rug and lots of big pillows. Let the children bring their favorite books from home to share during "R" week. Make certain they are properly identified so they can be taken home at the end of the week.

Try to find as many books as you can that have titles containing words that begin with the "R" sound. Read the titles to the children. Have them listen for the "R" words and identify them.

Extension Activity:

Have a Reading Race! Challenge another classroom to participate in a Reading Race and have parent involvement too! Send home a letter to parents explaining that you are having a Reading Race with another class. Each time they read a book with their child, they are to send in a slip of paper with the title and the author. Explain that their child then gets a footprint up on the wall helping his/her class to reach the Finish Line first.

Make multiple copies of the footprint below on construction paper. Record each book read on a footprint and attach it to the wall to win the Reading Race!

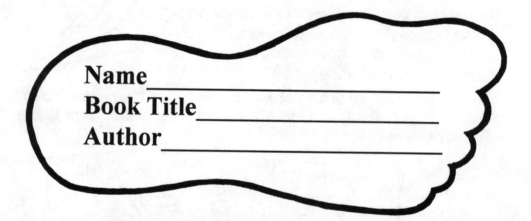

Name_____
Book Title_____
Author_____

Author Study - H.A. Rey

Objective and Directions: Refer to **Biography** page 11.

Background:

H.A. Rey, author of *Curious George*, has had his books published in at least nine languages. Before writing, Mr. Rey worked in Brazil for several years. He began writing and illustrating children's books after he met his wife, Margaret, who also loves art.

Suggested Reading:

Curious George
Curious George Rides a Bike
Anybody Home?

Curious George Takes a Job
Curious George Gets a Medal
Where's My Baby?

Rainbow

Science

Objective: To learn the colors of the rainbow in the correct order

Materials: 9" x 12" sheets of white construction paper, crayons, a prism, chalkboard

Directions: Help children discover a rainbow by shining light through a prism. The colors of the rainbow can easily be remembered by remembering a name - ROY G. BIV. Write the following on the chalkboard:

R - red
O - orange
Y - yellow
G - green
B - blue
I - indigo
V - violet

Have the children make their own rainbows using crayons and white paper. Start with a small violet rainbow shape and add each color on top of the violet arch in reverse order.

Suggested Reading:
Planting a Rainbow by L. Ehlert

Rockets

Objective: To demonstrate action - reaction rocket propulsion

Materials: a long cylindrical balloon, a straw, kite string (approximately 25-30 feet)

Directions: Attach a string to a hook or a similar permanent fixture at least five feet high, at one end of the room. At the end of the other end of the string, insert the string through the straw. Blow up the balloon, but do not tie the opening. Holding the opening closed, tape the straw to one side of the balloon. (See illustration.) Pull the string taut and release the balloon. The action is the air being released from the balloon. The reaction is the balloon traveling along the string.

reaction   **balloon**   **action**

Recycling

Science

Objective: To use recycled materials to produce a creative work of art

Materials: any materials students would discard (i.e. milk containers, foil, ribbon, wrapping paper, juice and cereal boxes, straws, etc.), the top or bottom of a gift box for each student, glue, scissors

Directions: Ask students to bring in materials. Lay materials out on a table or floor. Demonstrate how the students can glue the materials to create a robot, a house, a rocket, an animal, or any masterpiece of modern art. Give students the top or bottom of a gift box to use as a base for their work. Paint if desired.

Suggested Reading:
50 Simple Things Kids Can Do To Save the Earth by the Earthworks Group

Recycled Paper

Objective: To learn about recycling by making recycled paper

Materials: 3" deep pan (square if possible), piece of window screen to fit pan, newspaper, piece of at least 1/4" plywood (about same size as newspaper), water, blender, measuring cup

Directions: Follow the directions below. You may want to make the paper while the class watches.

1. Tear 2 1/2 pages of newspaper into tiny bits.
2. Put the torn paper into a blender. Add five cups of water, cover blender and turn on. Blend until paper turns to pulp.
3. Measure out one cup of pulp and pour it over the screen. Spread it evenly with your fingers. Fill a pan with about an inch of water. Put the screen into the pan.
4. Lift the screen and let the water drain off.

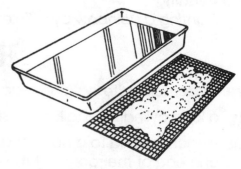

 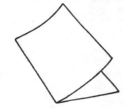

5. Open a section of the newspaper to the center page. Place the screen with the pulp on it onto one side of the open paper. Close the paper.
6. Place one of your hands outside the paper and under the screen. Place your other hand outside the paper but over the pulp. Carefully flip over the newspaper so the screen is now on top.

7. Place the plywood on top of the closed paper. Press down on it to squeeze out as much water as possible.
8. Open the newspaper. Carefully lift the screen off the pulp. Leave the paper open to let pulp dry for at least 24 hours. When pulp is dry, carefully peel it off the newspaper. Draw a picture on it.

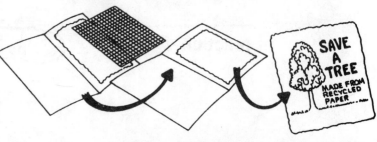

SAVE A TREE
MADE FROM RECYCLED PAPER

Number Rhymes

Math

Objective: To teach and reinforce how to form the numerals 1 to 10

Materials: copies of the number rhymes below, newsprint, crayons or pencils

Directions: Repeat the rhymes below with the children as you demonstrate how to form each numeral.

Have the children glue the rhyme for each numeral on a separate sheets of paper as you introduce each numeral. Keep the children's papers and when all ten are completed, let them make individual books to take home. They could make construction paper covers with the title, **My Number Rhymes**.

1. Start at the top
   to make a **one**.
   Go straight down.
   A **one** is fun.

2. Around the bend
   And then straight back.
   When you're through,
   you have a **two**.

3. Around and around
   What do you see?
   You see the way
   To make a **three**.

4. Down and over
   And down to the floor.
   Look at that,
   You've made a **four**.

5. Down and around
   That **five** looks fine.
   Don't forget
   to add the line.

6. Down and around
   Don't try any tricks.
   Just down and around
   Makes a **six**.

7. Across the top and
   Down to the ground.
   And you know
   Its a **seven** you've found.

8. Snake to the ground
   and back to the sky.
   There's your **eight**
   Ready to fly.

9. A circle first
   Then down the line
   Aren't you proud of
   This great big **nine**.

10. A one and a zero
    Ten is a hero.

Red Ribbon - Right Hand

Math

Objective: To reinforce right and left hand

Directions: Put a red ribbon on each child's right hand and repeat with the class several times during the day, "Red ribbon - right hand." Continue this activity for as many days as you consider appropriate.

Extension Activity:
Play games such as "Hokey Pokey" and "Simon Says" to reinforce right and left.

Ruler

Objective: To learn to use a ruler as a tool for measurement

Materials: ruler worksheet (page 207), pencil, ruler for each child, chalkboard, chalk

Directions: Explain the use of a ruler for linear measurement in inches and feet. Display rulers and yardsticks. Using the chalkboard, have children measure lines that you have drawn, being sure to place the "zero end" of the ruler at the beginning of each line. After the discussion, demonstration and chalkboard practice are completed, encourage the children to measure the lines on the worksheet themselves.

When finished, the children may want to use their rulers to measure books, desks, pencils, etc.

Extended Reading:
Inch By Inch by Leo Lionni

More Ruler Fun

Objective: To give practice in drawing lines with a ruler

Materials: copies of the R on page 194, a ruler for each child, crayons

Directions: Give children copies of the large R on page 194, preferably on light-colored construction paper. Have them cut it out and use their rulers to draw lines on it using all different colors of crayons. Display them for "R" week.

Name _____

Ruler Fun

Write the number of inches on each line.

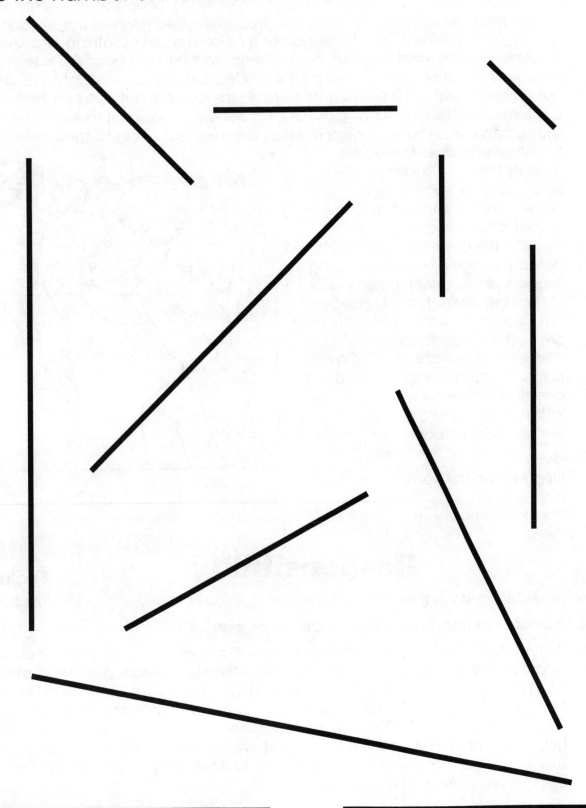

Red-Rover

Games

Objective: To play games using the "R" sound

Materials: large open area or gym

Directions: Line students up facing you against a wall or fence, or have them stand behind a line created with a jump rope. The teacher, or leader, stands in the center of the gym or play area. The leader calls out, "Red-rover, Red-rover, anyone wearing _____ come over." The leader names a color, a type of clothing, etc. Any students wearing what is called, must attempt to run to the opposite side of the play area without being tagged by the leader. If a student is caught, he/she becomes "frozen" in the spot where he/she was tagged, but can now help capture other students running by, as long as he/she does not move his/her feet. The students who make it across the play area without being tagged, remain at the other end while the leader repeats the call, "Red-rover, Red-rover, anyone wearing _____ come over." This time, the leader names a new color and students wearing this color must attempt to run across the play area without being tagged. The leader repeats the call until all the students are tagged or are safe on the other side of the play area. The leader then turns around, and repeats the call, naming a new color. The game ends when all but one student has been caught! The last student remaining may become the new leader for the next game.

Other Games:
Ring Around the Rosie
Ring Toss
Running Relay Races

Responsibility

Social Studies

Objective: To understand what responsibility means

Materials: a list of classroom chores/jobs, chart paper, pen

Directions: With students, make up a list of chores/jobs that need to be done in the classroom (erase board, empty trash, pass out paper, clean up centers, pull blinds, etc.). Each day/week, assign a group of students the chores/jobs with one student being responsible for one chore/job. On a chart that you hang on a wall, have each student mark off when he/she has done his/her chore. Each group should help its members remember to do their chore/job by checking the graph to make sure all chores/jobs are checked off. Reward each group that gets all of its chores/jobs done each day/week.

Raisins and Stuff

Cooking

Raisins make a very good snack that can be mixed with many things such as:

peanuts and walnuts

a dry cereal such as Cheerios or Rice Krispies

grated carrots (add a little vanilla yogurt)

peanut butter and spread on a cracker, stuffed in celery, or spread on apple sections

Raspberry Rounds

3/4 cup butter

1 2/3 cups unsifted flour

1 1/2 cups oatmeal

1 cup confectioners sugar

1 cup packed brown sugar

1/2 teaspoon baking soda

12 oz. raspberry preserves

Mix brown sugar and butter. Add baking soda, flour and oatmeal. Pack half the mixture in a greased 9" x 13" x 2" baking pan. Spread the raspberry preserves on top. Sprinkle the second half of mixture over the preserves. Bake 20-25 minutes at 400 degrees. When cool, use a round cookie cutter to cut into circles. Remove with spatula and sprinkle with confectioners sugar.

Rice Pudding With Raisins

1 1/2 cups cooked rice

1/4 cup sugar

1 small can evaporated milk (5 oz.)

2 eggs

1 1/2 cups milk

1 teaspoon vanilla

raisins

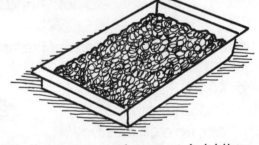

Cook the rice according to the directions on the box. Mix the eggs and sugar. Add the remaining ingredients and mix well. Grease a Pyrex pan with butter or margarine. Pour in mixture and dot with butter or margarine. Bake in a 350 degree oven until it is a golden brown. Sprinkle with nutmeg if desired.

You might what to use brown rice for a different taste.

Soaking the raisins in water first will make them plump and juicy.

My Child's Favorite Recipe

Recipes

Objective: To make a class recipe book

Materials: a recipe from each child, construction paper for covers

Directions: Send a note home asking parents to copy down their child's favorite recipe on a plain sheet of 8 1/2" x 11" paper. Suggest they allow their child to illustrate it.

Make enough copies of each child's recipe for the whole class. Compile the recipes into a class recipe book for each child. Encourage them to decorate the cover. Brainstorm with the class to come up with a title such as **Really Good Recipes**.

Little Red Riding Hood   Dramatization

Objective: See **Dramatizations** page 30.

Materials: book - *Little Red Riding Hood*, basket, red towel (cape), two strips (18" x 2") of flannel, needle and thread, cloth headband (preferable grey or brown), two brown flannel triangles (3" x 3" x 3")

Preparation:

Create Little Red Riding Hood's cape by sewing the strips of flannel to the red towel to create ties for her cape. Create the wolf's ears by sewing the flannel triangles to the headband.

Directions: Read the familiar tale to the children, *Little Red Riding Hood*. Children love familiar stories. Then, let the children act out the story. Change the characters often so all the children have an opportunity to participate.

Music

Rowing

Have two children as partners sit on the floor facing each other with soles of the shoes touching. Partners should hold hands and "row" back and forth singing, "Row, Row, Row Your Boat."

Then, make up new versions of the song using "R" words and let the children come up with the actions. Examples:

Read, Read, Read Your Book
Run, Run, Run Around
Rain, Rain, Rain Comes Down
Reach, Reach, Reach the Sky
Ride, Ride, Ride Your Bike

Read, Read, Read Your Book.

clap . . . clap clap

Rhythm

Using any music (such as piano, guitar or tape) have children clap to the rhythm. A march is a good rhythm to start with. After children can clap out a rhythm, use other body movements such as marching, skipping, hopping or jumping to the beat of the music.

Repeating Rhythm

Objective: To repeat a given rhythm

Directions and Materials: Refer to **Tom-Tom** page 229.

Book List

Bodecker, N.M. (1973). *It's Raining, Said John Twaining.* New York: Atheneum.

Brown, M.W. (1972). *The Runaway Bunny.* New York: Harper and Row.

Carle, E. (1987). *The Rooster's Off to See the World.* Picture Book.

Freeman, D. (1978). *A Rainbow of My Own.* New York: Penguin Books.

Galdone, P. (1985). *Rumpelstiltskin.* New York: Houghton Mifflin.

Ginsburg, M. (1974). *Mushroom in the Rain.* New York: Macmillan.

Hall, A. (1968). *The Remarkable Egg.* New York: Lothrop, Lee and Shepard.

Hoban, T. *Round and Round and Round and Round.*

Hutchins, P. (1967). *Rosie's Walk.* New York: Macmillan.

Kalan, R. (1978). *Rain.* New York: Greenwillow.

Lionni, L. (1982). *Let's Make Rabbits.* New York: Pantheon Books.

Lobel, A. (1984). *The Rose in My Garden.* New York: Greenwillow.

Potter, B. (1955). *Peter Rabbit.* New York: Grossett and Dunlap.

Spier, P. (1982). *Peter Spier's Rain.* Garden City, NJ: Doubleday.

Tresselt, A. (1946). *Rain Drop Splash.* New York: Lothrop, Lee and Shepard.

Williams, M. (1987). *The Velveteen Rabbit.* Avon Books.

R Pictures for Miscellaneous Activities

Enlarge the cards below to make flash cards throughout the study of the "R" sound.

Table of Contents

*Remember to check **B Chapter Table of Contents** (page 4) for additional activities.

Skeletons

Art

Objective: To paint a skeleton and to make the children aware that there is a skeleton inside their bodies

Materials: 12" x 18" black sheets of construction paper, white paint, paintbrushes, scissors

Directions: Have the children feel their head. Tell them this is their skull.

Have them feel their spine and identify it. Have them feel their ribs and identify them. Have them feel and identify their arm and leg bones.

Use black paper and white paint. Demonstrate for the children how you can paint the skull first. Then, paint the spine, ribs, arms and legs. Cut out the skeletons leaving some black around the white painting.

This is a great activity for Halloween.

Sponge Painting

Objective: To create sponge paintings of shapes beginning with the "S" sound

Materials: sponges, shallow trays of paint, white paper, scissors

Directions: Cut sponges into assorted "S" shapes such as sun, star, sailboat, snowman, snake, etc. Students dip the sponges into the paint tray and then place them on their paper to create prints. Students can create a scene or design.

Suggestion: Students could create their prints on large cutouts of shapes beginning with "S."

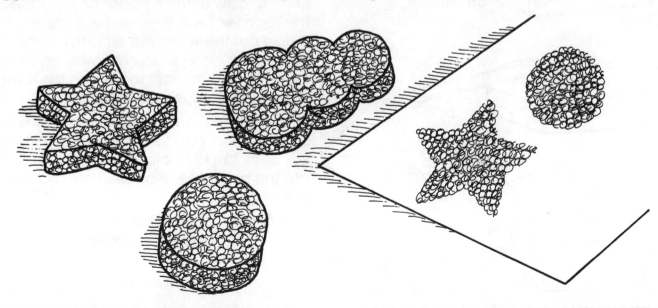

Silhouettes

Art

Objective: To create shadows to make silhouettes

Materials: overhead projector or film strip projector, 12" x 18" sheet of black and white paper for each student, white chalk or crayon, tape or magnets, chair, scissors, glue

Directions: Utilizing tape or magnets, secure a black sheet of paper to a chalkboard or wall. Face the projector toward the paper so that the light shines on the paper. Have a student sit in a chair near the paper so that his/her profile is evident on the black construction paper. (You may need to move the projector forward or backward to fit the child's shadow on the paper.) Using the chalk or white crayon, trace the student's profile and cut it out. If desired, mount it on white construction paper.

Extension Activity: See **Light** page 132.

Suggested Reading:

What Makes a Shadow? by Clyde R. Bulla
Mother, Mother I Feel Sick by Remy Charlip
My Shadow by Sheila Gore

Soap Sailboats

Adult cuts off corners.

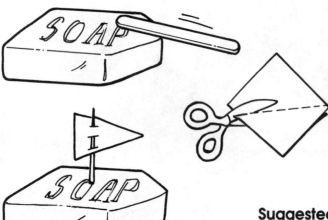

Objective: To create a sailboat that will float

Materials: Ivory soap, Popsicle or paste sticks, construction paper, toothpicks, pencils, scissors, knife (for adult use only)

Directions: Using the pencil, have the children draw the pointed bow of the sailboat on the soap. The teacher, aide or parent volunteer should cut these corners off with a knife for the children. The children, however, should use the Popsicle sticks to smooth the sides and pointed edges of the "boat."

Using construction paper, have the children draw and cut out a small triangle-shaped sail. Stick the toothpick through the sail and into the boat (See example.) and have a class regatta.

Stick figures using toothpicks to hold them can be put on the boats as well.

Suggested Reading:

Mr. Bear's Boat by Thomas Graham

Sign Design

Objective: To create signs

Materials: 9" x 12" sheets of white or yellow paper, pictures of road signs, event signs, sale signs, - *I Read Signs* by Tana Hoban, *I Read Symbols* by Tana Hoban

Directions: Show students a variety of signs. Discuss their purposes. Introduce children to simple symbols such as triangle, square, circle, rectangle.

Next, using some familiar symbols, or some of their own, students can design their own sign.

Suggestions:

Create signs for your classroom designating work areas, directions, (N, S, E, W), rules, etc.

Create signs advertising a favorite story.

Create signs dealing with a specific subject (drug awareness, courtesy, playground safety).

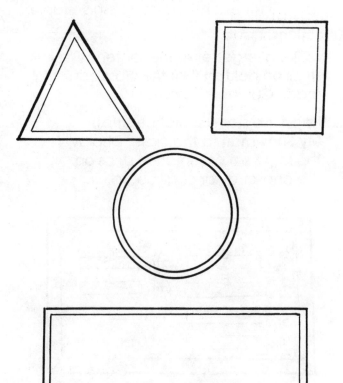

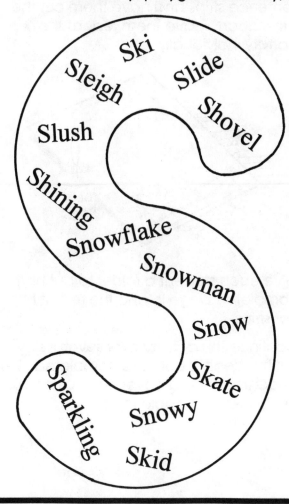

Ski
Sleigh
Slide
Shovel
Slush
Shining
Snowflake
Snowman
Snow
Skate
Sparkling
Snowy
Skid

Winter "S" Words

Objective: To create a chart of winter words beginning with the sound of "S"

Materials: chart paper, markers

Directions: Indicate to the children that winter is a special "S" time because so many winter words begin with the sound of "S."

Draw a big "S" on the chart and start with snow. Brainstorm other words with the children. If necessary, use riddles to elicit correct responses.

Note: See **Silly Snowman Book** on page 219.

Extension Activity:

Give students sheets of blue construction paper. Have them make a winter scene drawing pictures of as many "S" words as they can.

Story Sequencing Sentence Strips

Objective: To sequence and illustrate a story

Writing/ Reading

Materials: 9 sheets of 9" x 12" light blue paper and a folder for each student, glue, crayons (including white), a copy of the sentence strips on page 217 for each student, scissors, stapler

Directions:

1. Make a large set of the sentence strips on oaktag that the class can read. Cut them apart.

2. Read the story (sentence strips) **My Snowman** to the class. Display the large set of sentence strips on the chalk tray or chalkboard.

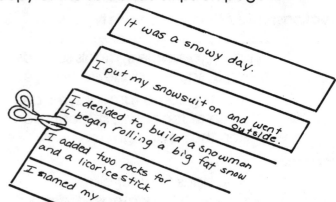

It was a snowy day.
I put my snowsuit on and went outside.
I decided to build a snowman
I began rolling a big fat snow
I added two rocks for and a licorice stick
I named my

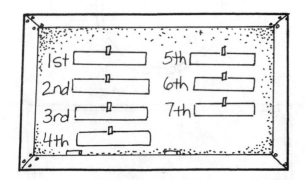

3. Ask the students what happened first, second and so on, numbering the strips and taping them in order on the chalkboard.

4. Next, give each student a copy of the sentence strips and have them cut the strips apart. Have them repeat the activity individually.

5. When the students' strips are numbered in order, have them glue the first sentence strip to the bottom of a sheet of paper. Discuss what might possibly appear in their illustrations (house, dog, car, clouds, etc.) and what not to include (a dinosaur, a flower, etc.).

6. Have students complete the illustration.

It was a snowy day.

7. Give each student a folder to put his/her completed page in and the rest of his/her strips.

8. Continue this activity over several days until students' books are completed. Let students design a cover, then assemble the books and staple them.

Suggested Reading:
The Snowman by Raymond Briggs
Snow Joe by Carol Greene

My Snowman

It was a snowy day. My house and yard were covered with snow.

I put my snowsuit on and went outside.

I decided to build a snowman. I began rolling a big fat snowball.

Next, I rolled a medium-sized snowball. I put it on top of the big fat snowball.

I rolled a small snowball for the snowman's head. My big sister helped me put it on top.

I added two rocks for the eyes, a carrot for his nose and a licorice stick for his mouth.

I named my snowman _____. What a great day!

217

Someone Said Book

Objective: To create a class book

Materials: construction paper, markers, stapler or notebook rings and hole punch

Directions: Discuss the use of speech balloons and quotation marks for words that characters in a story are actually saying. Have each child dictate a sentence to you that they will then illustrate. Begin each page with the words, "Someone said," at the top. Then, use quotation marks to complete the sentence with the child's words written at the bottom of the page. The child will illustrate his/her page. The repetition of words, "Someone said," and the child's illustration should simplify and encourage the reading of this class book. When all children have completed their papers, staple or bind them into a class book and enjoy! (See illustration.)

Suggested Reading:

The Grouchy Ladybug by Eric Carle - This book demonstrates the use of both quotation marks and speech balloons.

Something Special

Objective: To have a creative writing experience emphasizing the sound for "S"

Materials: paper, pencils, crayons, markers

Directions: Discuss nouns with the children that begin with "S" such as snow, summer, spring, school, swimming, skiing, etc. Have each child select one that he/ she thinks is special. Write the child's selection on a sheet of paper similar to the following: "School (or other noun) is special because . . ." Take dictation and have the child illustrate the "story."

All pages can be assembled into a class book called, "Something Special."

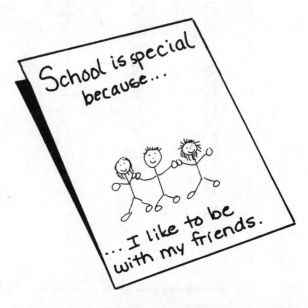

Silly Snowman Book

Writing/ Reading

Objective: To make a silly snowman book

Materials: 9" x 12" sheets of white paper, crayons, markers, notebook rings for binding

Directions: Using words that begin with the letter "S," have children finish and illustrate the following sentence starter:

The silly snowman saw a s_____ .

Collect and bind the papers together to form a class book.

Author Study - Dr. Seuss

Objective and Directions: Refer to **Biography** page 11.

Background:

Dr. Seuss, Theodore Seuss Geisel, was born in Springfield, Massachusetts, in 1904. He published over 45 books in several languages. His first book, *And To Think I Saw It On Mulberry Street*, was rejected 28 times before it was published in 1937. One of Dr. Seuss' many accomplishments included writing entertaining stories beginning readers could enjoy themselves. One of his most beloved books is *The Cat in the Hat*. Dr. Seuss died in 1991 in La Jolla, California.

Suggested Reading:

The Cat in the Hat   *The Sneetches*
Horton Hears a Who   *Fox on Sox*
Horton Hatches the Egg

Subtraction Story

Math

Objective: To demonstrate the subtraction process by having children role-play different subtraction stories

Materials: chalkboard, several identical magnetic objects

Directions: Select three children to role-play a subtraction story such as: "Three children were bouncing balls. Two of the children went home. How many children were left?" After you have modeled this type of story several times with different children, ask the children to take turns designing and directing a subtraction story.

Using the chalkboard and magnets, tell a subtraction story about the objects. When the children are comfortable with this activity, add numerals and explain the subtraction and equal signs. Encourage the children to make up their own stories using magnets and numerals.

Sight

Science

Objective: To introduce the children to the five senses in general and the sense of sight in particular

Directions: Explain to the children that there are five senses (seeing, hearing, smelling, touching, tasting). Ask them to name any they know. Talk about the fact that sometimes a person lacks one of the senses (i.e. a deaf person cannot hear and a blind person cannot see).

Explain that today you are going to concentrate on the sense of sight and the importance of the care of the eyes. This is a good opportunity to discuss playground safety as well. Ask the children to come up with some playground rules to protect the eyes such as: "Never throw rocks, pebbles, sticks, etc. at someone." "Never run with pencils, sticks, etc."

With the children sitting in a circle, invite one child to be the leader. He/she goes to the center of the circle. He/she selects an object in the room and then tells one thing about it saying, "I see something in the room (i.e. that is red)." Several children may try to guess what it is from this one clue. If they are unsuccessful, the leader adds another clue, i.e. "I see something in the room that is red and hanging." If no one guesses it, the leader adds a third clue, "I see something in the room that is red and is hanging and has two other colors." The next clue may be, "I see something in the room that is red and is hanging and has two other colors, and it begins with the sound for F." (flag) When a child finally guesses correctly, he/she becomes the leader and the game continues. Make sure the child repeats the cumulative clues each time. This is a good memory exercise as well as a lesson in observation.

I see something in the room that is red.

Smell

Science

Objective: To introduce the sense of smell

Materials: cotton balls, vinegar, vanilla extract, cologne, onion (cut), orange slices, flour, garlic clove (cut), 4 small plastic containers, aluminum foil

Directions: Discuss the sense of smell. Many things have distinctive aromas, and we can help identify objects by smelling.

Saturate one cotton ball with vinegar, one with vanilla extract and one with cologne. Put a cut onion, garlic, orange and flour in separate containers. Cover with foil and punch holes in the foil.

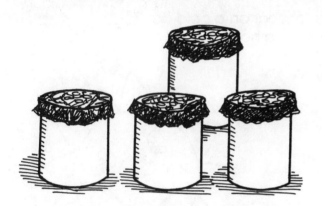

Have the children smell the cotton balls and the containers and try to identify the source of the smell. They should not put their noses too close to the objects. You may get answers such as salad, cookies, etc.

Stress that this experiment is a controlled school experiment. They should NEVER put their noses too close to any objects they are smelling. They should never do this experiment at home. Some things may he harmful to smell such as ammonia, bleach and other cleaning fluids or powders.

Seed Sort Game

Objective: To practice sorting seeds

Materials: several different kinds of seeds such as pumpkin, apple, grapefruit, watermelon, cantaloupe, lemon or orange, small containers to store the mixed seeds, egg timer

Directions: Spread out the small containers. The object of the game is to sort the seeds into containers before the time runs out. Turn over the egg timer and let the fun - and learning about classification - begin!

Extension Activity:
Have children bring in fruit. Remove and save the seeds. Make a salad.

Suggested Reading:
Seeds, and More Seeds by Millicent Selsam

Solar Energy

Science

Objective: To understand that the sun is, and can be used as, a source of heat energy

Materials: a sunny day, a wooden block, a metal spoon, a black or blue piece of material (such as a sock), a light piece of material, chart paper and marker

Directions: Discuss with students how the sun not only provides us with light, but also with heat. Ask students if they know how their classroom or home is heated when it is cold/cool outside. Explain that the sun could also heat our classroom or home, but we need to capture, or trap, the heat first. This heat from the sun is called "solar energy." Show students the materials listed above. Tell them that the class will conduct an experiment to find out which materials hold the sun's heat best. Place the items in a sunny location. After a couple of hours, have students test by feeling the objects to find out which items hold heat best. Which items feel warm? Which items feel cool? Make a class chart of your findings. Ask students:

1. What color jacket would be good to wear on a cold day?
2. What color would keep you coolest on a hot day?
3. On a hot day, which car would be warmer, a black one or a white one?
4. If you were stirring hot soup, which spoon would you rather handle, a wooden spoon or a metal spoon?

Note: This activity works best in spring or summer when the sun is strong.

Suggested Reading:
Solar Energy at Work by David Petersen

Sink/Float

Objective: To conduct an experiment to find out if various objects sink or float in water

Materials: a plastic bin or container of water, a box of various objects such as a wooden peg, bead, scissors, paper clip, ruler (wood and plastic), piece of string, pencil, crayon, straw, stone, paintbrush, etc., a chart divided in half - one side labeled **Sink**, the other labeled **Float**

Directions:
Have children take turns selecting an object from the box and predicting whether it will sink or float. Check the prediction by putting it in a bin of water. Then, place the object on the appropriate side of the **Sink/Float** chart.

This activity can culminate in a story describing the experiment and the results.

Steal the Snowman

Games

Materials: large open area, a plastic bowling pin or an empty plastic soda bottle

Directions:
- Divide the class into two teams. Line the students up at opposite ends of your play area facing each other.

- Give each player a number. (Each team should be given the same set of numbers so that two students, one on each team, have the same number.)

- Place the plastic pin or bottle in the center of the playing area between the two teams. The pin or bottle represents a snowman. You will then call out a word and then a number.

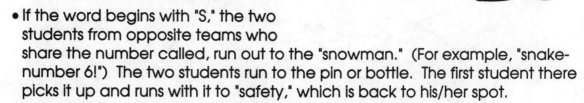

- If the word begins with "S," the two students from opposite teams who share the number called, run out to the "snowman." (For example, "snake-number 6!") The two students run to the pin or bottle. The first student there picks it up and runs with it to "safety," which is back to his/her spot.

- If the student who picks up the bottle reaches his/her spot without being tagged, he/she scores a point for his/her team.

- The student who does not "steal the snowman" tries to tag the "thief." If successful, he/she scores a point for his/her team.

- If a word is called that does not begin with "S," the players should remain in their spots.

- The game ends when every player has had a turn, or as long as time or interest permits.

Note: As young students become familiar with the game, explain that if they reach the pin first, they do not have to pick it up immediately, or at all. The player has the option to allow the opponent to pick up the pin with the hope to tag him/her, and gain a point for his/her team. Players may reach the pin at the same time. They can stand or circle the pin until they feel ready to surprise their opponent and run with the pin!

Other Games: Simon Says, Soccer

School Supper for Lunch

Cooking

Prepare an "S" menu with the children for a supper in school at lunch time.

An ideal menu might be:

Soup (Refer to "Bone Soup" on page 28.)
Sandwich (of choice)
Salad - grated carrots with raisins

Other foods to add might include strawberries, string beans, squash, spinach.

❀ **MENU** ❀

Soup . . . .
Sandwich . . . . .
Salad . . . .

"S" Rhythms

Music/Rhythm

Use body movements to music that suggest:
sailing
skipping
skating - ice and roller
skiing
shoveling snow
sliding

The Sights

Poetry

I saw the sights along the street
As I went walking by.
I saw a fly
And a baby cry
As I went walking by.

I saw the sights along the street
As I went skipping through.
I saw a view
And an old blue shoe
As I went skipping through.

I saw the sights along the street
As I ran up and down.
I saw a clown
And the whole town
As I ran up and down.

by Ada Frischer

Wah!

Book List

Ahlberg, J. and Ahlberg, A. (1988). *Starting School.* New York: Viking.

Briggs, R. (1978). *The Snowman.* New York: Random House.

Brown, M. (1947). *Stone Soup - An Old Tale.* New York: Scribner.

Bulla, C.R. (1962). *What Makes a Shadow?* New York: Crowell.

Carle, E. (1972). *Secret Birthday Message.* New York: Crowell.

Carle, E. (1984). *The Very Busy Spider.* New York: Philomel Books.

Charlip, R. (1966). *Mother, Mother, I Feel Sick.* Parents' Magazine Press.

De Paola, T. (1989). *Strega Nona.* New York: Simon and Schuster/Chardiet Unlimited.

Duvoisin, R. (1956). *The House of Four Seasons.* New York: Lothrop, Lee and Shepard.

Gag, W. (1938). *Snow White and the Seven Dwarfs.* Putnam Publishing Group.

Gibbons, G. (1983). *Sun Up, Sun Down.* Chicago, IL: Childrens Press.

Graham, M.B. (1978). *Be Nice to Spiders.* New York: Harcourt Brace Jovanovich.

Greene, C. (1983). *Shine, Sun!* Chicago, IL: Childrens Press.

Greene, C. (1982). *Snow Joe.* Chicago, IL: Childrens Press.

Hader, B. (1976). *The Big Snow.* New York: Macmillan.

Hoban, T. (1972). *Count and See.* New York: Macmillan.

Hoban, T. (1984). *I Read Signs.* New York: Greenwillow Books.

Hoban, T. (1983). *I Read Symbols.* New York: Greenwillow Books.

Hutchins, P. (1986). *Surprise Party.* New York: Macmillan.

Keats, E.J. (1962). *The Snowy Day.* New York: Viking Press.

Lionni, L. (1968). *Swimmy.* New York: Pantheon.

Mayer, M. (1986). *Just Me and My Little Sister.* Western Publishing.

Selsam, M. (1959). *Seeds and More Seeds.* New York: Harper.

Sendak, M. (1976). *Chicken Soup With Rice.* Weston, CT: Weston Woods.

Sendak, M. (1977). *Seven Little Monsters.* New York: Harper and Row.

Seuss, Dr. (1962). *Dr. Seuss's Sleep Book.* New York: Random House.

Seuss, Dr. (1953). *Scrambled Eggs Super!* New York: Random House.

Shaw, C.G. (1947). *It Looked Like Spilt Milk.* New York: Harper and Row.

Showers, P. (1974). *Sleep Is for Everyone.* New York: Harper and Row.

Steig, W. (1969). *Sylvester and the Magic Pebble.* New York: Windmill Books.

Tresselt, A. (1989). *White Snow, Bright Snow.* New York: Lothrop, Lee and Shepard.

Waber, B. (1972). *Ira Sleeps Over.* Boston, MA: Houghton Mifflin.

Zolotow, C. (1958). *The Sleepy Book.* New York: Lothrop, Lee and Shepard.

Tt

Table of Contents

*Remember to check **B Chapter Table of Contents** (page 4) for additional activities.

Tepees

Art

Objective: To create a class tepee

Materials: two bed sheets (preferably yellow, white or beige), five 6' to 8' poles or sticks, 5' of rope, assorted colors of paint, paintbrushes, open area, masking tape or small rocks

Directions: To decorate your tepee, lay the sheets out on the floor, or on the ground outside. (Fasten them to the floor/ground with masking tape or small rocks.) Talk with your class about Native American tepees. Tell them how they were made of poles cut from trees and buffalo hides. Explain the care of putting them up and taking them down. Ask why that was important. Discuss Indian sign language and explain how Indians drew pictures for written communication. Put some examples from below on the chalkboard. Explain that Native Americans often decorated their tepees with symbols.

After the discussion, tell the class they are going to make a tepee. Let them decide how to decorate the tepee, and have students paint the sheets accordingly. Let sheets dry. Next, arrange the poles or sticks in tepee fashion (see illustration) leaving an open area for an entrance/exit. Have students hold poles/sticks in place. If working outdoors, you can push the ends of the poles/sticks into the ground. Wrap the rope around the poles/sticks where they join, and tie.

Last, drape the sheets around the outside of the sticks or poles, leaving a space for an entrance/exit. The sheets can be secured with peel and stick Velcro, but it is not necessary unless there are strong winds in your area.

Indian Writing

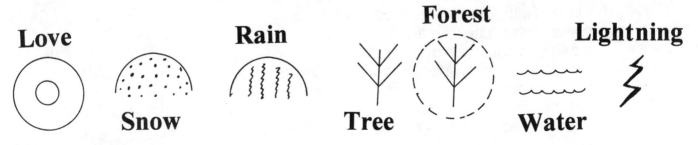

Love   Snow   Rain   Forest   Tree   Water   Lightning

Extension Activity:
Let the children play in the tepee pretending to be Native Americans of long ago.

Totem Pole

Art

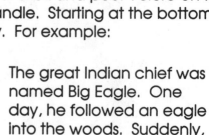

Objective: To create a totem pole and to extend students knowledge of Native American customs and legends

Materials: a long pole such as a broom handle, stick and peel Velcro, 12" x 18" sheets of construction paper, markers, crayons, scissors

Directions: Read a story to the children about Native Americans of the Northwest Coastal tribes. They are the tribes that make totem poles.

Show students pictures of a totem pole. Explain that a totem pole sometimes relates a story. Make up an "Indian legend" with the children using characters such as a chief, a warrior, a hunter, some children, parents, animals, birds, etc. After you have made up the story with the children, discuss the characters of the story. Have the children draw the various characters on large sheets of construction paper. Try to keep the drawings fairly large. Put stick and peel Velcro on the back of each character and on the broom handle. Starting at the bottom, place the characters on the pole as you tell the story. For example:

The great Indian chief was named Big Eagle. One day, he followed an eagle into the woods. Suddenly, he spotted a bear . . .

A totem pole can also be made by assembling various sizes of ice cream cartons (with lids). Students can paint different characters on them. You could also use construction paper scraps, paintbrushes; yarn, ribbons, scissors, markers, crayons, etc. to decorate the ice cream cartons. Stack the cartons on top of each other to create the totem pole.

Suggested Reading:
Three Little Indians by Books for Young Explorers, National Geographic

Tom-Tom

Art

Objective: To further enhance the study of Native Americans

Materials: oatmeal box or salt box for each child, markers or paint, construction or kraft paper

Directions: Cover the cylinder box with construction paper. Discuss and model various Indian designs. Have the children paint Indian designs on the box. Do not paint the top or bottom of the container.

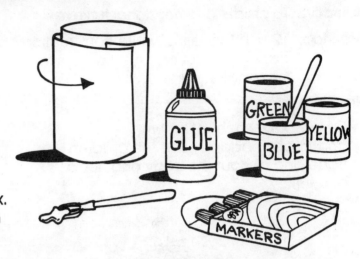

Alternate Directions:
Collect two pound coffee cans. Paint the cans and let them dry. Then, have the children paint the Indian designs on them.

Suggested Reading:
Three Little Indians by Books for Young Explorers National Geographic

Tom-Tom Rhythms

Music

Objective: To repeat rhythms that a student/teacher plays on a tom-tom

Materials: chart paper, markers

Directions: Explain to students how a tom-tom is played. Next, instruct students to sit "Indian style" with their hands on their knees. Tell students that you will play a rhythm on the tom-tom, and that when you raise your hand, they will clap the same rhythm back to you. Keep the rhythms short and simple to start. When children are comfortable with the procedure, allow students to play the rhythm on the tom-tom.

Clap, Clap . . .
Clap, Clap, Clap

Tissue Paper Turkey

Art

Objective: To create 3-dimensional turkeys

Materials: 12" x 18" sheets of white construction paper, 9" x 12" sheets of brown construction paper, pre-cut orange triangles for beak, markers, glue, pencils, tissue paper cut into small squares

Directions:

1. On a 9" x 12" sheet of brown construction paper, have the children trace and cut out the body and head of a turkey.

2. Glue the brown shape near the bottom of the 12" x 18" sheet of white paper held vertically. With markers, add feet, feathers and eyes. Glue on the triangular beak.

3. Add a 3-dimensional quality to the feathers with the tissue paper. Holding a square of tissue paper in one hand, place the eraser end of a pencil into the center of the square. Gather the ends of the square around the pencil. Dip the square with the pencil into glue and then onto the feathers of the turkey.

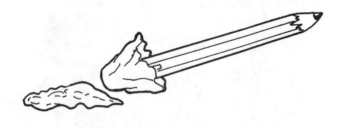

4. Remove the pencil, leaving the tissue paper square behind. Place the next tissue paper square close to the first one. The feathers look especially bright and colorful if each one is a different, but solid, color. When finished, the feathers appear to be ruffled.

Extension Activity:

This project may also be completed as a cooperative class effort. You may want to make one large classroom turkey and have each child work on part of the body feathers.

Tissue Paper Trees

Art

Objective: To use another application of tissue paper to create an apple tree

Materials: green and red tissue paper cut into 1" squares, green and brown crayons or paint, construction paper, flat top pencil with no eraser, paste or a small amount of white glue in a paste dish

Directions: Model for the children how to make a tree trunk using the brown crayon or paint.

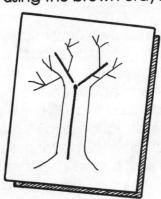

Tree A

Have the children find the middle of the paper. Put a dot in the middle of the paper and draw a straight line down. This will be the center of the trunk. From the center point, draw two arms up to form a Y with the trunk. This will create two branches. Have the children draw the other branches and twigs but no leaves.

To form the leaves, place the flat top of the pencil in the center of a square of green tissue paper. Wrap the square around the pencil. Dip just the flat part in the paste or glue and place it on a branch of the tree. Remove the pencil. The tissue leaf will remain on the paper. Place leaves on all the branches and twigs. To make the apples, form the red squares of the tissue paper into balls, dip them in the paste or glue and place them on the branches.

Tree B

Form the tree trunk in the same way as you did for Tree A. Using a green crayon, make a cloud sitting on the tree trunk.

Make the leaves in the same way except this time, cover the cloud completely with green leaves. The red apples on this tree may be made in the same way in Tree A.

T is for Turtle

Art

Objective: To make turtles, a favorite "T" animal

Materials: 9" x 12" sheets of brown construction paper, 9" x 12" sheets of green construction paper, white glue, markers, paintbrushes, tissue paper

Directions: Fold brown construction paper in half. Draw one foot. Cut out two at the same time. Open the brown paper and draw the turtle's head and tail. On the green construction paper, draw a large rainbow shape for the shell. Cut out all pieces and assemble with white glue. (See illustration.)

With markers, draw eyes, mouth and decorate the shell with boxes. (See illustration.)

Tear or cut tissue paper into small squares or shapes. Dip paintbrush into white glue and then onto tissue paper. "Paint" the tissue paper shapes onto the shell with the brush. The outline of the boxes will show through the layer of tissue paper. When dry, this gives the shell a nice, textured effect.

Read the fable, *The Tortoise and the Hare*, and *The Little Turtle* by Vachel Lindsay.

Extension Activity:

Encourage children to name their turtles with a name beginning with the "T" sound. Then, sit in a circle and let each child tell the name of his/her turtle and something about it. For example: "My turtle's name is Terry and he likes to sit in the sun." "My turtle's name is Tuffy because he's the strongest turtle around." "My turtle's name is Tippy because she walks around on her tiptoes."

Talking Totem Pole

Objective: To record an Indian legend on tape

Materials: tape recorder, totem pole or poles from the art activity on page 228

Directions: Record the legend developed by the class when it was making its totem pole. Have the children take the parts of the various characters.

Play the tape behind the totem pole.

Invite another class to see and hear your talking totem pole.

Top	Toad	Town
Tune	Tummy	Turkey
	Turtle	
	Toe	
	Twist	

A Terrific T Day

Objective: To think of things that begin with the "T" sound

Materials: several oaktag T patterns, construction paper

Directions: Brainstorm with the class all the things they can think of that begin with "T". Let them take turns drawing pictures of "T" words on the chalkboard for the class to guess. Write the word below each picture to help build sight vocabulary. Then, have the children trace and cut out a large T. Let them fill the T with "T" words.

Extension Activity:

As a follow-up activity, ask each child to bring a T item from home to share the next day at school.

Author Study - Brinton Turkle

Objective and Directions: Refer to **Biography** page 11.

Background:

Brinton Turkle was born in Alliance, Ohio. He uses all kinds of tricks like suspense, humor and even charm to capture his readers' attention.

Suggested Reading:

Thy Friend, Obadiah
Obadiah the Bold
Deep in the Forest

Rachel and Obadiah
The Adventures of Obadiah

Teeth

Science

Objective: To see the effect that different liquids have on teeth

Materials: baby teeth that have fallen out, a glass of milk, a glass of soda pop, a glass of grape juice, a glass of water

Directions: Tell the children that you are going to put a baby tooth in each glass and observe them every day for a week. Enlarge the chart at the bottom of the page to record your observations.

You might want to leave it over the weekend and make final observations on Monday.

Have the children draw conclusions about what effect drinking each of those liquids will have on their teeth.

Write a class story using the findings on the chart as the basis for your sentences. Be sure to include the conclusion: Healthy teeth require good nutrition and good eating habits!

Extension Activity:

See if you can get the school nurse to give a demonstration on the proper way to brush teeth.

Tooth Experiment	Mon.	Tues.	Wed.	Thurs.	Fri.	Final Mon.
water						
milk						
soda pop						
grape juice						

Taste Test

Science

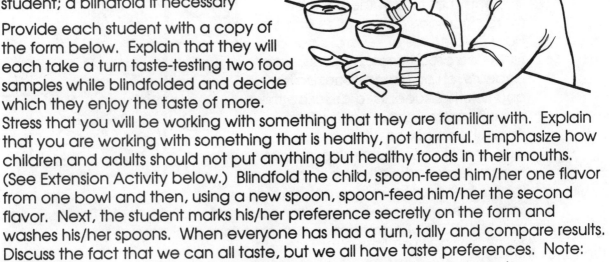

Objective: To realize that different people prefer different tastes and to continue the study of the senses

Materials: two flavors of one type of food, for example, two flavors of Jell-O, two flavors of pudding, two different kinds of crackers; two spoons for each student; a blindfold if necessary

Directions: Provide each student with a copy of the form below. Explain that they will each take a turn taste-testing two food samples while blindfolded and decide which they enjoy the taste of more. Stress that you will be working with something that they are familiar with. Explain that you are working with something that is healthy, not harmful. Emphasize how children and adults should not put anything but healthy foods in their mouths. (See Extension Activity below.) Blindfold the child, spoon-feed him/her one flavor from one bowl and then, using a new spoon, spoon-feed him/her the second flavor. Next, the student marks his/her preference secretly on the form and washes his/her spoons. When everyone has had a turn, tally and compare results. Discuss the fact that we can all taste, but we all have taste preferences. Note: Check student records for food allergies before choosing your samples.

Extension Activity:
Now would be a good time to discuss alcohol, drugs and poison.

I prefer the taste of:

1. ☐   2. ☐

Tasting With Our Tongues

Science

Objective: To identify foods with different tastes: sweet, sour and salty

Materials: pictures of food, magazines, scissors, three sheets of 12" x 18" construction paper, paste

Directions: Discuss the functions of our tongues: speech, swallowing, taste. Explain to students that today, there will be more discussion of the sense of taste. Hold up pictures of several kinds of food (ice cream, orange juice, peanuts, chips, lemons, sour balls) and ask the students to describe the taste of each. Label each of the three sheets of construction paper with one of three tastes. Next, have the students find pictures of food in magazines that have a sweet, sour or salty taste. Students can cut them out and paste them to the appropriately labeled sheet of construction paper to form a collage.

Optional Activity:

Have students sample the three tastes discussed. Supply each student with a piece of pretzel, a small cookie and a quarter of a lemon slice. (Be sure to check student records for food allergies first.) Discuss and record the tasting results.

Note: Be sure to discuss safety. Stress that children and adults should not put anything but healthy foods in their mouths.

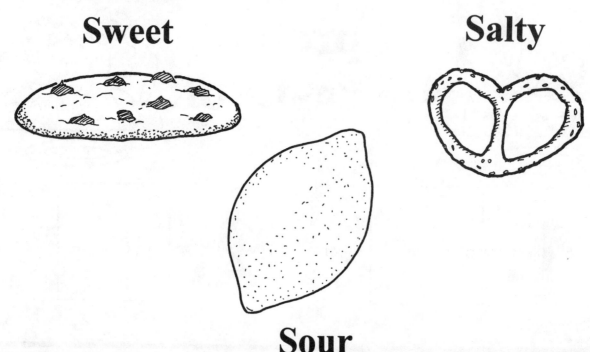

Sweet

Salty

Sour

Touch Box

Science

Objective: To explore the sense of touch as one of the five senses

Materials: a large box, a sock, glue, various objects to identify by touch

Directions: Cut a round hole large enough for a hand to fit into the side of the box. Cut the toe off the sock. Glue the sock to the outside of the box around the hole to form a sleeve. Now, push the "sock sleeve" into the hole. You have made a touch box!

Place an object in the touch box. Then:

1. Have a child place his/her hand in the sock and then try to guess what is in the box.

2. Have that child give the next child a clue as to the description of the object (size, shape, weight). If the child guesses incorrectly, he/she gets to use his/her sense of touch and provide a clue for the next child.

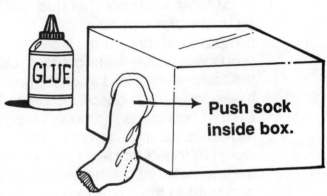

Push sock inside box.

It's very slippery!

3. Put several identical objects in the box and have children count or sort them.

4. Vary the textures of the objects in the box. Ask a child to find a soft object, a rough object, a slippery object or a sticky object. Children may take turns describing an object for the next child.

I found a pair of spoons!

5. Put part of an object in the box, such as the cap of a pen, and have children guess the whole object.

6. Mix a pair of objects with other objects and have children isolate and identify the pairs.

Suggested Reading:
Let's Find Out by Touching by Paul Showers

Temperature

Science

Objective: To use a thermometer to measure temperature

Materials: 2 thermometers, 2 cups warm and cold water, red and white yarn, cardboard or oaktag, hole punch, marker

Directions: Ask students if they've ever been sick and had their temperature taken. Ask them what their mom or dad used to measure their temperature. Discuss what temperature is. Tell students that air and water also have a temperature, and that it is also measured with a thermometer. Using the teacher-made demonstrative thermometer (as described below), explain how a thermometer's mercury moves up as it gets warmer and down as it gets colder. Next, place a thermometer inside the classroom and one outside the classroom window. Compare the temperatures. Place a thermometer in cold water and one in warm water. Again, compare the temperatures. Make a chart of the temperatures.

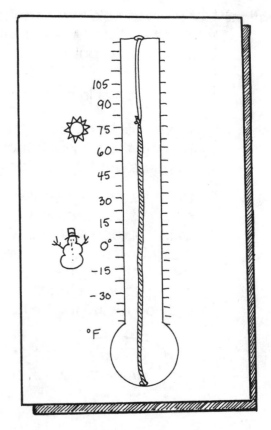

Demonstrative Thermometer

On oaktag or cardboard, draw a thermometer. Tie a piece of red and a piece of white yarn together at one end. Punch a hole at the top of the thermometer and at the bottom of the thermometer. String the red and white yarn through the holes, tying it in the back and cutting off the excess. Holding the yarn from the back, you can move the yarn up and down to demonstrate how a thermometer works. The red yarn represents mercury. To help students understand, draw pictures on the side of the thermometer to correspond with the degrees.

Tooth Graph

Math

Objective: To develop students' graphing skills

Materials: copies of the tooth cutouts, graph chart

Directions: Give each student a copy of the strip of teeth below. Along the left side of a graph chart you have prepared, write each student's name. Along the bottom of the graph, print numerals 0, 1, 2, 3 . . . Ask each student how many teeth they are missing, or how many teeth they have lost. For each tooth lost, have the students cut out and glue one paper tooth in the graph boxes next to their name. Examine the results.

Extension Activity:

Write a math story. You may want to include:

1. Who has lost the most teeth? How many?
2. How many teeth have been lost in all?
3. How many children have lost the same number of teeth?

Sue								
Chris								
Susie								
Jack								
Lisa								
Joe								
Sam								
Judy								
Linda								
Tom								
	0	1	2	3	4	5	6	7

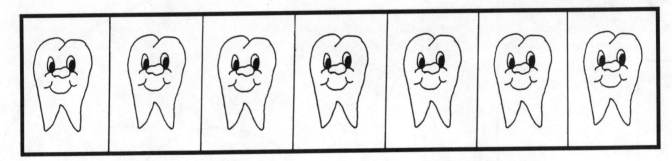

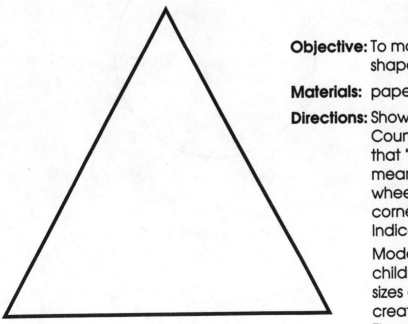

Triangle

Objective: To make children aware of the triangle shape and the prefix "tri"

Materials: paper, scissors, several triangle shapes

Directions: Show the children a triangle shape. Count the sides and the points. Indicate that "tri" at the beginning of a word means "three." A tricycle has three wheels. A tri-cornered hat has three corners. A triangle has three angles. Indicate the three points to the children.

Model how to make a triangle. Give the children several triangle shapes of various sizes and colors. Have the children create a picture or a free-form design. They can use crayons to complete their pictures.

T Is for Ten

Math

Objective: To become aware of what a 10 looks like and to learn how to count to 10

Materials: copies of the 10 below for each child, pencils, markers

Directions: During "T" week, provide ample opportunities for the class to count to 10, starting with their fingers. Write the numerals in sequence on the chalkboard. Use a set of flashcards with the numerals and a corresponding set of objects to practice with throughout the week. As a culminating activity, give the students copies of the 10 below. On the one, have them write the numeral 10 ten times. Then, on the zero, have them draw a set of 10 objects.

- -

T Is for Ten

Transportation

Social Studies

Objective: To make children aware of various means of transportation below the ground, on the ground, above the ground, on water, yesterday, today and tomorrow

Materials: stories, pictures, mural paper, paints, markers

Directions: Discuss the various means of transportation.

Ask students the following:

1. How do you get to school?
2. How do you think children long ago got to school?
3. How did people travel before there were cars, trains and airplanes?
4. How do you think people might travel by the time you are a grandmother or grandfather?

Use the mural paper to create a transportation time line and space line. Some examples are: walking, canoe, animal, bicycle, carriage, train, car, bus, sailboat, steamboat, submarine, subway, elevated train, dirigible, airplane, hot air balloon, rocket and space shuttle.

To stimulate imagination and creativity, make a futuristic transportation mural.

Extension Activity:

Divide a bulletin board into 3 sections as shown. Discuss which category all of the kinds of transportation that have been mentioned thus far would fall into. Ask children to bring a picture for the bulletin board of a kind of transportation. Encourage them to think of some different and unusual ways.

Suggested Reading:

Transport on Earth by Neil Ardley
By Camel or By Car by Guy Billout
Trains by Byron Barton
Train Song by Diane Siebert

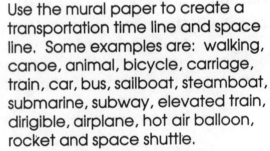

Kinds of Transportation

Land	Sea	Air

Telephone

Games

Objective: To help children understand how messages often get miscommunicated

Directions: Seat students in a circle. You become the telephone operator. Think of a message to be sent through the "telephone wire." The message is whispered from you the student on your right and then on to the student next to him/her and so on in a counter-clockwise direction until it reaches the last student, seated to the left of you. This last student relates the message out loud. His/her message is then compared with the original message.

Note: If a student has not heard the whispered message, he/she may ask, "Operator?" The message is then repeated once. If the student is still unsure, he/she must relay the message the best he/she can.

Tic-Tac-Toe

Objective: To practice recalling "T" words

Materials: chalk and chalkboard

Directions: Draw a large tic-tac-toe grid on the chalkboard. Divide the class into two teams. Make up riddles whose answers are "T" words. Ask a child on Team One a riddle, such as, "I am a striped, wild animal. What am I?" If the child answers correctly, he/she marks an X on the grid. If he/she does not answer correctly, Team Two gets a chance. Play continues until everyone has had a chance to participate. The team with the most tic-tac-toes wins.

Tag

Objective: To afford the class plenty of exercise

Materials: an open play area

Directions: Tag is a simple game. One child is "It" and chases the other children until he/she tags another child who then becomes "It."

Variation: To add a little spice, you could develop a process of elimination whereby each tagged child is out to see who is left as the ultimate winner.

Cooking

Suggested cooking activities:

tomato salad
tomato sauce
tapioca pudding
French toast

Suggested Trips

Train ride

Two Tigers   Poetry

Two big tigers
Were walking near a tree.
One's name was Rum Tum Tum.
The other was Ree Tee Tee.

Rum Tum Tum was hungry.
Ree Tee Tee was sad.
Neither one had had dinner
So, the two were very mad.

by Ada Frischer

Book List

Barton, B. (1986). *Trains.* New York: Harper and Row.

Barton, B. (1986). *Trucks.* New York: Harper and Row.

Beckman, B. (1985). *I Can Be a Teacher.* Chicago, IL: Childrens Press.

Brown, M. (1986). *Arthur's Teacher Trouble.* Little, Brown and Company.

Brown, M. (1986). *Arthur's Tooth.* Little, Brown and Company.

Galdone, P. (1986). *The Teeny-Tiny Woman.* Ticknor and Fields.

Gibbons, G. (1982). *Tool Book.* New York: Holiday House.

Gibbons, G. (1987). *Trains.* New York: Holiday House.

Gibbons, G. (1981). *Trucks.* New York: Holiday House.

Giff, P. (1984). *Today Was a Terrible Day.* New York: Penguin Books.

Lobel, A. (1976). *Frog and Toad.* New York: Harper and Row.

Mayer, M. (1981). *Terrible Troll.* Dial Books.

Parkinson, K. (1986). *The Enormous Turnip.* Niles, IL: A. Whitman.

Rockwell, A. (1974). *Toolbox.* New York: Macmillan.

Selsam. M. (1965). *Let's Get Turtles.* New York: Harper and Row.

Siebert, D. (1990). *The Train Song.* New York: T.Y. Crowell.

Silverstein, S. (1964). *The Giving Tree.* New York: Harper and Row.

Tresselt, A. (1969). *It's Time Now.* New York: Lothrop, Lee and Shepard.

Udry, J. (1956). *A Tree Is Nice.* New York: Harper and Row.

Ungerer, T. (1964). *One, Two, Where's My Shoe?* New York: Harper and Row.

Zolotow, C. (1963). *Tiger Called Thomas.* New York: Lothrop, Lee and Shepard.

Zolotow, C. (1986). *Timothy Too.* Oakland, CA: Parnassus Press.

Table of Contents

*Remember to check **B Chapter Table of Contents** (page 4) for additional activities.

V Vest

Art

Objective: To make a vest to reinforce the "V" sound

Materials: large grocery bags, scissors, markers

Directions: Work through the following directions with the class step-by-step.

1. Place a folded grocery bag flat in front of you, with the flap up.

2. Cut off the entire bottom of the bag at the fold end of the flap. (The bag will now be open at both ends.)

3. Next, to make the opening for the vest, cut straight up the center.

4. When you open the vest, the two sides will be folded in. Cut half circles into these folds for arm holes.

5. Turn the bag inside out to decorate. Form a V-neck at the front opening.

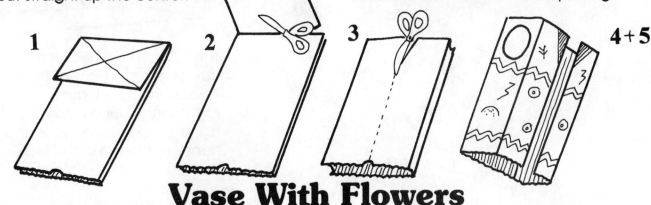

1   **2**   **3**   **4+5**

Vase With Flowers

Objective: To make a vase of flowers to use to decorate the classroom with

Materials: 8" x 11" sheets of white construction paper, pencils, black fine line markers, crayons, 9" x 12" sheets of black construction paper for mounting and framing

Directions: Have children find the middle of the paper and draw a horizontal oval with a pencil. This is the "water." Next, children draw a rounded line from one end of the water to the other end to form a vase. (See illustration.)

Working with a pencil, add many stems. All stems must dip into the water!

Now add a circle to every stem for the center of the flowers. Add petals, and finally, the leaves. (See illustration.)

When the drawing is completed, have the children trace every pencil line with a black fine line marker. The final step is the coloring. Then, mount the drawings on black construction paper, display and admire.

Valentine Person

Art

Objective: To create unique valentine cards to hang up for Valentine's Day

Materials: pink, white and red construction paper, 12" x 1" strips of construction paper, 4" round paper doilies, pencil, crayons, scissors, paste, red yarn, paper fasteners

Directions: Each child will need construction paper for two large hearts for the body and head, four small hearts for the hands and feet, four strips for the arms and legs, and two doilies. Mix and match the colors for each valentine person. Accordion fold the strips.

The children can either trace and cut, or cut pre-traced hearts. Attach the head, arms and legs to the body using paper fasteners. Paste the four small hearts to the arms and legs. (See illustration.)

Draw a face on the head. Write "I love you" on the body. Attach a doily behind the top of the head. Punch a hole near the top and attach a piece of red yarn to hang the Valentine People around the classroom.

Enrichment Activity:

Make a "Very Happy Valentine Town." Have children save various containers from lunch (milk cartons, yogurt containers, juice cartons) or have them bring one from home. Provide red, white, pink and purple construction paper and scraps to decorate their containers. Have them make hearts for windows and doors.

246

Video

Objective: To help instill pride in students' written work by videotaping to create a class tape (The tape can become part of your lending library.)

Materials: quiet room/area, video camera and tape, tripod, students' work, music stand, masking tape, volunteer parents or staff

Directions: Set up the video camera on the tripod in a quiet area or in the cafeteria. Place the music stand facing the camera. Place an "X" with masking tape on the floor where you'd like each student to stand. Each student will take a turn presenting his/her work. One by one, have students leave the room to be taped. (The parent or staff volunteer can operate the camera.) The student can read his/her story and place an illustration on the stand. Non-readers can explain their illustrations. When everyone has had a turn, watch the tape and allow students to take the tape home to share with their families.

Suggestions:

Prior to the taping, discuss and practice public speaking skills. Send a note home to parents with details of the activity so they can help their children practice. (Parental consent to videotape may be necessary in some districts.) Have students bring in props and/or wear clothing related to their story topics. (For example, if the story is about riding a horse, the students could wear a riding hat and hold a bridle.) Students could decorate the videotaping stage with a mural for the background. If desired, students could be assigned a topic, or stories could relate to a theme you are working on.

Parent Connection

Make copies of the letter to parents on page 248. (First, fill in the times and dates you plan to videotape.) This is an experience that can be shared and enjoyed by all!

_____
Date

Dear Parents:

Our class is creating a class videotape. Please help your child practice reading aloud his/her work. Speaking skills to focus on include eye contact and voice volume. When the tape is completed, your child will have the opportunity to bring the tape home to share with you.

We need your help at school! If you are available to help us videotape, please check and return the form below.

Thank you for your cooperation.

_____
Teacher

- -

I can help videotape on:

☐ _____ _____ _____
    date   day   time

☐ _____ _____ _____
    date   day   time

☐ _____ _____ _____
    date   day   time

_____
signature

Vegetable List

Writing/
Reading/
Cooking

Objective: To create a list of healthful vegetables to be used for making a vegetable salad or vegetable soup

Materials: chart paper, markers

Directions: Discuss the importance of vegetables to good health. Make vegetable lists on chart paper according to color.

Vegetables

Green	Yellow	Other
broccoli	squash	beets
peas	pumpkin	cauliflower
string beans	corn	red pepper
lettuce		carrots
celery		mushrooms
peppers		onions
cucumber		

Discuss which vegetables might make a good soup or a good salad.

Extension Activities:

1. Make vegetable soup.
2. Make a vegetable salad. Use lettuce, small pieces of broccoli and cauliflower and sliced zucchini. Toss in a bowl with vinaigrette dressing.

   Vinaigrette dressing recipe
   1 tablespoon wine vinegar
   1 tablespoon Dijon mustard
   3 tablespoons olive oil

   Use these proportions and increase as necessary.

   Optional: Add parsley, basil, diced shallots.

A Variety of Vegetables

Writing/ Reading

Objective: To recognize vegetables as menus are read and to improve listening skills

Materials: a month of school menus

Directions: Slowly read to the class the school menus for the past month. Ask the children to raise their hand each time a vegetable is mentioned. Write the name of the vegetable on the chalkboard. Keep a tally of how many times each vegetable is read.

At the end of the listening exercise, make a graph to show the frequency of the different vegetables being offered on the menu.

Extension Activity:

Re-read the menus and make lists of other food categories and determine their frequency, i.e. hot dogs, hamburgers, macaroni and cheese. The results could be very interesting!

Author Study - Chris Van Allsburg

Objective and Directions: Refer to **Biography** page 11.

Background:

Chris Van Allsburg's birthday is June 18. He grew up in Grand Rapids, Michigan. This talented man has won the Caldecott Medal, the medal awarded to the most distinguished American children's picture book of the year.

Suggested Reading:

Jumanji
The Polar Express
The Wreck of the Zephyr

Ben's Dream
Two Bad Ants
The Z Was Zapped

Violets

Poetry

Five purple violets in the flower store
I bought one and then there were four.
Four purple violets growing near a tree
I picked one and then there were three.
Three purple violets in the garden grew
I picked one and then there were two.
Two purple violets growing in the sun
I picked one and then there was one.
One purple violet growing all alone
I picked it and then there was none.

Those five purple violets met face to face.
There were all bunched together in my little vase.

by Ada Frischer

Volcano

Science

Objective: To become aware of the term, "volcano"

Materials: clay, baking soda, vinegar, red food coloring, small dish or tray, small container

Directions: Find a chart that depicts the parts of a volcano. Show it to the children, explaining the different parts and the concept of "eruption."

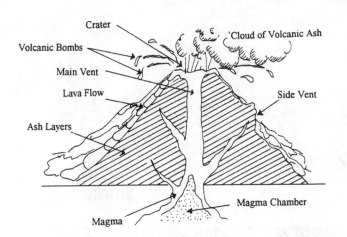

Crater

Volcanic Bombs

Main Vent

Lava Flow

Ash Layers

'Cloud of Volcanic Ash

Side Vent

Magma Chamber

Magma

Then, help the children make a volcano shape with clay. Be sure the opening at the top is big enough to accommodate and support the small dish or tray. Put two spoonfuls of baking soda into the small dish through the opening of the volcano. In another small container, mix a little red food coloring with some vinegar. Pour the vinegar solution into the small dish with the baking soda and watch the "lava" overflow!

Be sure to explain that the composition of lava is not vinegar and baking soda!

Vibration

Objective: To see and feel vibration, and to demonstrate how vibrations cause sound

Materials: a plastic ruler, cymbals, a musical triangle, tuning fork, rubber bands of varying widths, shoe boxes

Directions: Seat students around a table or desk. Place a ruler on the edge of the table/desk, with approximately eight inches of the ruler hanging off. Holding the ruler securely on the table/desk, gently lift the other end of the ruler and release it, causing it to vibrate. Ask the students:

1. What do you see?
2. What do you hear?

Repeat the process this time and ask a student to stop the ruler with his/her hand. Make observations.

Experiment with the cymbals, tuning fork, etc. Allow students to feel the vibrations.

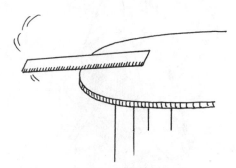

Ask students to bring in shoe boxes from home. Create a rubber band "guitar" by placing rubber bands of various widths around the open boxes.

Extension Activity:
Invite a violinist to your classroom to both explain how a violin works and to perform.

V-Formation - Bird Migration

Science

Objective: To become familiar with the V-formation in which some birds migrate

Materials: masking tape, pictures of migrating birds (if available)

Directions: Discuss why some birds migrate. Show pictures (or draw a sketch) of the migrating flight formation. Ask students which letter of the alphabet the formation looks like. Next, create a large "V" across your classroom floor with masking tape. Have students stand on the tape and pretend to be migrating birds!

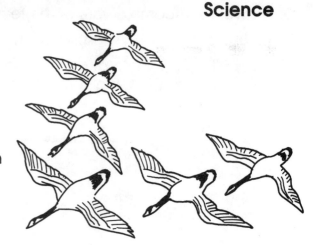

Vote

Social Studies

Objective: To help the children understand the concept of voting

Directions: As a follow-up to the listening activity involving the vegetable served during a month of menus (page 250) or to the videotaping (page 247), take a class vote. Either vote on students' favorite vegetable or on their favorite video. Explain that the concept of exercising the right to vote is the basis for our country's foundation.

Talk about some things students' parents might vote on, such as passing taxes, electing government officials, or allowing certain buildings to be constructed.

Veterans Day

Objective: To help the children appreciate what a veteran is

Directions: Explain to the children that a veteran is a person who has served his/her country in time of war. Ask if they know what a war is. Ask if they have heard their parents talk about war or if either of their parents ever fought in a war.

Explain that Veterans Day is set aside to honor all the people who have fought for America throughout history. Most towns have a parade that the children will probably see on TV or even attend. Tell the children that the Vietnam Veterans Memorial is in Washington D.C. as is a tomb known as the Tomb of the Unknowns for all the war dead. Perhaps a veteran could come and visit your class dressed in uniform.

Table of Contents

*Remember to check **B Chapter Table of Contents** (page 4) for additional activities.

Weaving - Paper and Finger Art

Paper Weaving

Materials: one 9" x 12" sheet of construction paper, twelve 1" x 9" strips of construction paper of a contrasting color

Directions: Do the following activity with the children.

Fold the 9" x 12" paper in half the long way. From the folded end, cut straight lines one inch apart to 1/2 inch from the end.

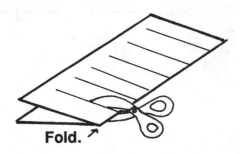

Fold. ↗

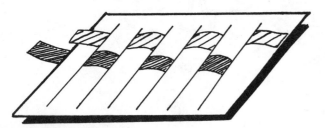

Open the paper. Weave the strips into the 9" x 12" paper going over and under the slits in a weaving fashion.

The first strip will go over and under.

The next strip will go under and over creating a waffle weave effect.

Finger Weaving

Materials: jersey loops

Directions: Model the following directions for the children.

1. Working with your palm facing you, place a jersey loop across four fingers (not your thumb) as follows:

   Put the loop over the pointer, twist it, put it over the next finger and twist it. Do this two more times.

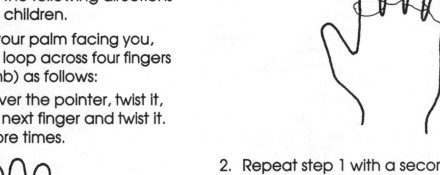

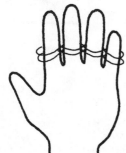

2. Repeat step 1 with a second loop of another color.

3. There are now two loops across your fingers. With your palms facing you, pull the bottom loop over the top loop and over each finger in turn.

4. Put on another loop as described in step 1.

5. Repeat step 3.

6. Continue repeating steps 2 and 3. The weaving will start to come down the back of your hand. Continue until the weaving is of the desired length for a head or a wristband.

7. To remove the weaving from your fingers, take another jersey loop and slip it through all four loops on your fingers before you take it off your hand. Knot this loop. Pull out one of the loops from the opposite end and tie together with the last loop to form a head or wristband.

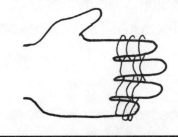

254

A Wonderful Witch

Art

Objective: To create a wonderful witch for Halloween

Materials: 9" x 12" construction paper in assorted colors, a supply of smaller construction paper in various sizes and colors, glue, colored Sunday comics torn in strips, markers, scissors

Directions: Have the children fold a piece of 9" x 12" colored construction paper in half vertically. Cut on a diagonal across the top open end. Save these triangular pieces to use as shoes. Open the folded paper and glue the triangular shapes under the dress as shoes. (See illustration.)

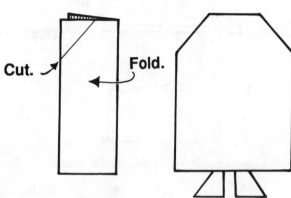

Have children draw and cut a circle for the head and a triangle for the hat. Glue these together with the hat on the top of the head. Draw a face on the head with markers. Tear colored Sunday comics pages into strips for hair. Glue the strips to the back of the head. (See illustration.)

Curl the hair strips around a pencil or leave them straight. Attach the head to the body. Make a broom out of a rectangle and a square and glue it on an angle to the front of the dress. Fringe cut the bottom of the broom. (See illustration.)

My witch's name is Weirdie!

Extension Activity:
When the children have completed their witches, have them sit in a circle with their witches. Let them take turns naming and introducing their witches, telling something about them. For example:

"My witch's name is Susie, and she is a kind witch who loves children."

"My witch's name is Weirdie, and she likes to do weird things."

"My witch's name is Wanda, and she loves to wander all over the sky."

Art

Wood Sculptures

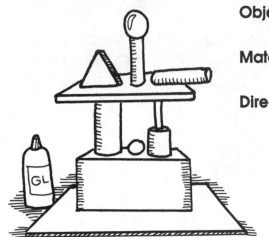

Objective: To encourage imagination by creating wood sculptures

Materials: small pieces of wood, glue, paint, paintbrushes, cardboard

Directions: Using the pieces of wood and glue, model for the students how the wood could possibly be arranged on a cardboard base to create a sculpture. Creations could be completely abstract, or they could be models of an object such as a building or toy. Next, allow students to create sculptures. Let them dry overnight. Paint if desired.

Note: The size of the cardboard will depend on the size and number of wood pieces used.

Wallpaper

Objective: To create a wallpaper mosaic

Materials: old wallpaper books, glue, large piece of butcher paper, tape

Directions: Gather old wallpaper books from wallpaper stores. Let the students look through the books until each one finds a pattern he/she likes. Let them cut out their pattern. Direct them to cut shapes out of their pattern.

Then, tape the butcher paper to a wall low enough so the students can reach it. Have them take turns gluing their creations wherever they would like to create a wallpaper mosaic.

Save the Whales!

Objective: To understand the term "endangered"

Materials: 12" x 18" sheets of construction paper, crayons

Directions: Explain to the children that sometimes there becomes too few of an animal left in the world which leads to the fear that the animal may not be alive anymore. When that fear arises about an animal, it is termed "endangered," which means it is in danger of becoming extinct like dinosaurs.

Explain that whales were hunted so much that they were endangered and people around the world fought to save them.

Write the words: SAVE THE WHALES on the chalkboard. Let the students copy the words on their construction paper using a black crayon. Then, show them how to draw a simple picture of a whale.

Winter Walk

Objective: To sharpen children's power of observation

Materials: 9" x 12" sheets of white construction paper, crayons, notebook rings for binding

Directions: Bundle up the children and go for a walk on a winter day! Tell them to bring along their five senses and their memory banks to help them remember the walk.

When you are back in the room, gather the children around you and encourage them to share their experiences. Next, give them each a 9" x 12" sheet of white construction paper and some crayons and let them draw and color from their memory. Circulate the room and take dictation from each child. Collect the finished papers, bind as a class book, and share the memory of a winter walk.

Suggested Reading:
Rosie's Walk by Pat Hutchins
I Went Walking by Sue Williams

If I Had One Wish

Objective: To encourage creative thinking and creative writing

Materials: construction paper, markers, crayons, books - *The Magic Feather Duster* by Will and Nicholas, *Sylvester and the Magic Pebble* by William Steig, *The Fish Who Could Wish* by John Bush, Korky Paul

Directions: Read one or all of the suggested books.

Ask the children to think about what they would wish for if they had one wish.

Remind them of what happened to Sylvester and tell them that they should think very carefully before they make their one wish. Have each child illustrate his/her wish and take dictation from the children.

These pages can be assembled into a class wish book.

Author Study - Brian Wildsmith

Objective and Directions: Refer to **Biography** page 11.

Background:
Brian Wildsmith was born in Yorkshire, England. He was the oldest of four children and ended up having four children of his own. Wildsmith likes to use lots of color in his books and likes to challenge his readers to put words to what they see on the page.

Suggested Reading:

Animal Shapes	*Bear's Adventures*	*Give a Dog a Bone*
Brian Wildsmith's Circus	*All Fall Down*	

What a W!

Writing/ Reading

Make several oaktag patterns of the W below to use for a variety of activities.

Objective/Activity 1: To identify things that are white

Materials: black construction paper, white crayons or chalk

Directions: Have children trace around the W on black construction paper using white crayon or chalk and cut it out. Then, they draw things that are white on their W's. Brainstorm these items first (snow, milk, stars, polar bear, goose).

Objective/Activity 2: To identify things that begin with the "W" sound

Materials: light-colored construction paper, crayons

Directions: Have children trace around the W on construction paper and cut it out. Have children draw 10 items that begin with the "W" sound.

Objective/Activity 3: To understand the questions: Who? What? Where?

Materials: light blue construction paper, black crayons

Directions: Have children trace and cut out the W. Then, write Who? on the chalkboard for children to copy on their W. Do the same for What? and Where? Talk about W questions and have children illustrate them.

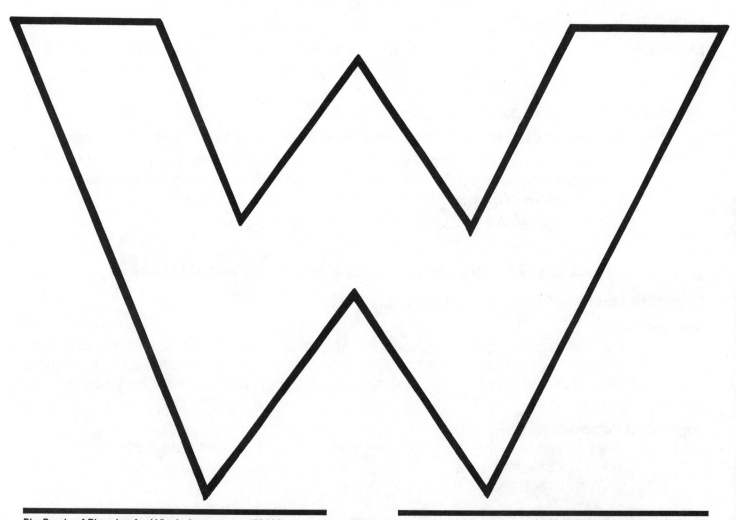

Wind and Water Experiment Science

Objective: To conduct an experiment to see if wind has any effect on drying a wet area

Materials: chalkboard, wet sponge or cloth, book

Directions: Before you conduct the experiment, discuss with the children the fact that wind is moving air. Have them create a windy atmosphere by moving a hand quickly back and forth in front of their faces. Then, let them try it with a paper or book.

Tell the children that you are going to put two wet spots on the chalkboard. One will dry by itself, the other will have wind blown on it. Have the children predict which spot will dry faster, or if they will dry at the same time. Tally the predictions.

To conduct the experiment, place two wet spots on the board at an arm's distance from each other. Fan one with a book. Observe the changes and draw conclusions.

Suggested Reading:
The Wind Blew by Pat Hutchins

Weight

Objective: To record and compare students' weights

Materials: a pound scale and if available, a kilogram scale, chart paper, marker, class list

Directions: On the chart paper, create two columns. Label one **Pounds** and the second **Kilograms**. Have each student weigh themselves on each scale. Record the weights anonymously on the chart paper, and then again on the class list. Repeat the activity in a month, or in several months. Compare individual and class results.

If using both the pound and kilogram scales, discuss why the students' weights are "different."

Extension Activity:

Write a "science story" about your findings. You may want to include the following:

1. How many students weigh more than 50 pounds? How many weigh less?
2. How many students gained weight? Why?
3. What is the difference between the heaviest student and the lightest?
4. Do any students weigh the same? How many?

259

Weekly Weather Watch

Science

Objective: To become familiar with the days of the week, the number of days in a week, and to become aware of the surrounding climate and season

Materials: a large sheet of posterboard with the days of the week written across the top, cotton balls, gray flannel, blue marker, sun cutouts, umbrella cutouts, snowman cutouts

Directions: Name and count the days of the week.
Each day, record the weather. Use:

cotton balls - fair weather clouds (cumulus)
blue marker - storm clouds (stratus)
sun cutouts - sunny skies
umbrella cutouts - rainy days
snowman cutouts - snowy days

Record weekend weather on the following Monday. Perhaps you could assign students to find out the weekend forecast. Compare the forecast and actual weather on the following Monday.

Extension Activity:
See **Clouds** on page 37.
See **In the Rain . . .** on page 197.

Suggested Reading:
Weather Watch by Gail Gibbons
Cloudy With a Chance of Meatballs by Judi Barrett
Weather by Mark Pelligrew
The Cloud Book by Tomie dePaola
It Looked Like Spilt Milk by Charles Shaw

Social Studies

Wheels

Objective: To begin to understand the importance of the wheel

Materials: newsprint, crayons

Directions: Ask the children to name things that have wheels. Lead them into the realization that without wheels, we would have a difficult time moving things.

Have the children draw five things with wheels that are part of their lives. Set aside time for them to share their drawings.

Washington's Life

Objective: To learn about the life of George Washington

Materials: 8 1/2" x 11" sheets of construction paper, crayons, glue, scissors, copies of the George Washington pattern, copies of the star pattern

Directions: Make enough copies of the pattern of George Washington for each student. Enlarge the patterns to fit on an 8 1/2" x 11" sheet of construction paper. Have students color their pattern and paste it at the bottom of a piece of construction paper. Write **Washington's Life** on the chalkboard. Have students copy it above their pictures of Washington. Using the star pattern, make enough stars so that each student has 6 of them. On each star, have the students number from 1 to 6. On another sheet of construction paper, students should glue the stars, in order, from top to bottom on the left side of the paper. (See example.) Copy the sentence strips below, one set for each student. Have students cut the strips apart and glue them in the correct order next to the stars.

> Washington was born on February 22, 1732, in Virginia.

> As a teenager, Washington worked as a surveyor.

> Washington led the army during the Revolutionary War.

> After the war, Washington was elected our country's first President.

> George Washington died in 1799 at the age of 67.

> Today, Washington is called "The Father of Our Country."

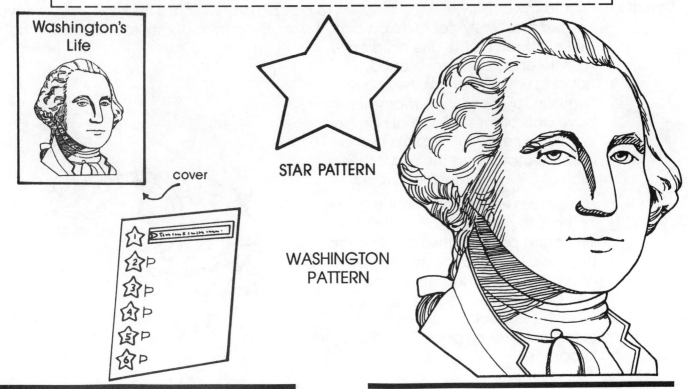

Washington's Life

cover

STAR PATTERN

WASHINGTON PATTERN

Watermelon Seed Counting Book

Math

Objective: To make individual counting books

Materials: red construction paper, several patterns for watermelon slices, pre-cut green "rinds," glue, black crayons, notebook rings, hole punch

Directions: Have children trace and cut watermelon slices from the red paper. They will need to do this for each page of their books. The more slices they make, the bigger their book will be!

Have plenty of pre-cut green "rinds" available for gluing. Children will glue the rinds onto the red slices. (See Illustration.)

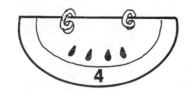

Punch two holes in the top of the slices and attach notebook rings. Have children write the numerals in order on the rinds and draw the matching number of seeds on the slices with a black crayon. (See illustration.)

Worth "Watch"ing

Objective: To observe different kinds of watches and ways of showing time and to become aware of their purposes

Materials: watches, copies of the practice sheet on page 263

Directions: Prior to this activity, ask the children to bring in any watches that they might have. You will most likely get quite an array - everything from Disney to spacecraft that make noises. Gather the children in a circle and pass them around, noticing whether or not they have numbers, and if so, how many, if they have dots or lines instead of numbers or if they are digital. Explain that a digital watch shows the exact time, such as 6:42 or sometimes 6:42:15.

Draw a big watch face on the board or use a toy clock. Explain that the little hand points to the hour and the big hand points to the minute. Draw hands in different locations and identify the time it reads together. Give the students the very simple practice sheet on page 263. Go over it together.

Name _____

Worth "Watch"ing!

Read the time on each watch. Color each watch.

11:00	red	6:00	brown
9:00	yellow	10:00	black
3:00	green	4:00	orange
2:00	blue	8:00	purple

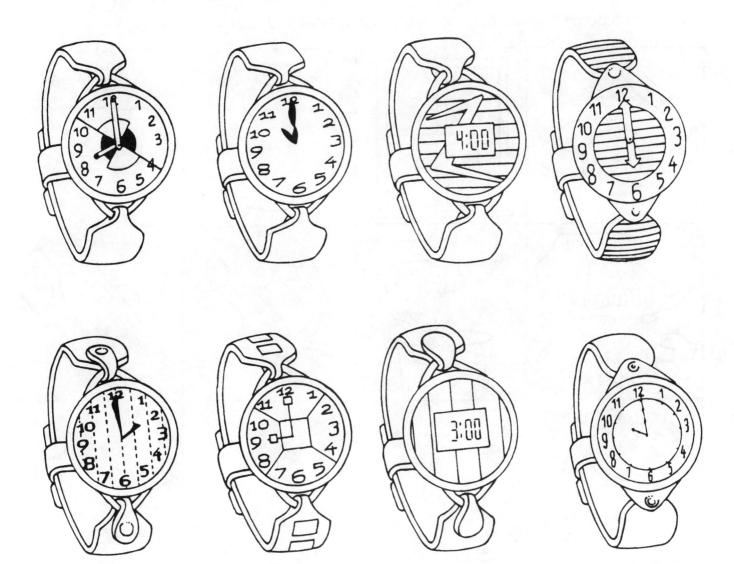

Cooking

Waffles - 12 Waffles

3 1/2 cups flour
4 teaspoons double-acting powder*
1 teaspoon salt
2 tablespoons sugar
6 egg yolks, 6 egg whites
8 tablespoons butter
3 cups milk

Mix the flour, double-acting powder, salt and sugar. Beat egg yolks well. Add the butter and milk to the yolks. When combined, add the liquid ingredients to the dry ingredients with a few quick strokes. Next, beat the egg whites until stiff. Fold them into the batter. For easy pouring, place batter in a pitcher. Fill waffle iron approximately 2/3 full. Close the iron and cook approximately 4 minutes. *In high altitude, 3 teaspoons.

W Pictures for Miscellaneous Activities

Enlarge the cards to make flash cards throughout the study of the "W" sound.

Poetry

Wishes

I wish it were winter
When the cold wind blows,
I like the way it tingles my nose.
I wish it were winter
When the white snow falls
I like to make white snowballs.

by Ada Frischer

Book List

Adams, A. (1985). *A Woggle of Witches*. New York: Macmillan.

Baker, J. (1991). *Window*. New York: Greenwillow Books.

Barton, B. (1972). *Where's Al?* New York: Seabury Press.

Barton, B. (1979). *Wheels*. New York: Harper and Row.

Graham. B. (1988). *Has Anyone Seen William?* London: Walker.

Hirschi, R. (1990). *Winter*. New York: Cobblehill Books.

Hutchins, P. (1967). *Rosie's Walk*. New York: Macmillan.

Hutchins, P. (1974). *The Wind Blew*. New York: Macmillan

Keats, E. J. (1977). *Whistle for Willie*. New York: Puffin Books.

Kerber, K. (1985). *Walking Is Wild, Weird and Wacky*. Landmark Editions.

Martin, C. (1987). *I Can Be a Weather Forecaster*. Chicago, IL: Childrens Press.

Milne, A.A. (1952). *When We Were Very Young*. New York: Dutton.

Milne, A.A. (1961). *Winnie-the-Pooh*. New York: Dutton.

Pollock, P. (1985). *Water Is Wet*. Putnam Publishing Group.

Reese, B. (1983). *Dale the Whale*. Chicago, IL: Childrens Press.

Rossetti, C. G. (1991). "Who Has Seen the Wind?" - *An Illustrated Collection of Poetry for Young People*. New York: Rizzoli.

Schenk de Regniers, B. (1961). *Going For a Walk*. New York: Harper and Row.

Sendak, M. (1984). *Where the Wild Things Are*. New York: Harper and Row.

Smith, K. B. (1987). *George Washington*. New York: J. Messner.

Stille, D. (1990). *Water Pollution*. Chicago, IL: Childrens Press.

Williams, S. (1990). *I Went Walking*. San Diego, CA: Harcourt Brace Jovanovich.

Wise, M. B. (1954). *Willie's Adventures*. New York: W.R. Scott.

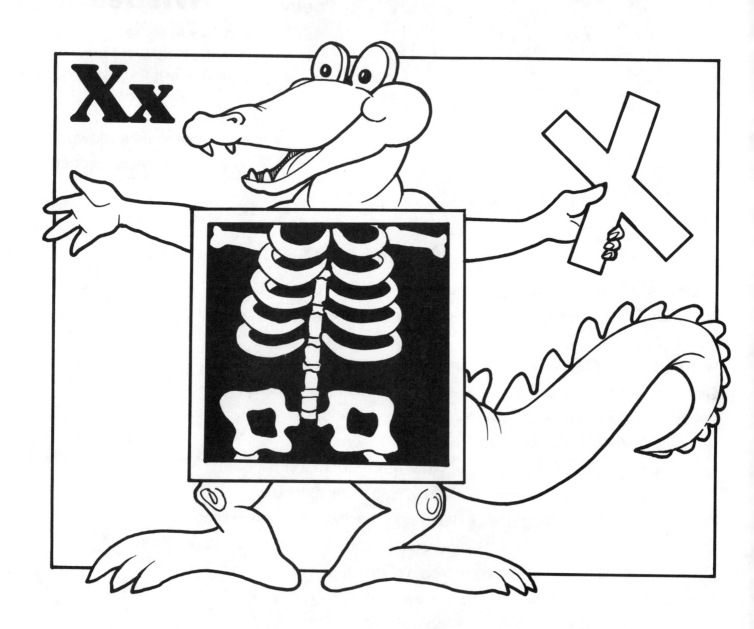

Table of Contents

*Remember to check **B Chapter Table of Contents** (page 4) for additional activities.

X-Ray

Science

Objective: To help children understand the purpose of an x-ray and what it shows

Materials: old x-rays, large black construction paper, white chalk or crayons

Directions: Borrow some old x-rays from a hospital or doctor's office. Show them to the children. Better yet, see if a radiologist or x-ray technician could come to your class for a visit.

Talk about the purposes of x-rays (look for broken bones, diagnose diseases, check suitcases at airports). Explain that an x-ray takes a picture when it hits a solid mass.

In our bodies, the x-ray goes through our skin and tissue and then hits the mass of the bones and takes pictures of our skeletons.

Give each child a large piece of black construction paper and white chalk or white crayon. Tell students that they are going to draw a picture of their skeletons as if they were taking an x-ray. Follow the directions below. Draw the skeleton on the board as you talk.

1. Have children feel their head. Explain that the inside bone is called a skull. Have them draw it at the top of their paper. Explain that their ears and eyes will not be there.

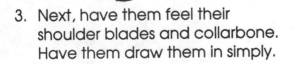

2. Have students feel the back of their neck. Explain that this is their vertebrae and that it extends all the way down to the end of their tailbone where they sit. Show them how to draw simple vertebrae.

3. Next, have them feel their shoulder blades and collarbone. Have them draw them in simply.

X-Ray continued

Science

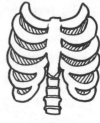

4. Next, have students feel their ribs and breastbone. Add them to the drawing, on top of their vertebrae.

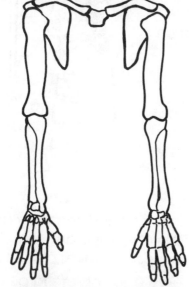

5. To the ends of the shoulder blades, add the upper and lower arms and then the bones in the hands and fingers. Have them feel the bones in their arms and arrive at the conclusion that the upper arm bones are larger than the lower arm bones.

6. Then, have students feel their hip bones and add the pelvis to their drawings.

7. Last, add the upper and lower leg bones, the kneecap and the feet and toes.

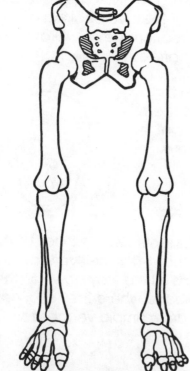

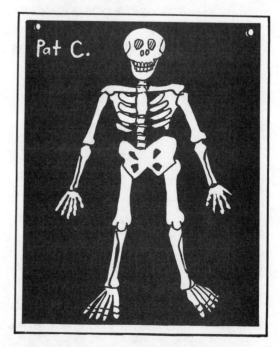

8. Display these classmade x-rays around the room.

Extension Activity:
Read *The Magic School Bus Through the Human Body* by Joanna Cole.

268

X Marks the Spot

Games

Objective: To participate in an "X Marks the Spot" treasure hunt

Materials: a sketched floor plan of the classroom, several small treasures such as stickers

Directions: Draw a floor plan of the classroom and make a copy for each child. Hide several treasures in various spots around the room. Mark one "X" on each floor plan to indicate where one treasure is hidden. Following "X Marks the Spot" directions, the children will search for the treasure indicated on their floor plan.

You can have a different location and treasure for each child, one treasure for the entire class to find, or one treasure for every 4 or 5 children to locate cooperatively.

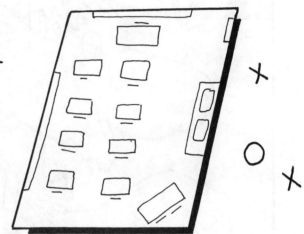

X and O

Teach the children how to play tic-tac-toe. Emphasize how to make an O and X as well as how to take turns.

The children take turns putting an X or an O in an empty box. Three X's or three O's in a row wins the game.

Start with an "X" in the middle. Have children practice writing winning combinations.

Table of Contents

*Remember to check **B Chapter Table of Contents** (page 4) for additional activities.

Yarn Picture Frame

Art

Objective: To create a yarn frame as a gift

Materials: oaktag circle about 5" in diameter or oval about 4 1/2" x 5" to create a similar-size frame, several pieces of yarn of various colors about 24" long, black construction paper

Directions:

1. From each circle or oval, cut out the center to create a one-inch border.

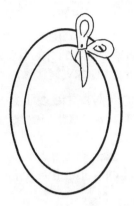

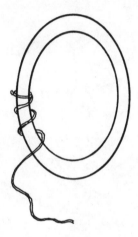

2. Tie the end of one piece of yarn to the back of the frame. Wrap the rest of the yarn around the frame being sure to keep each successive wrap close to the previous one so that no yarn overlaps.

3. As each strip of yarn is finished, tie on another color. Wrap over the knot. Continue until the frame is covered.

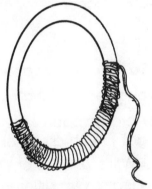

4. Tie the final end with the first knot. Make sure all knots are on the back of the frame. Tuck all loose ends under the yarn wrap. Attach a loop of yarn onto the back of the frame so that it can be hung.

5. Cut a piece of black construction paper the same size as the frame and glue this to the back of the frame. Glue a picture of the child to the black construction paper inside the frame. This makes a great gift.

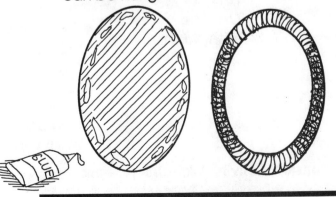

Yucky

Objective: To identify things that are yucky!

Materials: crayons, newsprint, scissors

Directions: Ask the children what it means to them when they say something is yucky. Brainstorm all the things that they find yucky. Ask them if everyone finds the same things yucky. (This is a good lead-in for a discussion about differences in people.)

Then, give the children a sheet of newsprint. Have them fold it 3 times to make 8 sections, and then cut the sections apart. On one page, they should design a cover. Write MY YUCKY BOOK on the chalkboard for them to copy on the cover. On each page, they are to draw something they find yucky. You might want to walk around the room and write the words for them.

Poetry

The Yak

One day a yak
Sat on a tack.
He didn't even hurt his back.
He was such a furry yak.

    by Ada Frischer

Acrostic Poems

Objective: To write a class poem

Materials: chalkboard, chalk

Directions: Acrostic poems are fun to write as a group. Here's a step-by-step approach to get the children going.

- Write YELLOW or YARN down the chalkboard.
- Brainstorm different words that begin with the letters in yellow or yarn. List them.
- Brainstorm sample lines for each letter.
- Put some lines together to make a poem.

    Yellow, yarn, yak
    Eating, eggs
    Love, lemons, like
    Let's, look
    On, one
    Wish, what

Yellow Things to Eat

Yellow Popsicles
Egg custard
Lemon ice cream
Lemon meringue pie
One of each for me
What yummy treats!

Extension Activity: Write the poem on paper.

Yellow

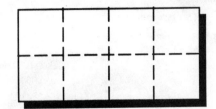

Objective: To make a book of things that are yellow

Materials: large sheets of yellow construction paper, old magazines and catalogs, glue, black markers or crayons, stapler

Directions: Give every child a large piece of yellow construction paper. Fold it three times to make 8 sections. (See example.)

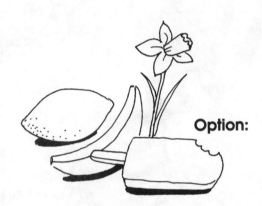

Have them use a black crayon or marker to divide their papers into sections. Hold a class discussion about things that are yellow (lemons, bananas, baby ducks, some raincoats, daffodils and daisies, some Popsicles, school buses, etc.). Write the list on the chalkboard. Then, make old magazines and catalogs available for the children to use to cut out things that are yellow. They are to glue one picture in each section.

Option: Have the children cut their sections apart and staple them together to make their "Yellow" books. Or, leave their papers together and make a class book, "Our Big Book About Yellow."

Yellow Yarn Y's

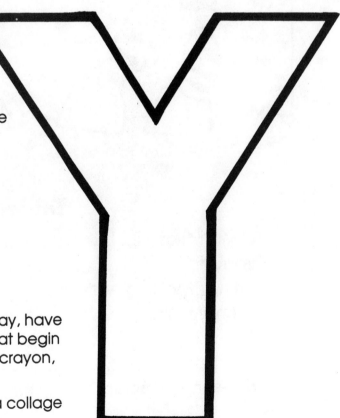

Objective: To make a yarn Y with y pictures

Materials: yellow construction paper, oaktag Y patterns, yellow yarn, glue, crayons

Directions: • Enlarge the Y pattern shown and make several Y patterns out of oaktag.

• Have the children trace around a Y pattern on a large piece of construction paper.

• Then, have them trace around their Y with white glue. Before the glue dries, they should take their piece of yellow yarn and put it on the glue to make a yarn Y.

• Let the yarn dry overnight. The next day, have the children draw pictures of things that begin with the "Y" sound (yolk, yo-yo, yellow crayon, yak, yams, yard, yardstick, yacht).

Optional: Have them cut out their Y's and make a collage with a caption that reads: **Y WEEK.**

Table of Contents

*Remember to check **B Chapter Table of Contents** (page 4) for additional activities.

Zoo Animal Bread Masks   Art

Objective: To make zoo animal masks out of dough

Materials: 2 cups flour, 3 tablespoons oil, 1/2 teaspoon salt, 1/2-1 cup lukewarm water, food coloring, bowl, cookie sheets, paintbrush, four 8" aluminum pie plates, metal table knife (adult use only), shellac, oven

Directions:

1. Measure flour and salt in bowl. Add oil and rub it in until mixture resembles coarse oatmeal.

2. Add 1/2 cup water. Blend with fingers. Add more water, if needed, to form a dough you can gather into a ball.

3. Knead for 10 minutes. Divide dough into 4-6 balls. Roll each to 8" in diameter.

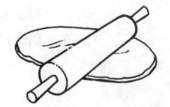

4. Place dough on the flat bottom of an inverted pie plate.

5. Cut in animal features with a metal table knife. Pinch features in dough with finger.

6. Form other features with pieces of dough. Attach dough to dough with water.

7. Place pie plates on cookie sheets. Bake in 350° oven for 10-15 minutes. Paint masks with diluted food coloring.

or

8. To display, place painted animal mask in 250° oven for 6-8 hours. Cool and then shellac.

E-Z Zebra

Objective: To make zebras for classroom display

Materials: 12" x 18" white construction paper, newspaper cut in strips, markers, glue, black yarn

Directions: Have the children draw a large zebra without stripes on the 12" x 18" white construction paper. Show them how to measure and glue newspaper strips on their zebra for stripes. Add some black yarn for a mane and finish the picture with markers.

Zippy Zoos

Objective: To give students the opportunity to dramatize being different zoo animals

Materials: a copy of the phrases below, a paper bag

Directions: Children love to act. They are wonderfully uninhibited at this age. How sad that they lose that magic as they grow older. For a fun activity that can be repeated again and again, copy and cut out the phrases below. Put them in a paper bag for children to choose and act out. If it would be easier for the children, you could let them work together in pairs.

zippy zebras	crying camels	sneaky snakes	angry anteaters	slippery seals
grumpy giraffes	happy hippos	preening peacocks	tiptoeing turtles	pesky parrots
bouncing bears	kicking kangaroos	terrible tigers	magical monkeys	leaping leopards
elegant elephants	lonely lions	dancing deer	crabby crocodiles	running rhinos

Writing/ Reading

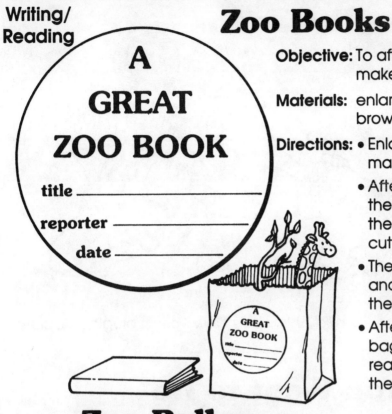

A GREAT ZOO BOOK

title _____

reporter _____

date _____

Zoo Books

Objective: To afford students opportunities to make "book" reports

Materials: enlarge copies of the pattern shown, brown paper bags, glue, scissors

Directions:
- Enlarge the pattern on the left and make multiple copies of it.

- After "reading" a book, students fill out the form with your help and glue it to the front of a paper bag. Drawings or cutouts can be added to the bag.

- The students could put their books and any other appropriate props in the bag.

- After the students share their paper bag reports, place them in the reading center so others can check them out.

Zoo Balloons

Objective: To let children make their favorite zoo animals

Materials: balloons, construction paper, string, black marker or crayons

Directions: Give students big pieces of construction paper to draw their favorite zoo animals. Help them write facts about their animals on their paper. Inflate the balloons and tie pieces of string to them. Punch a hole in the animals and attach the balloons through the holes with the string. Write the students' names on the balloons.

As a follow-up, do the **Zoo Graphing** activity on page 279.

Author Study - Charlotte Zolotow

Objective and Directions: Refer to **Biography** page 11.

Background: Charlotte Zolotow has written many books. She was born in Norfolk, Virginia, and now resides in Hastings-On-Hudson, New York. She loves to garden, read and go to the theater. She is now Harper and Row's editorial director for Charlotte Zolotow books.

Suggested Reading:

The Hating Book	*Timothy Too!*	*When the Wind Stops*
Something Is Going to Happen	*A Tiger Called Thomas*	*Sleepy Book*

The Zoo

Poetry/
Music

Zoo, zoo, zoo!
I went to the zoo.
I saw lions and tigers
And zebras too.

I liked the seals.
I liked the bears.
I liked the zebras.
That stood in pairs.

Zoo, zoo, zoo!
I went to the zoo.
I saw monkey and elephants
And zebras too.

by Ada Frischer

Suggested Reading: *Bronx Zoo Book of Wild Animals* by New York Zoological Society

Suggested Trip: The zoo

If You Want to Be

A fun song for the class to write as a group is a take-off on "Clap Your Hands." Some examples are shown:

If you want to be a monkey,
    grow a tail.
If you want to be a monkey,
    grow a tail.
If you want to be a monkey
    and swing from the trees,
If you want to be a monkey,
    grow a tail.

If you want to be a rhino,
    grow a horn.
If you want to be a lion,
    learn to roar.
If you want to be a chimp,
    make a face.
If you want to be a giraffe,
    stretch your neck.

What Do You See?

Children will enjoy coming up with variations of Bill Martin, Jr.'s book, *Brown Bear, Brown Bear, What Do You See?*

Assign each child an animal. Have them sit in a circle and take turns answering one another. Tell them they are to remember which animal they are and what animal they saw. Give them sheets of paper to draw their two animals looking at each other. Display the drawings in a row around the room.

Example:

Zebra, zebra, what do you see?
I see an elephant looking at me.

Elephant, elephant, what do you see?
I see a tiger looking at me.

Zoo Graphing

Math

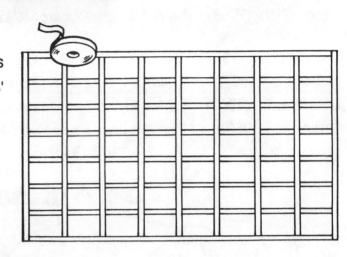

Objective: To make a floor graph

Materials: old shower curtain or drop cloth, masking tape, paper cut in squares

Directions: • Prepare a floor graph that is 6' x 3' using an old shower curtain or drop cloth. Flattened trash bags may also be used.

• Use masking tape to mark off squares.

• In the row of squares on the bottom, tape pictures of the zoo animals you think are your class' favorites. Use patterns on page 280.

• Give students squares of paper that will fit in the graph squares. Have them draw their favorite zoo animal on their square.

• Gather the children around the floor graph. Let each child tape his/her picture in the proper column. (You might need one column marked OTHER.)

• After each child has had a turn, talk about which zoo animal is the most popular, the least popular, the difference between the different animals, etc.

Zero

Objective: To help students understand the zero concept

Materials: tagboard, construction paper, zero patterns (below), rick rack, glue, counters

Directions: Bring the students to an area to sit around you. Alternate having groups of three students stand up. Give two of the students some counters. Then, have the group count what each one has. Ask them to count the third child's counters. Elicit responses as to how many the third one has. Write their responses on the board. Possible responses: not any, none, nothing. Explain that there is a number to represent nothing - a zero!

Write a large zero on the chalkboard or chart paper. Ask the students what is in the center of the number - NOTHING!

Then, have the students return to their seats and trace and cut out the zero patterns. Then, give them pieces of rick rack to glue to their zeros. Explain that rick rack makes a design that is another Z word. Ask if anyone knows what it is called - zig zag!

Optional: Show the children a large number line. Ask them where the zero comes on the number line.

Book List

Bridges, W. (1968). *The Bronx Zoo Book of Wild Animals.* New York: New York Zoological Society.

Gibbons, G. (1987). *Zoo.* New York: T.Y. Crowell.

Hoban, T. (1987). *A Children's Zoo.* New York: Mulberry Books.

Lopshire, R. (1960). *Put Me in the Zoo.* New York: Random House.

Seuss, Dr. (1950). *If I Ran the Zoo.* New York: Random House.

Van Allsburg, C. (1987). *The Z Was Zapped.* Boston, Massachusetts: Houghton Mifflin.

Zoo Animal Patterns

Culminating Activities

Now that all the consonant sounds have been addressed, it is time for review, reinforcement and evaluation.

The pages in this section include activities that work with all the letters of the alphabet. They include letter recognition of capital and lower case letters and letter/sound association.

Have fun while evaluating the progress of your children!

Alphabetical Order Game

Objective: To place letters in alphabetical order

Materials: 3 paper bags, alphabet chart, 3 sets of magnetic letters (If magnetic letters are not available, make copies of the lower case letters on page 289 and cut them apart. Don't forget to add the vowels!)

Directions: Separate your class into three teams. Place a set of letters in each paper bag. Each team will receive a set of letters. Each player places his/her hand into the bag and removes 2 or 3 letters (depending on team size).

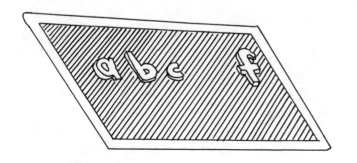

Instruct students to find out where their letter(s) appears in the alphabet. For students having difficulty, direct them to the alphabet chart. To play this game, each team must arrange all the letters in alphabetical order, with each player placing his/her letters. The player with the letter "a" in his/her hand would place the letter first. The player with the letter "b" would follow. The letters can be arranged on the chalkboard, a table or the floor. The team to be first in placing all the letters in order correctly, wins.

Riddle Game

Objective: To reinforce the letter sounds

Directions: After the children have become comfortable with the initial consonant sounds, make up riddles using any letter at random.

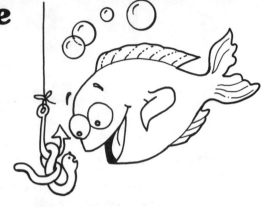

1. I'm thinking of a word that begins with the sound for "F". It's something that you might catch on a hook. (fish)

2. I'm thinking of a word that begins with the sound for "S". It's something that falls, and it is white. (snow)

3. I'm thinking of a word that begins with the sound for "Z". It comes before one. (zero)

4. I'm thinking of a word that begins with the sound for "P". It's something you eat and it has a crust and tomato sauce on it. (pizza)

After you have asked several riddles, have the children make up their own riddles.

An extension of this activity would be to talk about ending sounds.

1. I'm thinking of a word that ends with the sound for "T". It's an animal that purrs. (cat)

2. I am thinking of a word that ends with the sound for "R". It's something you ride in. (car)

3. I'm thinking of a word that ends with the sound for "L". It's something that you write with. (pencil)

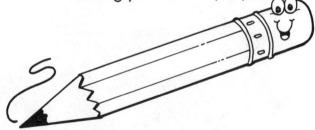

4. I'm thinking of a word that ends with the sound for "G". It's a pet. (dog)

Letter Games

Objective: To play a letter game stressing initial consonant sounds

Materials: 3" x 5" index cards cut in half so there is at least one 3" x 2 1/2" card for each child

Directions: Write an upper and lower case consonant on each card and turn the cards over so that the children cannot see what the letters are.

Have each child select a card and look at the letter it contains. Tell students not to show their card to anyone.

Each child has to think of a name and an item that begins with his/her letter.

For example, when it is his/her turn, a child may say, "My name is Bill, and I like bats. Can you guess my letter?"

The child that guessed the letter "B" has his/her turn and says a similar sentence using his/her letter. "My name is Mary, and I like meatballs." The game continues until everyone has a turn.

Some children may need some help. This can be provided by a friend or by you.

Fill in the Missing Letter

Objective: To listen for the missing consonant and fill in the missing letter

Materials: copies of activity sheets 284 and 285, pencils

Directions: Go over words on the activity sheets on pages 284 and 285. Say the pictures and have the children tell you the initial letter.

Illustrate on the chalkboard:

Say the name of the picture. Write the letter it starts with. Ask the children, "What word have I written?"

After you have illustrated several examples, go over the activity sheets with the class. Then, have the students complete the sheets on their own.

Make sure to stress that you can hear the sound best if you say the word aloud.

_____ at

Name _____

Fill in the Missing Letter

Listen to the word. Fill in the letter for the beginning sound.

__at

__at

__at

__at

__ish

__ish

Name _____

Fill in the Missing Letter

Say the word. Fill in the letter for the beginning sound.

Letter/Picture Match Bingo

Objective: To reinforce the letter sounds

Materials: capital letter boards - one for each child (page 288)
lower case letter boards - one for each child (page 289)
picture boards - one for each child (page 287)
capital letter cutouts (page 288)
lower case letter cutouts (page 289)
picture cutouts (page 287)
12 buttons for each child

Directions: Make 2 copies each of the capital letter boards, lower case letter boards and picture boards on pages 287-289. Have 2 sets for each child. Mount one set on oaktag or cardboard and laminate if possible. This set is the gameboard set.

The second set will be cut to separate the letters and pictures. These will be used by the "caller" in the game.

Either you or a child is the caller. Each child gets a gameboard. You can work with all capital letters, all lower case letters, all pictures, or you can mix and match depending on the abilities of your class.

It would be a good idea for the caller to use the letter pictures first. The children will then have a letter board. The caller says the name of the picture. The child then covers the picture that begins with that consonant with a button.

When the caller uses the letters, the children will have the picture boards. When the letter is called, the child will use a button to cover the picture word that begins with that letter sound.

Continue the game until the gameboards are covered.

Extension Activity:

Have the children make Bingo cards using pages 287-289. Each child can make his/her own Bingo card.

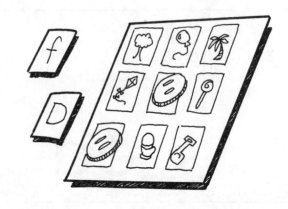

Picture Boards

Capital Letter Boards

B	V	Q	J
N	G	D	X
🙂	S	L	Z

M	C	T	P
K	R	W	H
Y	🙂	F	🙂

Lower Case Letter Boards

h	s	n	q
l	b	f	j
t	☺	z	v

c	g	w	d
m	p	k	r
x	☺	☺	y

Picture Find Worksheets

Objective: To locate pictures with initial consonant sounds b-m (Worksheet 1, page 291) and n-z (Worksheet 2, page 292).

Materials: a copy of both worksheets for each student, crayons, directions (below) to accompany the corresponding worksheet

Directions: Distribute the worksheets to students and name and discuss the objects pictured. Next, explain to the students that you will ask them to look for pictures that begin with certain letter sounds. Tell them to look at their worksheets while you speak. Read the following:

> Put a line under the object . . .

Worksheet 1 - Directions

1. Color the object that begins with the sound for b, blue. (boat)
2. Circle the object that begins with the sound for c. (cat)
3. Put a line under the object that begins with the sound for d. (dock)
4. Color the object that begins with the sound for f, purple. (fish)
5. Color the object that begins with the sound for g, green. (grass)
6. Color the object that begins with the sound for h, yellow. (hat)
7. Put a line under the object that begins with the sound for j. (jet)
8. Color the object that begins with the sound for k, red. (kite)
9. Color the object that begins with the sound for l, orange. (life preserver)
10. Color the object that begins with the sound for m, brown. (mountains)

Worksheet 2 - Directions

1. Color the object that begins with the sound for n, green. (nest)
2. Make an X on the object that begins with the sound for p. (puppy)
3. Circle the object that begins with the sound for r. (rabbit)
4. Color the object that begins with the sound for s, yellow. (sun)
5. Color the object that begins with the sound for t, brown. (tree)
6. Color the object that begins with the sound for w, blue. (water)
7. Put a line under the object that begins with the sound for y. (yak)
8. Circle the object that begins with the sound for z. (zebra)

Note: Be sure all the objects have been named before beginning. This activity could be used for evaluation.

291

ZOO

Alphabet Graph

Objective: To graph lower case letters; those with circles in their form, those with straight lines and those with both

Materials: three copies of the lower case letters on page 289 (cut apart), scissors, paste, prepared graph, chalkboard, chalk, alphabet chart of lower case letters

Directions: Ask the students to look at the alphabet chart. Explain that letters are made with straight lines, circles and curved lines. Tell them they are going took for letters that have circles, straight lines or both. As students supply answers, name the letter and print it on the board.

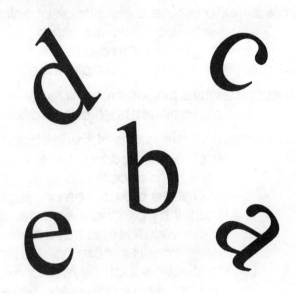

To graph, lay out one set of lower case letters across the chalk tray. Display the graph above it. Again, ask students to locate the letters that have circles in them. Ask students to pick them out, name them and paste them in the appropriate spot on the graph. Collect the remaining letters. Display a new complete set of lower case letters. Repeat the procedure, this time identifying letters that have straight lines. Again, collect the remaining letters. Repeat the procedure with a third set of lower case letters that have both circles and lines.

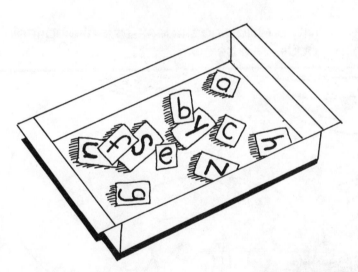

Alphabet Graph

O **circle**										
I **line**										
OI **both**										

Alphabet Animals - A Class Book

Objective: To create a class book of animals with each animal's name beginning with a different consonant of the alphabet

Materials: white paper, crayons, book rings or bindery, chalk, chalkboard

Directions: Print the letters of the alphabet on the chalkboard. Let students take turns choosing a letter. (As letters are chosen or assigned, mark it by printing the students' initials above it. This way, you and the children will know which letters have been "taken" and you will have a record of the assignments in case one has forgotten.) Next, brainstorm a list of animals. Explain to students that they will draw an animal that begins with the chosen letter. After the drawing is complete, write the letter and the name of the animal at the bottom. (i.e: F is for Fox.). Assemble the pages in order, create a cover and bind all together.

B is for Bear   C is for Cat

Additional Activity:

This book can be a very creative activity by allowing students to make up their own creatures by combining animal parts. See below.

Alphabet/Phonics Book

Objective: To make an alphabet/phonics book

Materials Needed per Child:

    13 sheets of 9" x 6" white construction paper
    1 sheet 9" x 6" colored construction paper
    1 sheet 9" x 6" oaktag
    scissors
    white glue
    1 shoe box
    3 worksheets - capital letters on page 297,
       lower case letters on page 29,
       pictures on page 296

Directions: Staple or bind together the 13 sheets of white construction paper, the colored paper for the cover and the oaktag for the back page. Have the children design their book covers and put their names on them. Have the children number all the pages first, using the front and back of each page. Explain to the children that they are going to make their own alphabet/sound book. They will do one page each day in consecutive order. If you have not worked with vowel sounds, you will have to help the children with the a, e, i, o, u pages.

Put a name on each shoe box and tell the children that they will each keep their own book and pages in their own box. Keep the boxes in an areas that is easily accessible to the children such as a countertop, cubby or desk.

Do the first two pages as a class activity to illustrate how the book will be made. After the first page, tell the children that they can now do the books on their own. Indicate the time frame in which they may select this activity. (Center time or free activity time is a good time for this selection.) However, they may do only one page a day. When they finish each page, be sure that they show them to you to make sure that they are doing it correctly, using consecutive order and not skipping any pages.

Now, you are ready to start the alphabet. Using pages 296, 297 and 298, each child will cut out and paste the capital A and the lower case a on page 1. Look at the picture worksheet (page 296). Help the children find the apple, cut it out and paste it on the A page. On the next day, work the B page in the same way.

From this point on, this should be an independent activity.

The letters on the capital letter worksheet are in consecutive order. On the lower case worksheet, they are placed at random, but in such a way that the letter students are up to will always be at the edge. It will not be necessary to cut all the letters at one time. The picture worksheet is arranged in the same manner.

F	L	R	X	:)
E	K	Q	W	:)
D	J	P	V	:)
C	I	O	U	:)
B	H	N	T	Z
A	G	M	S	Y

e	p	o	h	b	a
i	u	z	y	t	k
m	v	☺	☺	w	r
g	x	☺	☺	s	c
d	n	j	q	l	f

Have You Ever Seen . . . ? - A Class Book

Objective: To create a class book focusing on initial consonant sounds to describe a silly situation

Materials: white paper, crayons, book ring or bindery, chalk, chalkboard

Directions: Print the letters of the alphabet on the chalkboard. Assign students a letter or let them choose one. (As letters are chosen or assigned, mark the letter by printing the students' initials above it. This way, you and the students know which letters have been "taken," and you will have a record of the assignments in case one is forgotten.) Next, tell students they will need to use their imaginations. Write the sentence starter, "Have you ever seen . . . ?" on the board. Supply students with some silly endings to complete the sentence. Some examples may be:

> Have you ever seen . . .
> A. a boat in a bed?
> B. a shoe sail on a ship?
> C. a turkey talk on a telephone?
> D. a hippo in a helicopter?

Ask students to supply some endings. Next, tell students they will use the letters they chose or were assigned earlier to help them think of words to end the sentence. For example, if a student's letter assignment is "b," he/she will complete the sentence using "b" words. For example, "Have you ever seen a **bee** at **bat**?"

Have students illustrate their silly sentences. Create a cover and bind with book rings or bindery.

Have you ever seen a hippo in a helicopter?

Alphabet Books

Anno, M. (1975). *Anno's Alphabet.* New York: Crowell.

Duke, K. (1983). *The Guinea Pig ABC.* New York: Dutton.

Gág, W. (1933). *The ABC Bunny.* New York: Coward McCann, Inc.

Garten, J. (1964). *The Alphabet Tale.* New York: Random House.

Grossbart, F. (1966). *A Big City.* New York: Harper and Row.

Hoban, T. (1982). *A, B, See!* New York: Greenwillow Books.

Kitchen, B. (1984). *Animal Alphabet.* New York: Dial Books.

Lobel, A. (1980). *On Market Street.* New York: Greenwillow Books.

Miles, M. (1969). *Apricot ABC.* Boston, MA: Little, Brown and Company.

Neumeier, M. and Glaser, B. (1985). *Action Alphabet.* New York: Greenwillow Books.

Oxenbury, H. (1983). *ABC of Things.* New York: Delacorte Press.

Wildsmith, B. (1962). *Brian Wildsmith's ABC.* Franklin Watts.

Interactive Bulletin Boards

The following are bulletin boards for each of the consonants (except X). They are designed to be interactive to help reinforce each letter and the letter sound. The main theme and use of the bulletin board is indicated on each page. The use of materials such as paper, fabric, crayons, paint, yarn, etc. is left to your discretion.

Interactive Bulletin Board

Objective: To monitor progress in the study of letter sounds

Materials: construction paper, pictures, crayons/markers, paste

Directions: At the onset of the study of letter sounds, tell the children that you are going to start to construct a class flower. Each petal will represent a letter, and, as you learn about the sound each letter makes, you will add that petal to the flower. However, when you start, it will be a "naked" flower - just a center, stem and leaves, but no petals.

As you study each letter, add a petal to the flower. Put the letter on the petal with a marker. Have the children draw objects or paste pictures of objects beginning with that letter sound on the petal. Your flower will soon begin to blossom!

Balloons

Up, Up and AWAY!

Write each child's name on a balloon. When the child is able to identify the name of the beginning letter or sound, give the balloon to the child to take home.

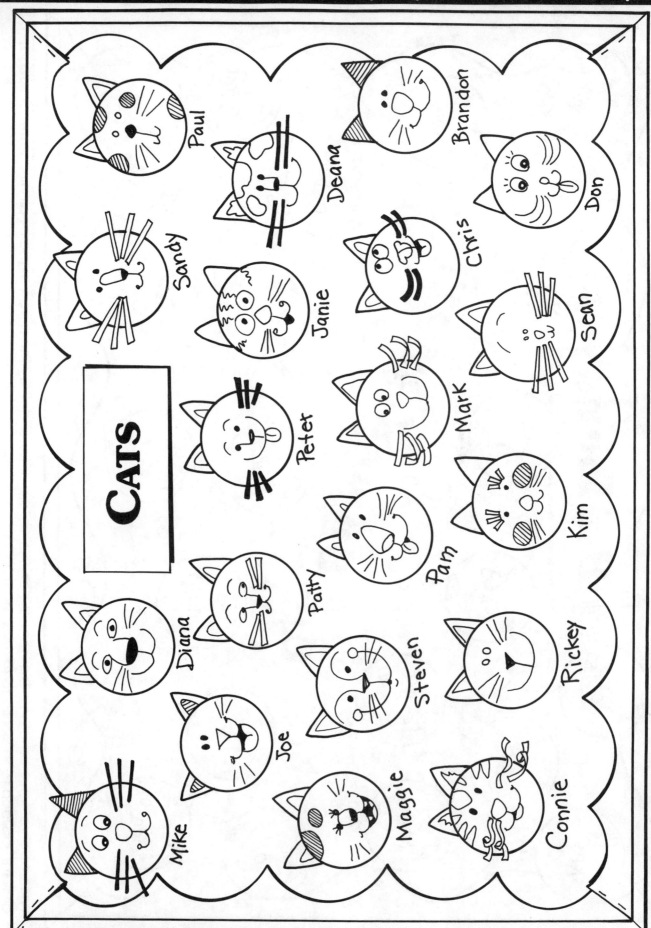

CATS

Have each child design and decorate his/her own cat head. Use paper plates for heads.

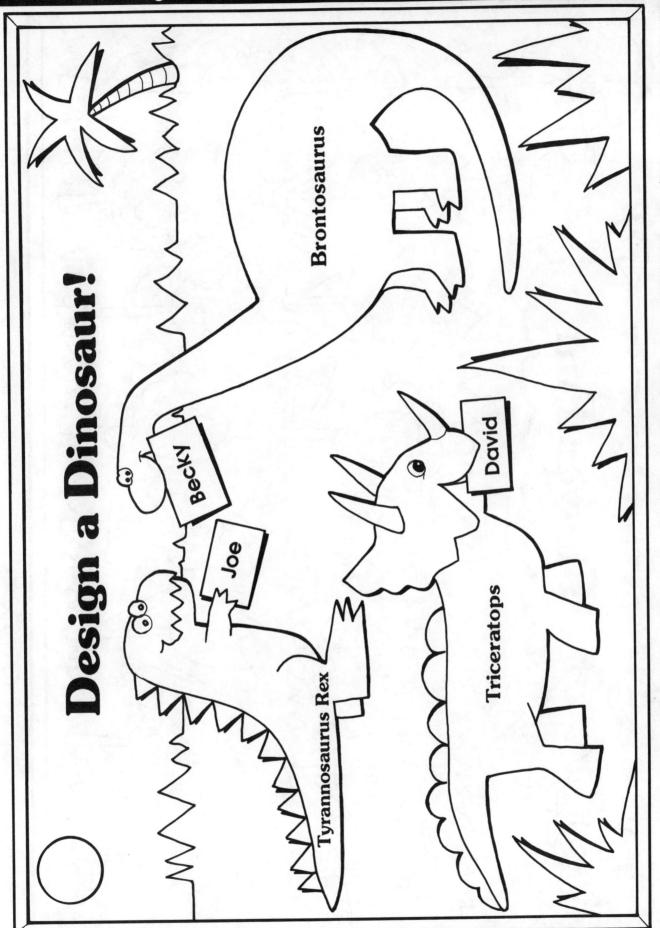

Design a Dinosaur!

Brontosaurus

Becky

Joe

David

Tyrannosaurus Rex

Triceratops

Have children design and draw their own version of a dinosaur with either the child's or dinosaur's name.

Flower Fun

Have each child design, draw, cut and paste a flower. Write each child's name on his/her flower.

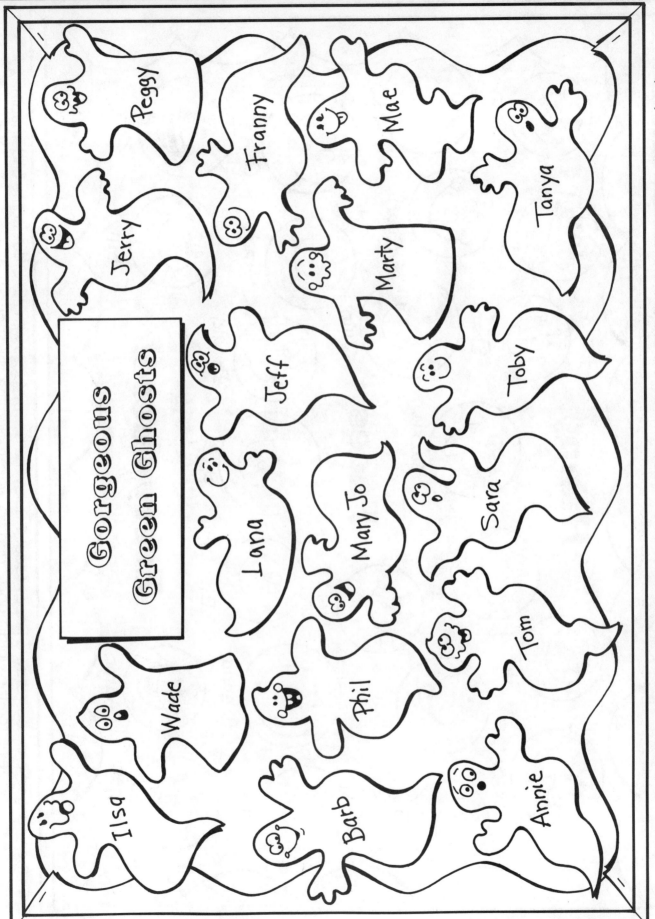

Gorgeous Green Ghosts

Using green construction paper, have each child draw, design and cut out his/her own gorgeous green ghost.

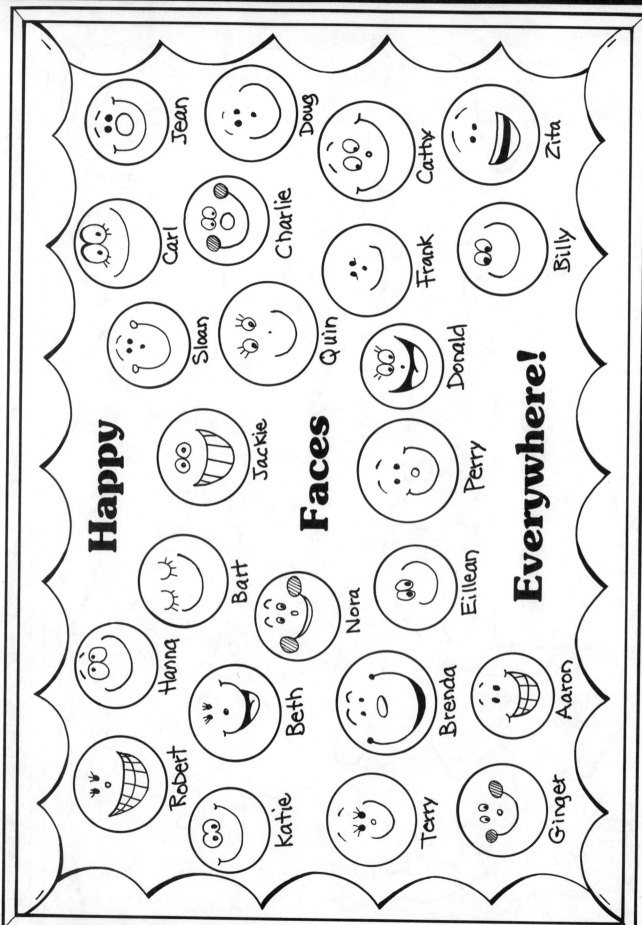

Happy Faces Everywhere!

Even the youngest child can draw a happy face! Display the happy faces with the child's name underneath. From time to time, reinforce the word "happy" and ask what makes the child happy.

Jolly

Jack-o'-Lanterns

Provide plenty of construction paper, paste, glue, scissors and markers and let the fun begin! The only rule is that the jack-o'-lanterns must be jolly!

Kites by Kids!

Have children design, draw and cut out their own kites. Encourage them to use many different colors and designs to decorate the kites. Use yarn for the tails.

Leafman

Laughing

Have children collect leaves from home and the playground to bring to school. Combine their leaves to make a large leafman - or encourage the children to make their own.

Monsters on the March!

Have children design their very own monsters! Read *Where the Wild Things Are* by Maurice Sendak and let their imaginations soar. Provide plenty of collage materials.

The
Number Net
Game

Use Velcro or stick pins to attach number nets to a bulletin board. Play games involving numeral recognition, numerical order, numerals before and after and addition or subtraction.

The Pumpkin Patch Match

Attach pumpkins to bulletin board with Velcro or stick pins. Children select pairs of pumpkins to make a match. This game may also be played with letters, pictures and sounds.

A Quilt of Queens

Have each child draw a picture of a queen using crayons and markers. Assemble and display the drawings together in the form of a quilt.

Rockets Away!

Have children draw, design and personalize rockets with their names. The sky's the limit!

Sailboats on the Sea

Harry · Grace · Ann · John · Shelly · Ben · Kevin · Nancy · Sid · Tom · Joel · Rosie · Stephen

Have each child trace or draw his/her own sailboat. Write the child's name on the sailboat.

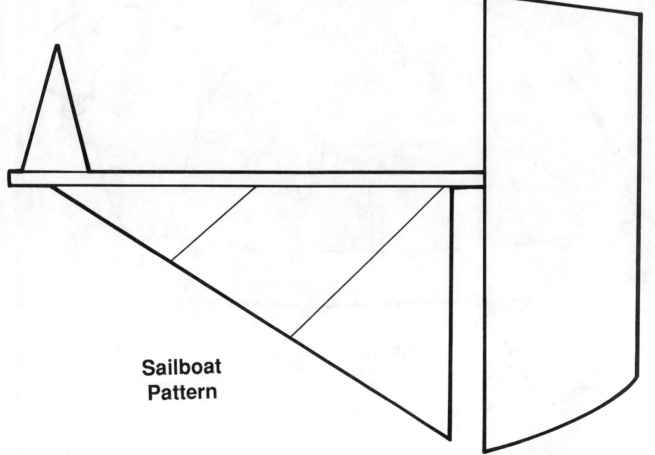

Sailboat Pattern

Turtle Talk

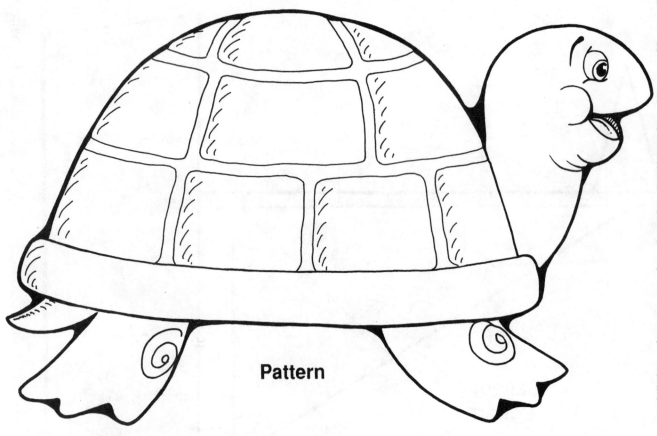

Pattern

Have children trace and cut out a turtle using the pattern. Introduce speech balloons and quotation marks. Write the child's name either on the turtle or in the speech balloon. Write the turtle's "talk."

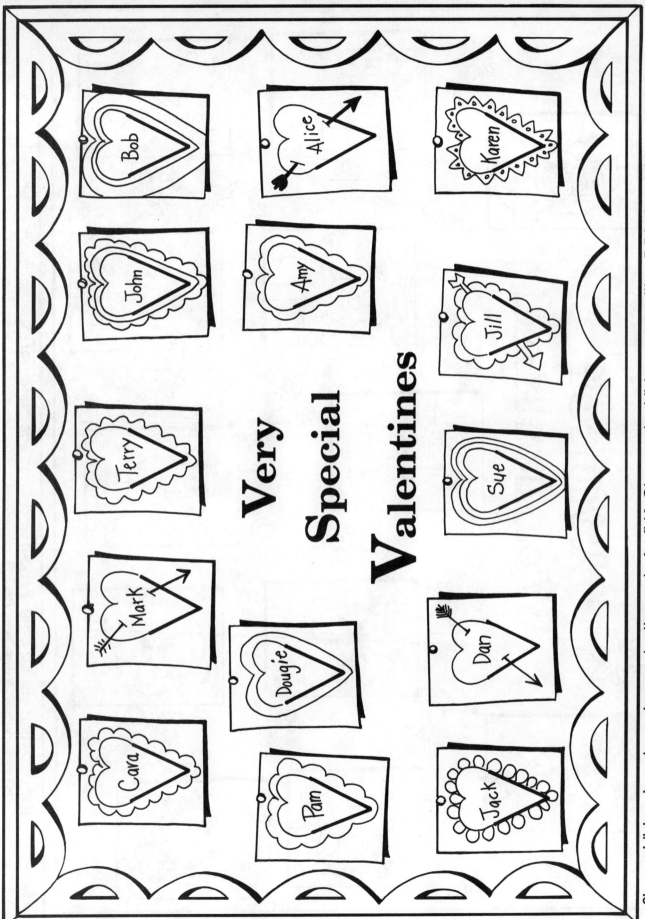

Very Special Valentines

Show children how to make a valentine out of a "V." Give each child a paper with a "V" to turn into a special valentine. Have each child write his/her own name.

Winter Wonderland

Have each child draw and color a picture about winter. Provide cotton for snow and pom-pons. Make snowflakes and sprinkle them around the drawings.